Verley and Eileen

With appreciation for your love
and friendship over the years.
God Bless.
Joe Aldred
21. 04. 06

Respect

Understanding Caribbean British
Christianity

Joe Aldred

 EPWORTH

British Library Cataloguing in Publication data

A catalogue record for this book is available
from the British Library

0 7162 0597 1

First published in 2005
by Epworth
4 John Wesley Road
Werrington
Peterborough PE4 6ZP

Typeset by Regent Typesetting, London
Printed and bound in Great Britain by
William Clowes Ltd, Beccles, Suffolk

Contents

Preface

This book aims to make a contribution to the growing awareness of the phenomenon that is the form of Christianity practised by Black people in Britain. However, in the same way that the writers of the Gospels display different emphases, so too my emphasis will differ from that of others writing in the same genre. My driving passion in adapting my PhD thesis for wider readership is that the Christian tradition that has nurtured me needs to have its story told by an 'insider' in a manner that is sympathetic yet rigorous. But the factors behind the book are not only personal, there are wider considerations too.

Christians from the Caribbean who have settled in Britain since the late 1940s have had to endure a low level of acceptance and understanding and, conversely, a high level of rejection and misunderstanding from the host Christian and secular society. In the midst of this, they have set about the construction of a new British identity that is dynamic, empowering and challenging. This identity as Caribbean British Christianity cannot be understood as peculiarly Caribbean, British, or Christian, but as all three combined and inseparable. This identity does not seek permission to be. It seeks understanding. Indeed, for a multicultural and multifaith society such as Britain to flourish, its different component parts need to understand each other. In the absence of such understanding, ignorance, prejudice, racism and patronizing behaviour poison the atmosphere and lead to disharmony. Understanding, though, requires diligence; and so this work explores one particular Christian community, and offers its method as a model and its findings as a catalyst for further explorations and understanding.

Chapter 1 sets the scene for the study. First, I discuss the research methodology used in the study, followed by an examination of the meaning of 'context' and the various influences that are at work within the context of Caribbean British Christianity. This is followed by an examination of theology in its various forms such as liberation and Black theologies. The chapter concludes with an analysis of my 'participant observer' role, reflecting upon my background and involvement in the research process.

Chapter 2 investigates ethnicity and religion in the Caribbean, examining how different ethnic groups contributed to the development of a 'Caribbean' ethnic identity, and summarizing the major contributories that impacted upon the development of Caribbean Christianity. Chapter 3 continues this ethno-religious theme by exploring the growth of Caribbean ethnicity and religious identity in Britain. It examines the socio-political and religious drivers for a new Caribbean British Christian identity.

In Chapter 4, three 'acts' of Caribbean British Christianity are analysed, which symbolize attempts to negotiate and appropriate its existence, and indicate how this community has managed to 'press along' in the midst of many adversities. In Chapter 5, the study analyses 'Incarnation' as a biblical antecedent for the experience of Caribbean British Christians. The role of the forerunner is discussed along with the pre-incarnation, incarnation, and post-incarnation phases of both *Logos* and Caribbean British Christianity.

Chapter 6 concludes the study by bringing together the personal experiences of Caribbean British Christians that have been related in the previous chapters, along with their resonance with the story of the Incarnation. This enables the development of a new theological interpretation, which the study calls 'respect'. I conclude that the ultimate meaning of respect is 'informed regard'.

Acknowledgements

During the period of this study, I lost both parents and one sibling. I honour them especially: my mother Iona, my father John and my brother Lester, all of whom meant so much to me in life and now in death. Without the support of several others, the project would have been impossible to sustain and complete. My immediate family have been extravagantly supportive, as I have so often missed my turn for chores and been unavailable at important times. To my darling wife Novelette, thank you and I love you totally. My thanks, too, to our daughters Marsha, Genelle and Alethea and son-in-law Andrew, for their understanding and love. Special thanks to my sister Gloria who generously funded my first three years of study. And thanks to my other siblings, James, Hosea, Paul, Timothy, Cynthia, Ruth, Jerry and Winsome, who have all been there for me.

I thank my PhD supervisors for their perseverance and advice, supporting me through difficult times. The Revd Dr John Vincent, Director Emeritus of the Urban Theology Unit in Sheffield, has been with me throughout. Thank you, John, for always believing in me. Dr Meg Davies co-supervised my work for a time, but it is to Dr Diana Edelman, who later replaced Dr Davies, that my special thanks go for providing the essential directional impetus for keeping my research on track and focused towards completion. I have benefited too from other associations, like the brothers and sisters and ministerial colleagues in the many churches I visited. I am indebted also to colleagues at the former Centre for Black and White Christian Partnership, the University of Birmingham, the Urban Theology Unit, the Editorial Board of the Journal of Black Theology and the Black Theology Forum. To the many friends I have been blessed with through the years, thanks for your companionship.

My thanks go to the staff at Epworth Press, and Dr Natalie Watson in particular, for working with me to transform the PhD study into a reading book. A basic fear that I had was that like so many before it, this thesis was going to sit silently on my shelf, never becoming available to a wider audience. Thanks to Epworth, this fear has been turned into my dream of publishing my first book. I have, of course, published some edited anthologies, and contributed chapters to others, but this is what I hope to be the first of many authored works of my own.

Finally, thanks to God for making it all possible.

I

Theology in Context

Introduction

I have heard many sermons in my time. One that stands out the most as a childhood memory is the one where the preacher kept repeating the words, 'Yes, but who do *you* say I am?' The sermon was based on the discourse between Jesus and his disciples concerning popular opinions about his identity (Matthew 16). Having heard their reports of the various perceptions held by the populous, Jesus asked them for their own views. Peter piped up, 'You are the Christ, the Son of God.' The preacher was adamant that we should all be like Peter was in the story; have a point of view and not be afraid to speak up about it.

The Gospel writer Luke appears to have been similarly challenged when he wrote:

> Since many have undertaken to set down an orderly account of the events that have been fulfilled among us, just as they were handed on to us by those who from the beginning were eyewitnesses and servants of the word, I too decided, after investigating everything carefully from the very first, to write an orderly account for you, most excellent Theophilus, so that you may know the truth concerning the things about which you have been instructed. (Luke 1.1–4)

My reading of this text indicates that a special responsibility rests upon those (of us) who know – by experience and association – our community's history, current state and aspirations for the future, to record it for present enlightenment and

posterity. That is to say, that I believe the informed insider is
the most reliable witness. It is in this spirit that I have sought
to discern and develop further a theology rooted in the experience of the Christian community in Britain of Caribbean
descent, to which I belong, which I have called 'Caribbean
British Christianity'.

This community has been a vibrant part of British Christian life, mainstream and Black-led, since the 1950s. During
that time, conflicting reasons have been advanced for the
movement's emergence and continued presence. I am left
with the deep feeling that the majority of commentators simply do not understand this phenomenon. And so, in Lukan
fashion, I have decided to add to this debate, as an 'insider'
with first-hand knowledge and experience of this community.[1] This study is not so much a theology 'about', but 'from
within', Caribbean British Christianity. Whatever others may
have said already, this is what I have to say as a contribution
to what has been and will be written in answer to the questions implicitly posed by Caribbean British Christianity: first,
'Who do people say we are?' and second, 'Who do you say
we are?'

Methodology

Four key themes provide the foci in this opening chapter,
which sets the scene for the study proper and its conclusions.
First, I explain the research methodology that is used.
Second, I examine some of the factors that influence contexts
generally and Caribbean British Christianity in particular.
Third, I provide an explanation of the nature of the theology.
Finally, I present an overview of my place within the context.
These themes set the scene for the development of this book
and they are discussed sequentially below.

The overarching methodology deployed in this work can be
best described as that of a 'participant observer', utilizing
ethnographic techniques, within a contextual theology framework. According to Claire Selltiz et al, the purpose of research
is to discover answers to questions through the application of

scientific procedures.[2] And this can be achieved through a variety of means, including structured, semi-structured and unstructured methodologies. In attempting to understand the context of Caribbean British Christianity, this study was conducted using semi-structured and unstructured research methods. Throughout, I played the part of a participant-observer, a role that Tim May locates within the discipline of ethnographic research. He states:

> Participant observation is about engaging in a social scene, experiencing it and seeking to understand and explain it. The researcher is the medium through which this takes place.[3]

This process was adopted because my personal, professional and ministerial proximity to the 'subjects' of this study rendered it most appropriate. Such has been the relationship between Caribbean British Christianity and myself that I have indeed been a listener to, observer and experiencer of it for many more years than this study has been in progress.

I began by asking, 'What is the nature of the theological underpinning of the Black Church Movement in Britain since the 1950s?' Although I had been part of this scene since the late 1960s and had completed a Master's degree which examined the future of a local 'Black majority' church, I had not specifically studied the theological underpinning of the movement as a whole. However, I found it necessary to make some decisions early on in order to guide the study. First, I narrowed my initial interest in the wider Black British Church Movement to focus on the narrower subject of Caribbean British Christianity. Second, I further focused the study on the ethno-religious experience of Caribbean British Christians, not on their entire life and experience. This is because in Britain it is the ethnicity and faith of Caribbean British Christians that are the two attributes that most define them and, therefore, the most pertinent to monitor and study. Finally, I decided that the study would work best if located overtly within the hermeneutical framework of 'contextual theology'. The particular model used in the study adheres to

John Vincent's theory of a three-part process for doing contextual theology.[4] Vincent suggests that 'in-depth situational
analysis', coupled with identifying a 'contextual biblical
antecedent', produces a new 'contextual theology'. I expected
that this narrower contextual focus upon Caribbean British
Christianity, rather than the wider remit of the Black Church
Movement, was more likely to produce the desired result.

To achieve my aim of discovering what I now call the 'holy
grail' of Caribbean British Christianity – that is, their sustain-
ing theological self-understanding – I pursued three research
initiatives. These were semi-structured initiatives, and are
highlighted in Chapter 4. In addition, unstructured initiatives
were undertaken, including visits to local church services,
regional and national conventions, concerts, seminars and
social events, involving a wide range of Black-led and mainstream denominations. From these, I got a 'feel' for what was
being preached, discussed and sung about. This has been very
helpful in providing supporting evidence for other information, which has been gathered by the previously mentioned
semi-structured method. As an insider, I have been mindful
of the potential dangers of the covert, or insider researcher, as
highlighted by Martin Bulmer. He warns against missing
some of the pertinent issues, or of being biased in the ones I
have chosen to include.[5] I believe that the outcome of this
work will indicate that a reasonable balance was struck in
terms of the issues highlighted and that the semi-structured
and unstructured methods were appropriate for the research
conducted in this context.

In working with Vincent's contextual model, first, there is
an in-depth study, critique and evaluation of Caribbean
British Christianity's situation 'from below'; that is, in a manner that draws upon the sources and resources of the people
in the situation. To do this I utilized literary, oral and personal
sources from within Caribbean British Christianity, as far
as possible. However, in order to ensure breadth and depth,
I sometimes utilized other reliable and relevant available
sources. My major objective was to ensure that the 'voices'
within the context are heard, understood and noted, thereby
ensuring the relevance of the research.

The call for in-depth critical research as a means to greater understanding comes from the Caribbean British Christians themselves. For example, Mark Sturge's plea, 'Don't dis me if you don't know me',[6] is one such demand for the kind of knowing that can only come from in-depth study, critique and evaluation. Sturge's words imply, for example, that a proper knowledge base needs to be in place before we make up our minds concerning the character of another person or group. And the popular viewpoint of Caribbean British Christianity is that this process of 'getting to know' is best facilitated by information that is provided by the people themselves. This is what Elaine Foster calls 'weh dem sey' – Jamaican patois for 'what the people say'.[7] That people need to tell their own stories cannot be overemphasized, and this study provided the opportunity for this to happen as a contribution towards greater understanding.

Throughout the study, the message contained in the words of Paul Grant and Raj Patel, embedded in the title of their anthology *A Time to Speak*,[8] has been a constant reminder of the degree to which Caribbean British Christians are determined to articulate their own stories. Getting a view from the grassroots of Caribbean British Christianity has been ensured by conducting parts of the study through a range of localized initiatives and sources, oral and literary. Some were set up specifically for this study, while others were drawn from existing sources. All in their own way highlight my determination to honour the call to self-articulation.

Another aspect of Vincent's methodology for contextual theology is to engage in an analytical, critical reading and discernment of an appropriate biblical or theological tradition. My aim is to find such an antecedent for the experience of Caribbean British Christians. This has been a significant pursuit for at least two reasons. In the first place, Black-led churches in general and Caribbean British Christianity in particular have an enduring love and deep regard for the Bible as their holy book. This has become abundantly evident in the unstructured research done on visits to various services and events where the Bible enjoys unchallenged supremacy and authority. As Selwyn Arnold makes clear, these churches view themselves as 'Bible-based', 'biblically-centred', or 'Bible-believing'.[9] This means that the Bible takes pride of place in determining the belief system and religious culture of this people as individuals and as Christian organizations. The esteem with which the Bible is held may not be unique among Christian communities, but it is certainly very evident here.

It was in these churches that I heard songs such as,

> The b-i-b-l-e
> That's the book for me
> I stand alone on the word of God
> The b-i-b-l-e.

Joel Edwards demonstrates well the degree to which the Bible is integral to Black worship when he writes about the in-depth knowledge of Caribbean British Christianity that is evident in both preacher and congregation.[10] He says that a responsive church will often read the preacher's text aloud and offer an appropriate concluding sentence or Bible verse. This and other expressions of love for scripture were evident in all the churches I visited. However, I found familiarity with the Bible should not be confused with theological understanding; although Caribbean British Christians knew well where to find biblical passages or stories, theological and doctrinal understanding sometimes lagged behind.[11]

The Bible seems to perform two key functions in the churches peopled by Caribbean British Christians. First, it is the book from which doctrines are developed for teaching people how to live. It is therefore very much in evidence during preaching and study classes. Second, it is used as a tool for meditation and reflection. People read it in the mornings and evenings, it will be with them on the bus and around the dinner table. And because this is the living Word of God, it is not thought necessary to have everything interpreted just right, because God the author will teach the reader what he or she needs to know and understand from the Bible.

A second reason why finding a biblical/theological antecedent has been important is that given the high regard in which Caribbean British Christians hold the Bible, to discover stories within it that resonate with their life is an affirming experience. This is particularly the case since Caribbean British Christians believe that they are called to 'tread where the saints have trod'.[12] All this has made demonstrating resonance between the biblical and contemporary experiences highly desirable.

The third aspect of Vincent's methodology is to bring together the two bodies of material, from the in-depth study of Caribbean British Christianity and the biblical antecedent, in a dynamic interplay to produce a new contextual theology. Clearly, when Caribbean British Christianity's experience is brought into dialogue with a biblical antecedent, the situation demands discernment as to what the one has to 'say' to and about the other. Caribbean British Christian experience has to be understood in light of scripture and vice versa, giving primacy to scripture without relegating experience to an irrelevance. This dialogue between Caribbean British Christianity's experience and theology, or the Bible, is what some Black theologians call 'Black God-talk'.[13] The main outcome of this interplay is the theology that has emerged as the sum of this discernment, producing 'God's Word' in and for our situation and our time. Having examined the methodology used in the study, my next task is to analyse the nature and various aspects that comprise the context of Caribbean British Christianity.

Context

In its root form, 'context' refers to the parts of a book or other writings that immediately precede or follow a quotation.[14] It is to condition a quotation within a text. By implication, therefore, context is the shared space in which different influences interact, in which old and new are reconciled. Relational challenges arise from the different influences within the contextual space, those which have been there of old and those which have newly arrived. Robin Petersen states that context reflects the inherently plural nature of life and its apparently irreducible differences.[15] It is a space of toing and froing, of competition and reconciliation of people and things. Diana Hayes points out also that within context there are sub-contexts to which people belong situationally.[16] This means that there is inter-contextual diversity and each person has premier and minor contextual belongings, which vary depending on their situation. This leads to a rotation of major and minor identities varying from individual to individual and from context to context. For example, I am a member of a minority ethnic group (in Britain), I am Black, Caribbean, Jamaican, male, Christian and a bishop; not to mention son, sibling, husband, father, friend and colleague. Although I am all of these and more, each of these takes its turn to be my premier identity. Contexts and contextual belongings with their many subtexts are, therefore, highly dynamic phenomena that pose real challenges to the process of reconciliation, or contextualization. Therefore, including the Caribbean British community, no one has any single identity all of the time.

The context of Caribbean British Christianity in which this study is conducted is a complex one that covers a wide range of experiences. In order to describe it in all its complexity I have taken into account traditional influences of social, political and economic factors.[17] While all three areas are of importance, the social dimension is central to the development of this study; and within this, religious and ethnic identities. It is by these two main characteristics that Caribbean British Christians are identified in British society as 'Black Christians'. Along with the triumvirate factors of social, political and economic influences, I consider 'time' to be an essential component in analysing the context of Caribbean British Christianity. As Musa Dube and Jeffrey Staley argue, in a 'post-colonial' era, former colonial subjects, now free citizens of the world, become travellers across space and time.[18] Given the degree to which Caribbean British Christians and their antecedents have travelled, and the close relationship between travel and time, it seems appropriate to highlight this as a key factor in discussing the context. In my analysis of the context of Caribbean British Christianity I look at past, present and future and add these factors to the traditional ones of political, economic and social. These act as windows allowing light to shine on the meaning of context. What follows is a brief overview of some of the influences that have impacted upon, and give a greater understanding of, Caribbean British Christianity's context. I begin with historic influences.

Past

As with all people, their history is of the utmost importance to Caribbean British Christians. Notably, the first theological journal emanating from Black Christians in Britain includes the word 'contextual' in its title and argues for the widest reach in defining the situation of Caribbean British Christianity.[19] In so doing, the journal signals a link between history and context. The context of Black Christians in Britain, according to its editor, spans a historical period from the third century to the present. A clear objective of the journal is to inform the reader concerning the proper context of Black Christian people in Britain, information that acts as a corrective to the popular belief that this presence dates only from the late 1940s with the arrival of the *Windrush*, for example. The *Windrush*, the troopship which docked at Tilbury in late 1948 with the first substantial 'cargo' of Caribbean migrants in modern times, has since come to symbolize the Black presence in Britain.[20]

In analysing the context of Caribbean British Christians, I have taken some cognizance of their past, recognizing that they appear proud of their history and keen to have it known that they are no 'Johnny come lately'. At least two inclinations of Caribbean British Christian existence are considered within the sphere of their historicity. The first is simply a commitment to embrace the past, in both its negative and its positive connotations, since the present is meaningless without it. Clodovis Boff, writing as a (Latin American) liberation theologian, argues that in relation to the 'oppressed', their present situation must be understood as a terminus of an entire, broad process and, therefore, part of the journey of history.[21] In other words, the present is not the whole story of a people;

it is merely the latest point of the life journey of that people with their ups and downs. There can be many reference points. For example, Doreen Morrison links Caribbean British Christians' past with the racism of the 1960s in Britain, that was fuelled by Enoch Powell and typified by his 'rivers of blood' speech.[22] However, Eric Pemberton prefers to recall the importance to contemporary religious expression of the Slave Religion of the Caribbean.[23] The historical journey of Caribbean British Christians is, therefore, of great significance when attempting to understand their context. The past must be embraced, but its reference points are open to interpretation. This study takes account of various experiences and influences, both secular and religious, that have shaped Caribbean British Christian lives.

Second, a holistic approach is adopted in considering the history of Caribbean British Christianity, thereby refusing to become sidetracked by single events such as slavery and colonialism, however significant these may be in their own right. Often the history of Caribbean people is equated narrowly with on the one hand slavery and colonialism, and on the other Pentecostalism as their designated faith. The reality is much more diverse and complex. Caribbean British Christianity is much more than the sum of slavery, colonialism and Pentecostalism. The whole of this people's history, not just a selective part, has to be considered in any analysis of their context. Anthony Browder makes this point in his recounting of the history of Black contributions to world civilization.[24] We cannot truly embrace a present that is divorced from our past.

Present

The present is regarded as only one part of the context of Caribbean British Christianity, not the whole. However, it is important to form a proper view of the present situation, that is, not one that is disproportionately rooted in a romantic past or in an idealistic future. To do this, the analysis of Caribbean British Christianity needs to be grounded firmly in the actual social, political and economic realities of the present; even as we have learned from the past and anticipate the future. A good example of a commitment to understand people in their current state is articulated by Inderjit Bhogal in his writing about his year as President of the Methodist Conference in 2000/1. Bhogal contends that in order to gain an accurate understanding of the plight of those in difficult situations in Britain, he needs to meet real people in real situations, particularly those who are hurting, who feel disadvantaged, or who are on the periphery of society.[25] When this is applied to Caribbean British Christians, I bear in mind the reality that their contemporary experience is multi-dimensional. For example, while in overall terms minorities suffer disadvantage, are excluded, or are on the periphery, not all of them suffer in these ways. Some appear to do well and are very much a part of the mainstream, while others really are excluded. A challenge for this study, therefore, is to gain an understanding of Caribbean British Christianity that is a true reflection of their diverse setting in the current British situation. Contemporary experience is about immediate realities, yet not without reference to the past and the future.

Future

The future impacts upon, and in a real way is part of, the context of Caribbean British Christianity in that contemporary experiences are affected by their hope for the future. Mostly, this is evident in their belief that irrespective of the conditions of life in the here and now, heaven awaits the faithful. Indeed, it has been a common saying among Caribbean British Christians that some are 'so heavenly-minded that they are no earthly good'. The eschatological debate among Caribbean British and other Black Christians takes various forms and has a significant effect upon their behaviour. African American theologian James Cone criticizes the idea of heaven with its emphasis on reward in the next world as irrelevant.[26] Caribbean British Christians certainly do not regard heaven as irrelevant, but they would agree with Cone that eschatological hope must also be inseparably linked to what God has done, is doing and will do in the world. Based upon faith in what God has done and is doing, Christians can speak meaningfully of the future.[27] In terms of how Caribbean British Christians perceive the link between their context and the future, S. E. Arnold highlights the need for them to develop a better balance between 'this-worldly' and 'other-worldly' concerns, in a study that highlights and promotes the need for greater social responsibility by Caribbean British Christians.[28] Arnold, however, envisages significant challenges in making this shift to focus on the social, physical and emotional aspects of Caribbean British Christians, while maintaining a real belief in and hope for heaven in the life after this one. Getting a correct balance between being 'this-worldly' and 'other-worldly' is a perennial challenge for Caribbean British Christianity, but it is evident that one way or another, hope for the future is an important aspect of their context.

Social and political issues

The term 'social' covers a wide range of issues that have impacted upon the experience of Caribbean British Christians in past, present and future. Some of these social categories are education, employment, housing, health and religion. While this is by no means an exhaustive list, it is widely accepted that minority ethnic people in Britain, of which Caribbean British Christians are a part, are adversely affected by almost every measurable social indicator.[29] This poses real challenges to Caribbean British Christianity and their attempt to co-exist in Britain on an equal footing with the majority culture.

The context of Caribbean British Christianity is influenced by politics in a number of ways. For example, political decisions opened up the opportunities for them to be in Britain in the first place. As Peter Fryer points out, changes to the 1948 British Nationality Act granted Caribbean people the right to come and stay in Britain as citizens of Britain's colonies and former colonies.[30] Politics also affects their lives as religious communities. Roswith Gerloff argues that White American church headquarters were engaged in (politically inspired) divide and rule practices that influenced the development of Caribbean British Christianity, as those headquarters seized the opportunity to get footholds in Europe.[31] There is little evidence of this, much more of Black fellowships and individuals willingly aligning themselves to overseas denominations. But the reality for Caribbean British Christianity is that in myriad ways politics influence their existence outside and inside the Church. Another aspect to contextual politics is that which asks questions concerning the willingness, or not as the case might be, to challenge principalities and powers, or what Maxine Howell-Baker and Tonya Bolton call 'structural evil'.[32]

There is growing evidence of involvement in politics beyond the narrow confines of church members' immediate interests. For example, whereas it has been true that Black Christians seemed averse to political engagement, many are involved with local politics as counsellors, some are involved with the judiciary as Justice of the Peace, and the Council of Black-led Churches is engaging political and civic leaders about their concerns in education, health, housing and employment. The leaders of Caribbean British churches are not yet as politically active as their American counterparts, but there are signs that things are leaning in that direction.

Economy

Economics have impacted on the experience of Caribbean British Christians, going back to their very origin. The coming together of Europeans, Africans and Asians in the Caribbean from the fifteenth century onwards was, among other factors, economically driven. According to Eric Williams, this influence has its root in the economic greed that was the impetus for slavery and colonialism.[33] Then the 1950s people movement from the Caribbean was certainly an economic migration, as young people came to Britain in search of a better life for themselves and their families.[34] Even today, where Caribbean British Christians live is largely economically determined, with the majority living in Britain's inner cities and former industrialized centres. However, during the study it has become apparent that some Caribbean British Christians enjoy a kind of redemption and lift whereby, though they may be on relatively low pay, their aspirational and frugal attitudes mean that they enjoy greater financial prosperity than might otherwise be the case. From that position, Caribbean British Christians support their churches, allowing Black-led denominations to be self-sufficient, acquire buildings, and to exist in secured spaces. Economics have therefore always played a key role in the experience of Caribbean British Christians.

Culture

As in other areas of their existence, the culture of Caribbean British Christians is part of a wider phenomenon that determines the manner of their behaviour and the response of others towards them. 'Culture' is used here to imply the popular expressive behaviours of Caribbean British Christians. For example, the degree to which cultural difference in worship styles makes it difficult for Caribbean British Christians to settle easily among White British worshippers, and vice versa, should not be underestimated. Some of these characteristics are very evident, such as a greater propensity to dress up for church, livelier forms of expressive communal worship, a stricter approach to discipline in family and religious circles, to name but a few. In analysing Caribbean British Christianity then, due regard has to be paid to the cultural aspect of their experience. Many Caribbean British Christian writers provide exposés of Caribbean British Christian culture, none more so than Joel Edwards' anthology, to which I will refer later.[35] Another key social-cultural area of Caribbean British Christian experience that warrants closer examination within the study is ethnicity.

Ethnicity

Ethnicity receives special attention in this study as a key area of research and analysis. I use the term 'ethnicity' in preference to 'race' in an effort to convey my understanding that the latter is an unhelpful and divisive, largely Western, terminology.[36] This work proceeds on the basis that there is only one race: the human race, which is made up of different ethnic groups. 'Ethnic' is a derivative of the Greek *ethnos*, signifying a people, nation, or what Theo Tschuy calls 'blood and belonging'.[37] The term has come to mean people of a common culture, language and sometimes religion, though not in any exclusive sense. As Immanuel Wallerstein points out, these categories are dynamic and not easily subject to boundaries of definition.[38] Wallerstein shows that ethnic groups do not easily conform to particular nation-state boundaries because culture expressed as language, religion and customs often occurs across national boundaries. Indeed, the concept of the nation-state is one that occurs relatively late in history.

Paul Gilroy emphasizes this sense of the dynamism and fluidity of ethnicity by saying that it is neither fixed nor impenetrable; rather, it is syncretistic. Its forms change, develop, combine and are dispersed in historical processes.[39] Ranjit Sondhi describes trying to pin down ethnicity as like attempting to divide a globe of mercury into three equal parts.[40] So, while to speak of ethnicity is to speak generally of 'blood and belonging', it is an imprecise terminology. People's identities are fragmented, multiple and situational, in which, according to Sondhi again, ethnicity is not the one difference that makes all the difference. Stephen Small comments that in racialized relations, the language employed is not only imprecise but entails a series of assumptions that may be false and misleading.[41] Notwithstanding these limitations, I am arguing that the ethnicity of Caribbean British people today is linked to the coming together of different ethnic groups in the Caribbean over the past 500 years.

The term 'ethnic' has emerged in a pluralistic British society as a premier means of articulating difference between people groups, especially between the majority and minority

ethnic groups.[42] The press, media and people in public life
make frequent references to Britain's 'ethnic' communities,
sometimes describing individuals or groups as being from 'an
ethnic background'. This inference was particularly evident
in the reporting and analysis of the 2001 social disturbances in
Bradford, Oldham and Leeds in which Asian and White
youths featured. In a recent television interview, I heard the
Conservative leader of the Opposition say, 'One of my deputy
chairmen is from an ethnic background.' This was said
against the backdrop of the Conservative Party attempting to
improve relations between them and the minority ethnic communities in Britain. I wondered whether the others were without ethnicity. In this and other instances, 'ethnic' is used as a
signifier for 'not White', which reintroduces an old British
imperialist application dating as far back as the fifteenth century, whereby non-Christian foreign nations and their people
were termed 'ethnic people', meaning pagan or heathen.[43]

Because of these associations, I find that politically sensitive African, Asian and Caribbean-descended people in
Britain are often antagonistic towards the term 'ethnic' when
used in the manner described above. It was in response to this
misuse of the term in mainstream British culture that, in a fit
of righteous anger, I used the headline 'Give Whites back
their ethnicity' in an issue of *Partnership News*.[44] The article
sought to point out that everybody has an ethnicity and that
use of the term by the majority to describe 'other' minorities
is inappropriate in a multi-ethnic society. Because ethnicity is
a major identifier in Britain, and in one form or another one
that often impacts negatively upon Caribbean British people,
it is made a major topic of inquiry in this work. In Britain,
there is an ethnic majority in the same way that there are
ethnic minorities. Ethnicity is located in the context of
Caribbean British Christians' humanity, within which addi-
tional facets of gender, sexuality and age are also at work.
While these aspects of human existence are worthy of exploration, within this study they are not major identity deter-
minants for a people popularly known as 'Black Christians',
for the reasons cited above.

Gender

In terms of gender, the battle of the sexes still rages. The work of women like Valentina Alexander[45] and several contributors to my anthology *Sisters with Power*[46] testifies to their discontent with the degree to which British Black women in the Churches are not viewed and embraced as the equal of the 'brothers'. The 'sisters' clearly feel that Caribbean British Christianity is a patriarchal space in which matriarchy is subdued and has little if any legitimate existence. This resonates with the view of African American womanist theologian Jacquelyn Grant, who argues that the locus of womanist theology is to be found in the context of their experiences and struggles in the church and wider society. Grant lists some of the experiential factors that affect women and which must impact their theology as historical, political, psychological, social, and religious circumstances.[47] Unless these factors are taken into account, it cannot reasonably be argued that any emergent God-talk represents women's concerns. Grant's call for the inclusion of the female voice within the Black American context resonates with that of Black Christian women in Britain. There may have been a time when Caribbean British women accepted the status quo, but they no longer do so.

Sexuality

Caribbean British churches teach and attempt to uphold a high moral standard in sexual and all other matters to do with the body. Yet in many respects, this is a highly sensual space with lots of dancing to rhythmic music, indulgence in sometimes ostentatious dress sense, and great emphasis upon marriage and child-bearing. There are areas of tension too, such as teaching on abstinence from sexual activity outside of marriage. Probably the most problematic area is that of homosexuality. In almost every circle that I have been in, Black-led church practitioners, if given the slightest opportunity, will expose their disapproving attitude towards same-gender sexual relationships. Homosexuality is regularly preached against in pulpits. During the row that flared up about the proposed appointment by the Church of England of a gay bishop in Reading, although they did not speak publicly, there is little doubt about where Caribbean British Christianity in general and Black-led churches in particular stood on the issue. It will be interesting to observe how the relationship between the Church of England and Caribbean British Christians evolves in the years ahead, particularly if the Church of England were to change its view on the ministry of clergy in gay relationships.

Robert Beckford, in his first book, *Jesus is Dread*,[48] calls for a more liberal approach towards homosexuality in Black churches. As of now, there is no evidence that his call is being heeded. Sexuality in Caribbean British Christianity extends beyond homosexuality, also, to the sexual norms of single people who are expected to be celibate, and married people who are expected to be monogamous. Caribbean British Christians' general position is that the only legitimate expression of sexuality is that between male and female within the framework of marriage. A strict code of dress, such as 'high enough neckline and low enough hemline' is reflective of attempts to moderate the expression of sexuality in the Churches.[49]

Age

The influence of age cannot be overestimated when considering the Caribbean British Christian situation. Historically, it has been young people who have ventured out in patterns of migration, settling down, rearing children who then become the youths who challenge the norms of their elders, thereby keeping the generational cycle moving. They were young people who travelled to Britain in the 1950s and launched the Black Church Movement, of which Caribbean British Christianity is a part. In a recent work, Anthony Reddie offers some powerful insights into this cyclic development in Britain, depicting some of the challenges of inter-generational dialogue and relationships, such as passing on to succeeding generations a sense of their culture and heritage.[50] Several other writers have developed themes around the way ahead for Caribbean British Christianity's young people, with the usual call for greater focus upon Afro-centricity as a means of providing a relevant and historically rooted social identity for them.[51] However, my central point here is that progression of life is a significant factor in the context of Caribbean British Christianity.

What I have been describing is the scope and extent of the context of Caribbean British Christianity within which their experience takes place. While all the above are important for this study, much of it is only implied in the detailed analysis, because the study has to be kept within manageable limits. Because of this, in the next chapter the analysis of the situation of Caribbean British Christianity will focus primarily on developments in the area of their ethnicity and faith. Having looked at the nature of the context within which they operate, I turn to an exploration of the nature of the theological project which is under way.

Theology

What follows is an examination of 'theology' and its forms within Caribbean British Christianity's context. That this study is called 'contextual theology' is indicative of the Caribbean British setting within which the study has been conducted, not that this is something 'other' than theology as such. Alister McGrath reminds us that the technical meaning of 'theology' can be seen by breaking it down into the two Greek words from which it is derived: *theos* (God) and *logos* (word).[52] Although words are not the only medium of reflecting upon God, they are highly significant in human communication. This composite meaning implies the use of words about God. Therefore, theology is the discourse humans engage in when attempting to make sense of the God Christians believe made the world and the relationship between that God and God's creation, including humanity.[53] McGrath states that at the heart of the theology project lies a human attempt, however inadequate, to speak about the divine being.[54] This project might be called, therefore, the God-talk of Caribbean British Christianity.

However, *logos* also alludes to wisdom and reason, as discussed later in Chapter 5. This indicates that 'God-talk' needs to be appropriately informed if it is to be more than empty babble. It also points to a second aspect of theology as discussed by Karl Rahner, who emphasizes the intellectual and academic elements of theology stating that theology is the science of faith, the conscious and methodical explanation and explication of the divine revelation received and grasped in faith.[55] This may take the form of a systematic analysis of the nature, purpose and activity of God, whether engaged in orally or literarily. In reality, theology as informed God-talk is little contested, if at all. What is not always embraced is the understanding that theologizing takes place in different settings and that the setting, including quality or lack of quality of information, largely determines the nature of the emergent theology. The theology that is presented in this study can be described as informed God-talk, and the information that directs the debate is taken from the context of Caribbean British Christianity's experience. This is what is implied by the term 'contextual theology' which has been developed here: a reflection upon God, using words, that is informed by the experience of the people engaged in the reflection.

Contextual theologies

As John de Gruchy points out, all theology is contextual, including Western European Theology, because every theology develops within a particular historical, political and cultural context and has been shaped by it.[56] This is said against a background where theology that has been done in the West by westerners has tended to be regarded as normative. Yet, clearly, 'Western Europe' is a particular context and the theology done there is a contextual theology. This work has deliberately and explicitly sought to add to traditional western sources like scripture, reason, tradition and revelation other sources of contextual significance to Caribbean British Christianity. As indicated above, some of these are time (past, present and future), social and politics issues, economics, culture, ethnicity, gender, sexuality and age. In this study, the contextual interplay corresponds to what Bevans calls an 'unabashedly subjective' space.[57] In this contextual space, new ideas are introduced into old situations, thereby creating relationships in which the new is reconciled with the old, bringing about something more new. Contextual theology, then, is the informed God-talk that takes place with full cognizance of the circumstances that inform a person's or people's experience within their situation. As Walter Elwell suggests, contextual theology grows out of the historical and contemporary scene and thought of a people.[58]

John Vincent argues that since all theologies are contextual, to make 'contextual' an up-front prefix to 'theology' is to make virtue out of necessity. Contextual theology, he says,

> is determined by, answering to, and hopefully making distinctive contributions within, a then current human and historical situation, a context describable in social, cultural, class, psychological and historical terms.[59]

Each context, because of its particular circumstances, will articulate an understanding of God and the world that answers the questions posed by its particular setting. Vincent offers the following working definition:

> A contextual theology sets out a version of Christian faith, discipleship and philosophy produced by the practice of specific Christians, and their reflection on that practice, within a certain historical, social, cultural, political and class situation.[60]

This is precisely what this project sets out to achieve by conducting the study of Caribbean British Christian theology within the framework of their experience in the social, political, economic and other appropriate spheres.

Modern 'theology' uses suffixes like Liberation, Black, Asian, African, Third World, thereby demonstrating difference. So too, 'contextual' expresses the difference of settings in which the appropriate models or approaches are advocated. David Ford states that there are three main arenas within which contextual theologies, or God-talk, occurs and is shaped; these are the academy, the churches and society.[61] In the academic context, practitioners are necessarily concerned with critique and textual correctness; however, the academy also needs to connect with the realities outside the study centre. In the churches clergy and laity are concerned with doctrinal norms and codes for living. Again, churches are challenged to move beyond their four walls and narrow communities to address the issues of concern to society at large. In wider society, a theology is needed that makes sense to people who may not go to church. A contextual theology will speak to people where they are, in their context. Again Ford argues that

> Nineteenth- and twentieth-century historical and sociological insights urge theologians to take fuller account of the situation in which theology is done and for whom and by whom it is done. The history of ideas is not enough. Theology needs to be seen in relation to the many forces and events helping to shape it.[62]

Because theology is not best conducted and produced in a vacuum, untouched by contextual factors, this thesis is deliberately 'contextual' by adhering to the principle of taking seriously the forces and events affecting the lives of Caribbean British Christians. It takes for granted that theological analysis is never conducted outside of a particular context, or, contexts, however narrowly or broadly defined. As Emmanuel Lartey makes clear, when some argue, 'surely there is only one theology', they are correct in that every theology is contextual, but they are incorrect in that there are multiple contexts in which individuals, groups and communities exist and theologize.[63]

The idea that any theological form is something pre-packaged, supra- or a-cultural and therefore beyond influence, is alien to the sentiments of this work, which believes that contextualization is no modern neologism but a necessity rooted in the very concept of doing theology.[64] In every situation where theology is done, there are explicit and implicit factors that shape the realities of that space. What is sometimes missing is a consciousness of the degree to which what is being done in the name of theology is influenced by the circumstances of the space within which the theology is being developed. It is important that theology is owned by and resonates with the real experience in the context in which it purports to be set.

Finally, in addition to the work of 'outsiders', I believe that there is an invaluable work that is to be done by 'insiders', and this study is primarily an insider's view. It is an objective and subjective attempt to understand better, and assist in shaping and making explicit the theological infrastructure that sustains this egalitarian community, by an examination of its historic and contemporary experience and future hope. As Ford suggests, the better way to do theology is by being in touch with the issues that affect the people in the situation or context in which that theology is being discovered and or constructed. When people's contextual experience is taken seriously, the resultant theology stands a good chance of being owned by the context that has contributed to shaping it. There has been a certain distance between the Black Church and the theologies that have been developed around and about them in recent years. The context of Caribbean British Christianity that is under discussion here, then, seeks to embrace their historical and contemporary experience and future hopes, focusing particularly on the crucial area of ethno-religious experience. Contextual theology has parallels with, but is different in form and emphasis from, other similar theologies, of which two are worthy of significant mention: liberation theology and Black theology. Indeed, I argue that both are forms of contextual theology.

Liberation theology

Liberation theology operates by making the experience of the poor and oppressed its central tenet, and in turn makes liberation its central goal.[65] This, then, is essentially a theology of and for the poor and oppressed. But it is more than that. Liberation theology is the theology of those who accept 'poor and oppressed' as their defining identity, and liberation as their defining life goal. In contextual theology, the experience of people within the context similarly takes centre stage and directs the theology that emerges, but it does not assume its subjects' primary identity to be that of 'poor and oppressed' and therefore necessarily in need of liberation. That is a matter to be discovered, not assumed.

A theology of liberation may emerge from a contextual theology, if that is what naturally emerges in that context. The need to keep an open mind is exemplified by the work of Wang Hsien-Chih in discussing the Taiwanese situation. The people Wang speaks of have been dominated, suppressed and exploited by foreigners, especially the Japanese and Chinese, and have as a result developed a 'homeland theology' out of their longing for peace and security at home. For the Taiwanese context, four key homeland theological themes have emerged: people, land, power and God.[66] These 'sources' may not fit easily with the liberation theology model of utilizing sources such as social, political and economic, or traditional western theological sources of scripture, reason, tradition and inspiration, but in the Taiwanese context, Wang believes them to be relevant in developing an appropriate theology.

Vincent states that for liberation theology to be done there must be both the experience of oppression and the perceivable reality of oppression.[67] There needs also to be an acceptance within the context that a primary relationship of oppressor and oppressed exists. It is the contention of this writer that although there exist in British society significant elements of racism, to describe the situation of Caribbean British Christianity as primarily one of oppression is to overstate and exaggerate the case. As will be demonstrated later, their existence as Caribbean British Christians is certainly not one that is defined exclusively, or overwhelmingly, in terms of their experience of and response to oppression. Rather, oppression is but one of their experiences, and it is not *the* one that defines them. Although some of my contemporaries take a different line on this and speak much of a concern for 'Black liberation',[68] I argue that what they often do is to transpose uncritically US concepts of Black (Liberation) Theology into the British context. A Black theology of liberation can only ever be one strand of Black theology in Britain, not its only focus. It certainly is not the main focus of Caribbean British Christianity, I argue.

James Cone insists that the definition of theology and the issues to which that theology addresses itself must emerge out of the life of that society and be subjected to re-analysis in every age and, I may say, every context.[69] To understand the British context as an exact parallel of Latin American or the US contexts reflects a kind of transatlantic mismatch such as happens when British people appear to use the term 'African Caribbean' as a simile for 'African American'. Evidently, African American quite properly describes the ethnic and historical place of Americans of African heritage. However, African Caribbean does not speak similarly for Caribbean people in Britain of African heritage. This is because the term African Caribbean falls short by not referring to their present location in Britain and the obvious British identity that goes with it. It is therefore inappropriate for Caribbean descended people in Britain who have been twice, not once, removed from Africa, to be simply named African Caribbean, since the term clearly omits reference to people's British identity. African Caribbean also assumes a homogeneous African identity for all Caribbean people. This is clearly not the case since as will be shown, Caribbean identity is heterogeneous in almost every way.

As stated above, to suggest, as some of my colleagues do, that the contemporary context of Caribbean British Christianity is defined overarchingly in terms of neo-slavery and neo-colonialism is to be disingenuous to the relational reformation that has taken place in society at large and to the 'upstandishness' of the descendants of former slaves and colonial subjects since the 1950s.[70] The practice of utilizing the slave-master/slave dialectic in the twenty-first century perpetuates the unworthy concept that what Caribbean people are at their core is rooted in that relationship and that their world-view is defined by it. It also risks making the descendants of slaves damagingly slave-minded, always having to understand their human existence through the prism of a negative identity. Slave heritage is part, not the whole, of the human experience of Caribbean people, whose antecedents predate the European slave trade in Africans by thousands of years. Such a historic people would be ill advised to perpetuate an existence that is describable only by reference to their slave heritage. They were and are, first and foremost, human beings: mothers, fathers, sisters, brothers, entrepreneurs, inventors, ministers, doctors and a whole lot beside: not just slaves, colonized and oppressed. The oppression/liberation dialectic is, therefore, not to the fore of this work. The struggle against racism and oppression can be engaged in by adopting a different focus, as this study will show.

Black theology

In addition to liberation theology, Black theology is another discipline with which this work naturally resonates, yet differs. Although 'Black theology' is now used more universally, it is generally applied to the form of theologizing that has emerged in the US context since the 1960s. It is itself a contextual theology. Cone reminds us:

> From the beginning, Black theology was understood by its creators as Christian theological reflection upon the Black struggle for justice and liberation, strongly influenced by the life and thought of Martin Luther King, Jr.[71]

The background to this development, according to Cone, consists of three major phases. The first phase was the Civil Rights movement of the 1950s and 1960s that campaigned for equal rights of Black people in American society. The second was the publication of Joseph Washington's book *Black Religion*, which argued that Black religion was the illegitimate 'child' of Black exclusion from the genuine Christian faith. Washington regarded this as mere folk religion. The third phase was the Black Power Movement spearheaded by Malcolm X, which pursued a militant strategy, arguing that the dream of multi-ethnic integration was a nightmare for Black people. For X, the overthrow of White power must be achieved by 'any means necessary'. Aspects of this beginning resonate with the British context, but the two are not the same. For example, the laws of Britain do not support racism in the way that US society operated at the time in which Malcolm X and Martin Luther King worked for liberation. The theological developments that emerged in the United States came straight out of the difficult social melting pot that was the nation of that time. Therefore, a theology fit for Britain in the twenty-first century cannot simply mimic the United States of the nineteenth and twentieth centuries. While these were legitimate responses to the US context that led to the unearthing of Black theology, as Vincent points out, 'contextual theology cannot be done by "applying" a theology from outside, even another contextual theology'.[72] This study in contextual theology leaves open possibilities as to what imperatives emerge, including liberationist ones, but the starting point is different from that of Black theology, US style, and its outcome can be expected to be different too.

As happened in the United States, so in Britain also a Black theology has emerged that is distinctively both Black and British. It responds to the forces and events of Black life in Britain and is a theology 'made in Britain' by Black Christians. It is indeed a Black British Theology! However, it does not divorce itself from Black theology elsewhere in the world, rather it is a branch of Black theology in general. Because of this, I place the words in the order that indicates that the British version is a localized version of a greater phenomenon; hence 'Black British theology'. Emmanuel Lartey, editor of the flagship journal *Black Theology in Britain* (now renamed, *Black Theology: An International Journal*), describes this theological phenomenon as Black God-talk, or Black God-expression. This journal explores and reflects upon what Black people in Britain are thinking, feeling, saying and expressing about their experience of God.[73]

Black British theology is greatly influenced by Caribbean British Christianity, but the latter is only one expression of the former. Ideally, this operates alongside other expressions of British Black theologies such as African British theology and Asian British theology, to name two. This work is one expression of Black British theology as Caribbean British Christianity is one expression of Black British Christianity. In so far as I am aware, no one has previously attempted to articulate a Caribbean British theology. However, attempts at developing a Black British theology have been many, and in Chapter 4 I examine some such attempts with particular reference to the major study by the central figure in contemporary Black British theology, Robert Beckford.[74]

The above provides a sampling of the theological project that is the basis of this work. Before closing this first chapter on theology in context, I need to say something about my own place within the context.

The writer in the context

I am a male Caribbean British Christian, a bishop in a Black-led Pentecostal church, who currently works in the field of intercultural ecumenism and as a local pastor. I am an active participant in the context, being both intellectually and emotionally involved. My role as a contextual theologian resonates with Gramsci's notion of the 'organic intellectual'. Gramsci describes such a person as one who is a product of his or her community and who works from within it as a constructor, organizer, and persuader, helping to create a counter-hegemony, a new norm, in the midst of a hostile or ill-informed environment.[75] Every church and context needs its own organic intellectuals to speak prophetically inward and apologetically externally.

However, I have tended to be a critical-prophetic voice inside and outside the Church calling for the total liberation of the people of God. James Cone argues:

> The Black church has always had outside critics from the time of its origin in slavery to contemporary Black and White scholars, especially amongst sociologists, psychologists and historians. But seldom has the Black Church created the context for prophetic criticism from within.[76]

I believe that the same is true for Black and other churches in the British context. The Caribbean British Christian community as expressed in Black-led churches in Britain, my own included, takes a dim view of what Cone calls 'self-criticism', that is, prophetic critique from within the church. It is often perceived to be an expression of disloyalty, because it is not confessional and uncritically affirming. In my experience, while Black-led churches have tolerated criticism from outsiders, those who have dared to be critical from inside have suffered hostility and sometimes outright ostracism and exclusion. Such intolerance poses a challenge for me as a bishop from within this context as I seek to subject my own tradition to critical analysis yet to remain in a position of leadership within it. I need to explain how I have got here and will do so by focusing upon five key areas of my own identity as Caribbean British, Christian, male, bishop and ecumenist.

First, my Caribbean British status begins with my birth in Jamaica to parents who typify, in many respects, the Caribbean identity espoused in this work. According to our family's oral tradition, my mother's immediate progenitors were of Asian and African stock. She herself was quite diminutive, light of complexion, with a straightish nose – a mixture of Asian and African in appearance. My father, like myself, on the other hand, was of pronounced African heritage and features. At the time of my birth Jamaica was still a British colony. This island country, widely vaunted as one of the most beautiful in the world, is described by Michael Manley, a former prime minister, as a microcosm of the Third World in terms of its colonial history, and as an 'abject object of imperial domination and exploitation' at around the mid

1900s.[77] At the time of my birth in the early 1950s, Jamaica's beauty was matched only by its economic poverty, and my family's surroundings in a deep rural part of the parish of St Catherine typified this condition. Without being aware of its full implications, I was one of two million flag-waving Jamaicans on 6 August 1962 when we became an independent country from Britain. However, by this time my father had become an economic migrant in Britain, and was soon followed by some of my ten siblings and later by my mother. In common with thousands of Caribbean minors, in 1968 I, too, made the journey to join my parents in England.

Being born in Jamaica under British colonial rule is one thing; living in England proved to be quite another. For example, it was not until my arrival in Birmingham at the age of 15 that I became aware of the significance of my skin pigmentation. Suddenly I was not just a boy, but a 'coloured boy'! Now, in 2005, I have been living in England for 37 years and am married with three daughters, all British-born. Having acquired British citizenship and a social status that this society regards as middle class, I no longer relate to Jamaica as 'home' in the way I did when I first arrived in England.

Neither, however, does England or Britain feel like 'home' in the way Jamaica did when I was a child. In the words of a Jamaican comedian of long ago, I am now a 'nowherian'. Put more positively, in the words of Yasmin Alibhai-Brown, I am part of the British Empire that has come home to the motherland; here, because White Britons did not resist the temptation to go out to the rest of the world to see, trade and conquer.[78] Part of living in Britain is the struggle to reconcile the hybridity of my Jamaican or Caribbean Britishness, knowing that this has come about because of the exploits of the progenitors of the White British majority-ethnic population. I, like many others, have lived in Britain for more than twice as long as I lived in the country of my birth and, determined to retain ownership of all my geo-history identity, I see myself as being of Caribbean British ethnicity. I am, however, acutely aware of the shortcomings that Alibhai-Brown points to when we see ourselves only as racial and ethnic creatures.[79]

Second, my Christian identity is also of great significance to whom I perceive myself to be and, I hope and believe, how others perceive me. This story begins in Jamaica also, where my parents, even before I was born, were members of the Bible Church of God, which later became known as the Church of God of Prophecy, a Pentecostal church with its international headquarters in the United States of America. According to Desmond Smith,[80] historian and son of the spiritual father of the denomination in Jamaica, R. C. Smith, this denomination was formalized around 1929 as a cluster of local indigenous congregations known as the 'Bible Church of God'. Soon, Smith Sr was being courted by the Pentecostal denomination from the United States, known as 'Church of God', which was anxious to gain a foothold on the island, and in the entire Caribbean and beyond.

The expansionist tendencies of the Church of God of Prophecy, based in Cleveland, Tennessee is well demonstrated in the denomination's history book.[81] In 1935 Smith had his airfare paid to attend the Church of God's international meeting in the USA, during which he was ordained a bishop. After many years of internal dispute between two factions of the Church of God concerning ownership of the name of the denomination, in 1952 the one with which Smith had affiliated was officially designated by court action to be called the Church of God of Prophecy. Smith, however, was allowed to continue to operate in Jamaica under the name Bible Church of God until 1964, when it officially adopted the international title Church of God of Prophecy.[82]

Having become a full member of the Bible Church of God in Jamaica at the age of 11, my memories of those early times revolve around my attempts to avoid some of the worst excesses of the restrictions my church attached to what it meant by 'living holy'. Much of this I perceived, and in some cases still perceive, as unnecessarily restrictive due to poor hermeneutics. It appears that the church's determination to demonstrate visible holiness traits introduced a supra-biblical culture that was given the same authority as scripture. For example, I fell in love with the game of cricket at an early age and discovered that the Bible Church of God believed that ball games fell into the category of 'worldly pleasure', not to be engaged in by those who were 'saved'. I would not, or could not, stop playing cricket with my mates and resorted to setting up the most elaborate evasion strategies to avoid being 'caught' playing by the church leaders. The church's 'Advice to Members'[83] reinforced this and many other taboos. For me, this brought about early reflection upon church teachings and what might be considered appropriate response to those ones that I found unreasonable, even oppressive. Later, as I became more theologically aware, I also became inclined to challenge church teachings that did not make sense to me.

I now can discern the historic shaping of my tendency to dissent as a reaction against a foreign power imposing in-appropriate rules that were policed by uncritical local cadres. This is akin to what Lewin Williams calls succinctly 'neo-colonialism', describing that as economic, social and political control by outside forces, yet often through the agency of inside privileged classes.[84] But, while my church 'taught' me to become machiavellian in my relationship with its teachings, by having to constantly seek ways of avoiding being caught breaking its rules and dissenting in trying to effect change, there was another impact on my understanding of Christian-ity that was developed in a parallel relationship: that with my mother. My mother radiated a quiet strength that provided care and protection of her children in the absence of her hus-band and an aloofness that rose above much of the triviality of church affairs and which found its sustenance in an unswerv-ing belief in God as Jehovah-Jireh, the one who will see to it, or fix it (Genesis 22.14). She would often sing a popular chorus,

> Let Jesus fix it for you
> He knows what to do
> Whenever you pray
> Let God have his way
> And he will fix it for you.

I do not recall hearing my mother pray any of the powerful and audible prayers that were commonly heard in our church in Jamaica and later in England, but none of us siblings could miss those she prayed in her bedroom, during which the names of all her children would be mentioned passionately to God. It was as though she created God's throne room in her bedroom, to the extent that her prayers and life of faith did not depend only upon what happened in the church, although she did not lightly miss church services. This appeared to be more about fellowship with fellow Christians, less about meeting God there. It is little surprise to me that I have developed and retained both my dissenting and challenging attitude to church where it appears not to liberate but to bind, as well as an unswerving faith in God as the providential sustainer who transcends yet embraces my humanity and that of my fellow humans.

Third, I am male, and in most Pentecostal settings this simple and unearned fact provides me with more privileges than the majority of members, who tend to be female. Although Pentecostal churches perceive themselves as 'Bible-believing' and ostensibly purport to be committed to the Pauline teaching that in Christ there is neither 'male nor female' (Galatians 3.28), they mostly understand this to be a spiritual truth which does not affect the actual lives of women in the church. In my own denomination women have progressively been given more responsibilities and privileges, but the church starts from the premise that men are its natural leaders. Dionne Lamont states:

> Speaking recently with numerous women in ministry, the general consensus is that today in the Church, women, particularly those in ministry, are still faced with a degree of discrimination, dogmatism and narrow-mindedness.[85]

I have to admit to being one of the beneficiaries of this slight against women. Many who, in my opinion, have been my equal and some probably better than me, have not been promoted and encouraged as I have been. Far more men, some of limited or of no real ability, have forged ahead of talented women just because they are members of the male gender. Again from the United States, even James Cone testifies repentantly to falling into the trap of an assumptive male hegemony in his ground-breaking work in Black theology as an instrument of liberation for Black people.[86] Being male in my Pentecostal church has meant privilege, a privilege I would like to believe I use for the liberation of all God's people, male and female. Here, however, my 'sisters' and 'mothers' are necessarily my judges.

Fourth, I am a bishop in a Black-led Pentecostal church, another position of privilege. Walter Elwell says that a bishop is one who is an overseer, pastor and shepherd of a flock of God.[87] This can be interpreted as a defender of the faith, a guardian of the flock and of what the flock gets fed. I first served in the office of bishop at the age of 30, young by my church's ecclesiastical norm, and was ordained when I was 36. The reason for the gap is that I was appointed as a District Overseer in 1983, but resigned after one year. I then served one year as National Evangelist from 1984, before being appointed as pastor in Oxford from 1985 to 1989, at which time I was appointed as District Overseer for a second time and ordained shortly afterwards.

I served as a bishop until 1997, but left my 'see' to become involved in wider ecumenical affairs. I now describe myself as a 'bishop at large', enjoying the privileges the title brings without its recognized institutional responsibilities. The Church of God of Prophecy does not revoke a bishopric even after one has ceased to serve in a 'see'. The ordination is for life, except in the case of gross misconduct resulting in one being 'deposed'. Rather than be a gatekeeper of what is inside the gate, I have tended towards seeking to improve the quality of what exists there. This has meant a prophetic public ministry with a strong emphasis on the salvific nature of faith. In other words, I seek to speak out against those aspects of church life that appear to me to bring people into bondage. Salvation means the freedom of the children of God. As in the words of Jesus in Mark's Gospel, 'the Sabbath was made for humankind, not humankind for the Sabbath' (2.27).

This prophet-bishop role refuses to side with the institution and seeks unerringly to aid the individual to struggle against institutional abuse, even or especially when it is being done in

God's name. Possibly the best example of this tendency is to be found in the manner in which in apartheid South Africa the church was used by Whites as a tool to oppress Blacks.[88] Variations on the theme are present in the history of the church also, here and there, and a shepherd's role is surely to protect the flock from ravenous 'beasts', wherever they come from and in whatever shape or guise they appear – even be that in the sheep's clothing of being church. I have found that this work is not best done in a corner, but territorially across denominational boundaries, because the work of poor theology and thirst for power is not denominationally determined or executed. Neither is the need for the prophetic voice exclusively found within churches; probably to a greater extent injustice and unrighteous deeds perpetrated upon fellow human beings are to be found outside of the church and in the wider world structures. Here too, I have not refrained from speaking and acting in seeking justice and equity in the fields of education, employment, health, housing and political representation, to name some.

Finally, in the past decade I have specialized in the work of intercultural ecumenism. Churches involved in the ecumenical movement have not only been divided, they have been divided over what it would mean to be united.[89] The different forms of Christian ecumenism (oikoumene) that are espoused in this text, be they 'organic union', 'plurality of types', 'communion of communions' or 'unity in reconciled diversity', provide some insight into possible ways of working. However, what disturbs me is the sight of Christians from different cultural, ethnic, denominational and para-denominational backgrounds purporting to serve the same God in Jesus Christ, yet rarely if ever speaking to each other as offspring of the same parents ought to do. I have grown increasingly perturbed by the pursuit to redefine Christian unity and prefer to work on the assumption that Christians are already one by being Christians. We should build upon this reality by getting to know one another and enjoying our God-given unity in diversity. In this sense, I am close to the concept mentioned above of unity in (reconciled) diversity.

My particular concern has been about the fragmentation that has developed among Black-led churches, many of which are of Caribbean origin. Greater co-operation between these groups has been my objective particularly since the early 1990s. Given the sameness of the social and political difficulties faced by minorities in Britain, collaboration to tackle them seems common sense. Such collaboration may emerge out of the common life experience of minority ethnic people in Britain in the period since the arrival of the *Windrush* in 1948.[90] Since that time, like other minorities, Caribbean British Christians have built congregations across the country that have become havens and creative spaces for many. People have not generally become members of these denominations due to their doctrinal purity: rather, they have felt the love of God in existing members and have settled among and become part of them. It is therefore to be bemoaned that church leaders have a tendency to become territorial, locking up within their ecclesiastical structures those God has given into their care and often refusing to allow them freedom of association.

My personal ecumenical remit aims to secure the freedom for all to relate, share and enjoy the company and friendship of fellow brothers and sisters in Christ. I believe that Christians living on the 'blind side' of each other is intolerable and a waste of good company and mutual enrichment. My ministry of reconciliation, based primarily upon the pretext of the need to get to know and appreciate one another, has taken me into pulpits, conventions, offices and retreats of all the major and many minor Christian and other faith organizations across Britain. From this I have gleaned an enormous amount of insight into, particularly, Caribbean British faith in Britain.

The foregoing provides a sketch of where I am in the British church scene and of some of the motivations that drive my life, ministry and academic work. It is an existence tailor-made for the 'participant observer' research methodology that is applied in this study. My personal story is but one piece of a major jigsaw, which is the context of Caribbean British Christianity.

Summary

This opening chapter has sought to indicate the nature of the research project that is presented here. I have proceeded on the basis that the application of an appropriate research methodology will lead to an examination of the key factors that influence the context of Caribbean British Christianity. By so doing, I believe we can come close to both identifying the community's central theological assumption and assisting in its development and enunciation. My own role in the context has been made explicit because it is one that functions as an integral spoke in the wheel of this work. The book is indeed an exposé of my life and that of the community to which I belong.

Because this work focuses upon Caribbean British Christianity and seeks to discover its theological core based upon a study of its context, it is important that we begin at the beginning. I have already decided to focus on the twin foci of their ethnicity and faith, bearing in mind all the other contextual and theological caveats mentioned above. So in the next chapter I explore the development of this people's ethnicity and faith.

Ethnicity and Christianity in the Caribbean

Introduction

The ethnic and cultural background of people of Caribbean descent living in Britain today is complex and often camouflaged by their being described as African Caribbean. This description does not properly articulate the diversity and complexity of the people concerned. Below I seek to unmask the true Caribbean identity, beginning with the original Indian people of the Caribbean and ending at the point of mass migration to the UK at the beginning of the Windrush epoch. The lineage of today's Caribbean British Christians can be traced to the multiple ethnic and religious communities that have inhabited the Caribbean area from the time of the original Indian people, the arrival of European explorers, entrepreneurs and missionaries, the forced introduction of Africans as slaves and Asians as indentured labourers, and the consequential mixed-heritage descendants born of mixed ethnic relationships. All this, I argue, has led to a Caribbean identity that is the sum of all of the above in general and none of them in particular.

Original Caribbean people

The story of Caribbean people as a distinct ethnic group begins with the original Indian people of the Caribbean. The original Indian people belonged to several different ethnic groups. There were, *inter alia*, the Algonquins in North America, Aztecs in Mexico, Incas in South America, Mayas in Yucatan, Syboneys and Arawaks in the Caribbean and the Bahamas, and Caribs in the small islands of the Southern Caribbean.[1] We can assume a fair degree of mingling between the people of these nations. This multi-faceted nature of Caribbean identity is worthy of note as it is a feature of Caribbean identity to this day.

Opinions vary concerning when and from where the original Indian people came. P. Sherlock states that based upon credible archaeological and other scientific evidences, people settled in the Caribbean and the Americas as many as 35,000 years ago.[2] Clinton Black suggests that the earliest people came between 15,000 and 20,000 years ago.[3] He believes that over a period of thousands of years they wandered out of Siberia, across the Bering Strait to Alaska, spreading slowly southwards, eventually occupying the entire hemisphere. However, Dale Bisnauth locates the arrival of Arawaks and Caribs as late as 200 AD.[4] He believes that around that time the Arawaks migrated southwards from the Orinoco basin in South America and settled in the south-eastern Caribbean. Bisnauth further believes that during the same period the Caribs migrated from the Amazon/Brazil region to settle in the north-western parts of the Caribbean area. There is therefore no consensus about when the original Indian people first settled. Equally, there is no contention that the original Indian people lived there. As Robert Stewart confirms, the Arawaks tended to live in the south and east, with Caribs in the north and west of the Caribbean area.[5] Stewart points out that what has come to be known popularly as 'Arawaks' were Tainos who spoke Arawak.

This demographic presence in the Caribbean of the original Indian people represents an important fact because Eurocentric historical accounts tend to begin the history of the Caribbean with the 'discovery' of the area by Christopher Columbus; as though only land, not people, was 'discovered'. I do not subscribe to the view that Columbus 'discovered' the Caribbean, because people were already living there when he arrived. He may have been the first European to visit the area, but it had been discovered long before he stumbled upon the area. The indigenous people of the Caribbean were themselves the first immigrants who travelled many miles, eventually settling in the area over a period of many centuries. We know that little regard was shown by the so-called discoverers towards the culture and humanity of the indigenous people. Yet, clearly, the original Caribbean people predate Columbus by some considerable time.[6] It is one of the many tasks of theology in a Caribbean context to acknowledge and affirm the presence and dignity of the original Indian people as human beings in the image of the Triune God.

As with the difficulty of dating the presence of the original Indian people in the Caribbean, exemplified by the contrasting dates given by Sherlock, Black and Bisnauth above, estimates of their numbers vary widely also. For example, Eric Williams estimates the presence of the original Indian people in the Americas, including the Caribbean, in terms of tens of millions by the time of Columbus' trip.[7] Yet Leonardo Boff and Virgil Elizondo state that in 1492 when Columbus arrived in the area, the indigenous population of Latin America and the Caribbean was approximately 100 million.[8] It may be impossible to gauge the precise population size of the original Indian people. Nor is that of overwhelming importance to this study, since it is possible to demonstrate their presence and demographic spread in the area. Across the Americas, the original Indian people population can safely be estimated in the millions and their presence estimated over centuries.

Writers point, too, to the levels of civilizations that were attained by the original Indian people. Augier et al make the point that these people had lived undisturbed by outsiders for centuries, developing their ways of life.[9] For example, they say the Algonquins of North America were hunters, fishermen and maize growers. The Arawaks were peace-loving and skilled sea people, building and using canoes that were manned by up to 70 people. They developed a social system based around villages in which small industries flourished by making nets, pots, lines, spears and cotton fibre, and even bred barkless dogs! In contrast the Caribs, so named because they are believed to have been cannibals, were a hunting and warring people who terrorized the Arawaks and were to provide the Europeans with their toughest resistance.[10] The Aztecs of Mexico developed an elaborate way of life, building great stone temples, and connected their towns by roads and causeways across the Lake of Mexico. The Incas of South America built an empire comparable in size and efficiency with the ancient Roman Empire, stretching from Ecuador to Chile. So we find original Indian societies that were at various stages of development throughout the Americas, including the Caribbean, and clearly making social and economic progress.

A rude awakening lighted upon the original Indian people with the arrival of the Portuguese explorer Christopher Columbus and his companions, sailing under the authority of the king and queen of Spain, Ferdinand and Isabella. Columbus' arrival in the Americas in 1492 marked the beginning of the European invasion and domination of the Americas.[11] The European appetite for economic wealth and the spread of their Catholic faith quickly led to the colonization, subjugation and enslavement of the original Indian people. According to Boff and Elizondo, the colonized indigenous people of the Caribbean were virtually wiped out within a relatively short space of time by the combination of forced slave labour and contagious diseases brought into the area by the Europeans. Kortright Davis states that the Spaniards eventually 'eliminated' the Arawaks, while the British and French had more trouble with the Caribs, who often attacked attempted settlements.[12]

A measure of the 'genocide' that was inflicted upon the natives is illustrated by noting that following Columbus' landing in 1492, by 1570 the number of original Indian people had dropped from the supposed 100 million to approximately 10–12 million,[13] a reduction of approximately 90 per cent in less than 80 years. However, these original Indian people of the Caribbean were not completely wiped out and original Indian people communities are still to be found across the Caribbean today, especially in places like Suriname. I discovered a website that espoused the virtues of tourist visits to

Suriname, including a glimpse of the life of the original Indian people of the Caribbean (see www.surinfo.org/homeeng. htm). Some of these people are currently present in Europe, mainly through French immigration.

Some of our contemporaries are directly descended from the original Indian people. Philip Potter, former General Secretary of the World Council of Churches, is partly of Caribs descent.[14] One member of the West Indies cricket team in 2002, Adam Sandford, is also said to be a descendant of the Carib people. Haydn Gill, writing in the *Barbados Nation* newspaper, says Sandford is the first ever Carib descendant to represent the West Indies at cricket.[15]

So, Caribbean original Indian people, mainly Caribs and Arawaks, have been living in the Caribbean area for centuries, long before Columbus' arrival in the area. They were the first people of the Caribbean and are therefore, at least in part, the antecedents from whom today's Caribbean British Christians are descended. Their numbers may have been drastically reduced, but they have survived inter-original Indian people rivalry followed by European invasion and colonization to remain an integral part of the ethnic fabric of the Caribbean to this day. In mapping Caribbean ethnic identity, therefore, the original Indian people cannot be overlooked, since it must be taken for granted that they also cross-bred with later arrivals in the Caribbean, thereby further perpetuating their ancestry.

European Caribbean

A second ethnic group upon which Caribbean ethnicity has been built are the Europeans, whose 'intrusion' into the Americas, including the Caribbean, abruptly interrupted the pattern of historical development of the original Indian people.[16] Eric Williams points out that their entrance into the region was accidental, since Christopher Columbus had really intended to sail to India in search of gold, spices, other exotic substances and expensive materials believed to be indigenous to that region.[17] Having sailed with his crew west-wards from Europe, Columbus believed that the land upon which they alighted after weeks of sailing was that of mainland India and its surrounding islands. The original Indian people they met, initially Arawaks whose languages they did not understand, only served to confirm the mistaken view of the Europeans that they were in India. Having sailed west and believing he was in India, Columbus named the area the 'West Indies'.

Gordon Lewis highlights how the European presence in the area developed:

> The first three great voyages of Columbus had ended before the close of the fifteenth century; Cortes entered Aztec Mexico in the same year, 1519, of Charles V's accession to the Spanish imperial throne; and by 1700 the four great powers of Caribbean economic and military aggression – the French, Dutch, Spanish and English – had established flourishing island and mainland colonies.[18]

Consequently, increasing numbers of Europeans migrated to the Caribbean as human resources for the growing trading and colonial enterprise. For example, as early as 1502, some 2,500 European colonists arrived in Hispaniola (modern Haiti), including 73 families.[19] Within a short space of time, however, many died from their failure to acclimatize, and generally Europeans did not cope well with the Caribbean heat. By the end of the trade in slavery in the nineteenth century, the Europeans had established themselves, albeit as an ethnic minority in all Caribbean countries.[20] In the early nineteenth century, the following approximate White representations prevailed in the Caribbean:

Less than 5% White	Less than 10% White	More than 10% White
British Guyana	Anguilla	Bahamas
Grenada	British Honduras	Barbados
Jamaica	Montserrat	Cuba
Nevis	Saint Kitts	Curacao

continued

Less than 5% White	Less than 10% White	More than 10% White
Saint Vincent	Saint Lucia	Dominican Republic
Tobago	Virgin Islands	Guadeloupe
		Martinique
		Puerto Rico
		Saint Eustatius
		St Martin
		Trinidad

There was, therefore, a significant minority European presence across the Caribbean. By the mid twentieth century, the largest White presence in the Caribbean was to be found in Barbados, constituting 5 per cent of the population, whereas in Jamaica Whites were only 1 per cent.[21] For over half a millennium, then, Europeans have had a notable presence in the Caribbean, arriving there from several countries in Europe.

It is easy to presume that the Europeans who went to the Caribbean were exclusively invading soldiers, well-to-do merchants and evangelizing missionaries and their families. However, as Williams points out, many poor Whites entered the area as indentured labourers, redemptioner servants and convicts. White 'indentured labourers' went to the Caribbean of their own volition, voluntarily contracted to work for fixed periods. 'Redemptioner servants', by contrast, were those who went or were sent as payment for indebtedness to a lender; 'serving time' to repay the debt. 'Convicts' were taken there as the place in which to serve their sentence profitably for the state. Williams concludes:

> This emigration was in tune with mercantilist theories of the day which strongly advocated putting the poor to industrious and useful labour and favoured emigration, voluntary or involuntary, as relieving the poor rates and finding more profitable occupations abroad for idlers and vagrants at home.[22]

White indentured labourers, redemptioner servants and convicts fared as badly as other Europeans before them under the hot conditions of the Caribbean weather. Their White masters and mistresses, the plantation owners, subjected them to impossibly hard labour backed up by frequent beatings, even killing the worst non-compliant or inadaptable ones. All in all, thousands were brought to the Caribbean as part of the early labour force.[23]

So, in one way or another and of one sort or another, European migrants added to the presence of the original Indian people and to the developing complexity of the milieu of Caribbean ethnicity. Even today in the Caribbean, and in Britain there are some White people who speak with a discernible Caribbean accent. And in the Caribbean the phenomenon of the 'poor Whites' is well known. We can therefore say that Caribbean ethnicity is inextricably linked to Europe ethnicity.

African Caribbean

After the original Indian people and the Europeans, the third ethnic group to enter the Caribbean arena, and ultimately the most influential in determining the Caribbean ethnicity, originated from Africa. As it became clear to the conquering Europeans that neither the native original Indian people nor the newly recruited White workforce of servants and convicts could meet the growing demands for forced labour, they sought a different, more robust kind of people who could withstand the rigours of the climate and the heady aspirations of greedy plantation owners.[24]

The European trade in slavery in Africans, which Hugh Thomas rightly calls 'an iniquity', began tentatively in the mid fifteenth century, even before Columbus' voyage to the Caribbean, with an expedition into Africa led by the Portuguese, Lancarote de Freitas, to find gold and other valuable materials. However, instead of bringing back the gold that was their main objective, he and his crew brought back to Europe 235 Africans as slaves; and paved the way for 400 years of hideous traffic in human stock as chattel.[25] Soon, the

European appetite for exploring foreign seas and lands that had led some to Africa led others to the Americas and Caribbean. The apparently endless reservoir of Africans as slaves became an attractive answer to the Caribbean labour shortage.

The trade in slavery developed in a triangular pattern that went from Europe to Africa, Africa to the Americas/ Caribbean and the Americas/Caribbean back to Europe, taking people to and fro. This sea route facilitated the transportation of an estimated 10–20 million Africans to the Americas.[26] Eric Pemberton estimates that approximately one quarter of these were taken to the Caribbean area.[27] This means that with the decline of the original Indian people, and the relatively low number of Europeans, Africans quickly became established as the largest ethnic group in the Caribbean. Because of the triangular nature of the trade in slavery, from the earliest time some Africans ended up in Britain also, usually becoming either servants or entertainers. It is not possible for me, of African and Caribbean heritage, to make reference to this issue without pointing to the inhumane nature of this trade in slavery enterprise. Such was its involvement in the trade in slavery that William Pitt the Younger said in the House of Commons in April 1792 that no nation in Europe had plunged so deeply into this guilt as Great Britain.[28] Many Africans did not even survive the voyage across the Atlantic, dying from disease, from overcrowding, being packed like sardines in ships, murder or suicide. Some preferred to throw themselves overboard and drown than endure their living death.

Commentators are agreed that the majority of the Africans held in slavery came from the western coastal areas of the African continent. However, according to C. L. R. James, the catchment area was much wider than the western coast. In a graphic description of events, James says of the intense search for slaves:

The slavers scoured the coasts of Guinea. As they devastated an area they moved westward and then south, decade after decade, past the Niger, down the Congo coast, past

Loango and Angola, round the Cape of Good Hope, and, by 1789, even as far as Mozambique on the eastern side of Africa.[29]

For 400 years this despicable crime against Black humanity persisted, drawing its victims from across Africa, and as Dale Bisnauth reminds us, engulfing Africans of several nationalities, tribes and language groups.[30] Of course, Africa in geographical terms refers to a continent of many different countries, nationalities and languages. Yet Mervyn Alleyne argues that the reality of African heterogeneity tended to be negated by their ability, probably born of necessity, to homogenize in the interest of survival, given their repeated displacements.[31]

The situation, therefore, was one in which a reduced original Indian people, augmented by thousands of Europeans, was joined by millions of Africans who were brought to the Caribbean as slaves. It is believed, too, that after the abolition of the trade in slavery, some Africans voluntarily migrated to the Caribbean as indentured labourers, thereby adding to the already substantial African presence. By the time the trade in slavery was ended, people of African descent easily represented the most numerous ethnic group in the Caribbean context. Indeed, according to Williams, as early as the middle of the sixteenth century so numerous were Africans on the Caribbean island of Haiti that one historian described it as an effigy of Ethiopia itself.[32] Once slavery was incrementally abolished during the nineteenth century, the majority of Africans had little or no interest in continuing to work for their former masters. A new source of cheap labour became necessary to maintain plantation life and servitude to Whites in the Caribbean. This ushered in another dimension to Caribbean ethnicity.

Asian Caribbean

By the nineteenth century Europe had not only colonized the Caribbean, it had colonized much of the East as well. India and the surrounding areas were under European, mainly British, administration and influence. The extent of the hegemony of the British is epitomized in the writing of J. M. Roberts, who says the following about a census taken in 1901 in India:

> There were just under 300,000,000 Indians. They were governed by about 900 European civil servants. Usually there was about one British soldier for every 4,000 Indians. As one Englishman once put it, had all the Indians chosen to spit at the same moment, his countrymen would have been drowned.[33]

Of course, the Indians, along with other colonial subjects, did 'spit' in ways that led eventually to independence, but only after a long period of foreign rule. This European rule over their Indian subjects would have acted as grist to the wheel of compliance with the invitation extended to Indians and other Asians to work as indentured labourers in the Caribbean. The call to work as short-term labourers in the Caribbean attracted takers from a wide variety of places in addition to India, including China, Java and Manderia.[34] According to Williams, Asian economic migration to the Caribbean commenced in about 1838 and ended around 1924, during which time their number totalled well in excess of one million.[35]

The vast majority of Asians who travelled to the Caribbean went ostensibly on a three- or five-year indentured contract very similar to the situation that pertained to the Caribbean people who travelled to Britain later. However, for a range of social and economic reasons, the majority of the Asians never made the return journey; instead, they settled disproportionately across the Caribbean.[36] The majority of them made their home in Guyana and Trinidad, and to a lesser extent Guadeloupe, Martinique, Suriname, Jamaica, French Guyana, Saint Lucia, Grenada, Saint Vincent and Saint Kitts. While, as described above, the European presence in the Caribbean remained relatively low, the Asian presence in Guyana has reached as high as 51 per cent, with 43 per cent designating themselves as 'Afro-Indian'.[37] According to Sherlock, 35 per cent of the population of Trinidad are of Asian descent, and in Suriname, East Indians almost completely dominate the national population in recent times.[38] After the original Indian people, the Europeans, and the Africans, this fourth ethnic group of Asians brings an added dimension to the growing ethnic diversity of this area. An altogether understandable by-product of this ethnic diversity sharing the same Caribbean space is that cross-breeding occurred, resulting in a significant number of mixed heritage offspring.

Multiple heritage Caribbean

The development in the Caribbean of a group of people designated 'mixed', or multiple heritage, demonstrates the extent to which different ethnic groups cross-bred with one another. Bridget Brereton states that this co-mingling of the 'races' occurred in the Caribbean despite strenuous efforts by some in all ethnic groups, but particularly among Whites, to prevent it and thereby preserve their 'racial purity'.[39] However, the narrow zeal of the essentialists is frequently superseded by human nature in which sexual passion refuses to recognize ethnic boundaries. My observation suggests that there are 'mixed' offspring probably of all combinations of ethnic groups present in the Caribbean, of which the best known has been the offspring of African and European parentage: Black and White producing what has been called variously 'half-caste', 'mixed-race', 'dual-heritage', 'multiple-heritage' and in recent times just plain 'Black'. But in addition, there are many people descended from other combinations, such as Asian-White, Asian-African, African-White and to a less evident extent, all of the other groups with the original Indian people. Sherlock states that 'mixed' has become the second or third largest ethnic group in the majority of Caribbean nations and in Dominica it has been the largest group.[40] During the second half of the twentieth century, 'mixed' was the second largest ethnic group in Antigua, Barbados and Jamaica; third largest in Guyana and Trinidad; with 'African' as the largest ethnic group in all except Trinidad and Dominica. However, the ethnic story of the Caribbean is even more complex than this.

Of Jamaica, with 90 per cent of its population laying claim
to an African ethnicity, and from where came the majority of
Caribbean migrants to Britain, Rex Nettleford says that as a
social entity, it has been in protracted creolized formation for
centuries.[41] And although African ethnicity is the visible and
recorded majority in the Caribbean, it is indeed doubtful that
any Caribbean person, whether of original Indian people,
European, African or Asian appearance, could describe themselves as belonging to just one ethnic group. Therefore, even
though a substantial number of Caribbean people may identify themselves as belonging to particular ethnic groups, some-
where along their lineage they most probably have 'blood'
relations in at least one other ethnic group, sometimes more
than one. Black British theologian and cultural critic Robert
Beckford, for example, avowedly self-defined as 'African-
Caribbean', acknowledges having a White European as his
great-grandfather.[42] This is by no means unusual among
Caribbean descended people.

I referred above to the multi-ethnic dimension to my
mother's and therefore to my ethnic identity; this applies also
in the case with my wife, who is of African Indian, or 'Afro-
Asian', heritage. Her father was half-Indian, half-African; she
is the product of his relationship with an African featured
Caribbean female. My wife's family is an object lesson in
Caribbean identity, whereby on her father's side they are visually Asian, and on her mother's side they are visibly African.
The picture gets decidedly complex were I to mention that
she is a 'love child' whose mother and father never married.
Her mother later married someone of part Chinese heritage!
The legacy of the Caribbean, therefore, is one of a co-mingled
ethnicity that leaves little if any ethnic absolutes. Jamaica's
national motto sums up the situation well: 'Out of many, one
people'. Mike and Trevor Phillips, in describing the Caribbean region's ethnic make-up, state that the routine condition
was a 'multi-racial' polyglot; a crossroads of people, cultures
and languages.[43] This is, of course, a reference to both the
multiples of single ethnic groups as well as the dynamic nature
of their mixing. And Hilary Beckles cites the legendary West
Indian author C. L. R. James, insisting that the history of the

Caribbean shows that a pioneering and unique human type developed there:

> Within the Caribbean a new mindset was created; a new people, who are carriers of European, African, [original Indian people] and Asian ancestry. Almost every civilisation in the world was brought to focus upon the Caribbean in order to create the conditions for economic growth. This resulted in a creolising sociological mixture that has produced this new Caribbean person called the West Indian.[44]

My central point here is that prior to the period of 'mass' migration from the Caribbean to Britain during the mid twentieth century, Caribbean people had become inextricably ethnically interwoven. Accepting that 'African' was their most obvious heritage numerically and visually, a new ethnicity emerged.

This background is essential to understanding the ethnicity of Caribbean people as people of multiple heritage, given birth to in the Caribbean. As we would say in Jamaica, Caribbean people 'mix-up'. Within the context of this study, therefore, these are the people – of original Indian Caribbean, European Caribbean, African Caribbean, Asian Caribbean, and multiple heritage Caribbean – to whom I refer as 'Caribbean'. It is my contention that this new ethnicity evolved in the Caribbean and takes precedence over other ethnic identities such as European, African, Asian, and mixed heritage. While this human development may bring dismay and disapproval to those who believe in ethnic essentialism, it is nevertheless an affirmation that there is only one race, the human race, and that this race is naturally drawn to each other even across ethnic, cultural and other boundaries.

It is against this ethnic background that Caribbean people travelled to Britain since the 1950s. Next I examine the religious traditions that prevailed in the Caribbean, especially Christianity in many forms, and that were destined to be carried to Britain.

Religious traditions in the Caribbean

As alluded to above, Caribbean people can be viewed as one discrete, richly diverse, ethnic group of humanity. And they are clearly identifiable also as people of faith. Their faith is primarily Christian, though shaped in a particularly Caribbean way. My task here then is to examine the development of the faith of Caribbean people, which they took with them to Britain. Elaine Foster, writing from the Caribbean British context, states that migrants from the Caribbean who settled in Britain since the 1950s were deeply spiritual people who had a dynamic faith *before* (emphasis mine) they left their homes to journey to Britain.[45] In other words, the specific characteristics of Caribbean British Christianity have their roots in the context of Caribbean life and have been shaped by it. Therefore, alongside the development and evolution of Caribbean ethnicity, the development of their faith is another major contributor to their identity. Indeed, their faith is as 'mixed up' as their ethnicity.

Elizabeth Thomas-Hope, referring to the complex developmental patterns of Caribbean religious life, says:

> Religion, more than any other cultural phenomenon mirrors the heterogeneity of the Caribbean. It reflects the differences in the traditions and colonial practices of Spain, Britain, France and Holland, and while it highlights the common experience of slavery and indenture, it magnifies the racial, ethnic and socio-economic complexities of the region, revealing both the sharp distinctions and the blurred overlaps, the blends and conflicts characteristic of a Creole culture. Elements of traditional West African religions, chiefly expressed in neo-Christian sects, exist side by side with orthodox forms of Christianity, the Hindu and Muslim faiths, and a representation of Judaism.[46]

As is evident in Britain today, the expressions of Caribbean British faith are multi-faceted, a feature that can be traced to the roots of Caribbean British faith in the Caribbean. I will go back to the beginning of this complex development, noting the religions of the various ethnic groups identified above and how they feed into a Caribbean faith system, the antecedent of what now exists in Britain since the mid-1950s, and which is primarily Christian. I begin with a look at the religions of the original Indian people of the Caribbean.

Religion of the original Caribbean people

Although there were several original Indian people groups, I will focus here upon the Arawaks and Caribs as they are the most historically traceable. According to the writers cited below, the history of the original Indian people has been uncovered mainly through archaeological finds and oral tradition among remaining descendants. Robert Stewart argues that the religious beliefs of the original Indian people of the Caribbean are important, not least because although their numbers diminished with the increasing dominance of other ethnic groups in the area, the striking similarities between African and Caribbean original Indian cosmologies have led scholars to conclude that Caribbean original Indian religion has been preserved and has syncretized with the folk religion of the newcomers to the area, Europeans, Africans and Asians.[47] There is evidence of some validity in the theory of syncretism, as we shall see.

According to Bisnauth,[48] Arawaks believed in a hierarchy of deities. At the top of their pecking order of deities was the Creator, Jocahuna, to whom they ascribed the virtues of being the one, supreme, invisible, immortal and omnipotent. Jocahuna was by nature well disposed towards the Arawaks and therefore was not deemed to need placatory worship or intercession. Beneath Jocahuna were lesser deities who were understood to have been left in charge of running the natural world, having been given delegated powers of governance by Jocahuna. Among these subordinate beings, Hurakan was associated with great storms, Guabancex with wind and water; then there were other gods and goddesses of fertility, disease and death. These lesser gods were perceived as having a penchant for mischief, especially turning good into evil.

Worship and supplications were necessarily made to them to ensure their good disposition towards the supplicant worshipper. We can say that one ancestor of today's Caribbean British Christian viewed worship as appeasement of God and God's 'deputies'. The intensity of worship would therefore be linked to the desperation or seriousness of the moment.

Because of the machinations of the mischievous and malignant spirits, or lesser deities, Arawakan 'worship' chiefly took the form of exorcisms, for which there was a human exorcist/healer called a Bohito. All ill-fated occurrences were put down to the work of these 'evil' spirits, and the Bohito had the religious responsibility to appease them. To assist in their worship, the Arawaks made images reminiscent of toads, reptiles and distorted human faces to represent these gods and goddesses, which, we are told, were as horribly conceived as the deities were believed to be malignant. These images, or *zemis*, were worn around the Arawaks' necks or worshipped in the consecrated village house in attempts to court the pleasure of the deities in the hope of warding off catastrophes. Other Arawak religious practices included taking certain natural medicines, decorating their bodies and wearing special jewellery for protection against these spirits.[49] And in a striking resemblance to the later practice among Rastafarians of using marijuana as a type of 'sacrament', the Arawak priests smoked tobacco as a sacred weed used to induce a state of communication with the spirits. Some zemis images, worn around the neck or placed in houses, were of departed ancestors, adopted to provide spirit protection against hostile zemis. The mediatorial role of the exorcist/healer priest, or Bohito, was central to the hoped for well-being of the Arawaks.

The Arawaks believed in life after death, in which good Arawaks went to reside in a pleasant place of peace and tranquillity called Coyaba. Here the spirits of departed ancestors enjoyed cool shade, delicious fruit, and safety from droughts and hurricane – heaven indeed! From this spirit outpost, free from the threat of malevolent zemis, ancestors were thought to be capable of intervening to counter the threat of the zemis to the living. Much of Arawakan religion resembles contemporary Caribbean British and other Christian religious practices. For example, the grading of deities reminds us of the Father, Son and Holy Spirit, which, although not officially thought of in hierarchical terms, is hierarchical in all but name: first, Father; second, Son; third, Holy Spirit. The mediatory place of the priest is a reminder of the degree to which Black Christians depend upon and look to their pastors and overseers. The belief that whatever happens is the result of God's anger, or indeed pleasure, and the appeasement of God through sacramental worship also resonate with today's Caribbean British Christians in a profound manner. These Arawakan theological/doctrinal positions are not necessarily exclusive to them, or to Caribbean British Christians today, but they certainly exist among both.

The Caribs, like the Arawaks, believed in a supreme Creator being, but they had no name for him or her.[50] How like the early Jewish nation of the Bible! This great and irresistible power did not require lavish worshipful attention from the Caribs, but again, like the Arawaks, they reserved their placatory worship for the lesser gods who were thought to control natural forces like water, disease and death. Worship aimed at appeasing these gods included creating effigies and making propitiatory blood sacrifices to them. The way Caribbean and other Christians relate to Jesus as the gateway to God and wear images and other relics with Jesus in mind, is interesting too. Then there are Jesus' ministers on earth who are not unlike the Caribs' priests who were called the Boyez. They were responsible for conducting sacrifices on behalf of the people.

Caribs were warlike people and attached much virtue to bravery. Believing that the spirit could inhabit the living, à la being baptized in the Holy Spirit in Pentecostal traditions, some would perform ritual cannibalism in the belief that through consumption they acquired the courage of war captives, similar to the Christian sacrament of eating the body and drinking the blood of Jesus. The Caribs' idea of heaven was that it was where the virtuous and brave went, with their wives and amid great felicity and enjoyment, being served by their captives, usually the Arawaks. A place of damnation awaited cowardly Caribs, where they would be in captivity and live a life of servitude to the Arawaks. We are reminded here also of the belief of some Caribbean Christian denominations, that they were the true church and that lesser Christians, if they made it to heaven at all, would be there as guests.

The religions of the original Caribbean people can be regarded as primitive, but they were the products of the environment in which people lived. Bisnauth highlights the contextual nature of this belief system:

> A hostile environment bred hostile spirits. Whether or not those beliefs would have changed if and when those people tamed their environment, I can never know. The intrusion of the Spanish into the Caribbean halted any further evolution of Arawak and Carib beliefs.[51]

So, at the time of Columbus, the original Indian people of the Caribbean held religious concepts that showed belief in a supreme being, lesser spirit beings, the need to placate the malevolent tendencies of these lesser spirits, priestly mediatorial functions and an understanding of a hereafter in which the 'good' enjoyed fullness of life, while the 'bad' were punished, or vanquished. It can be readily seen that many of these practices resonate with practices identifiable within Caribbean British Christianity. Whether they are carry-overs from the religions of the original Indian people, or just similar religiosity is unclear. Based upon the closeness of the similarities, I propose that these represent a religious continuum, at least in part. The next religious tradition to be brought into the Caribbean was that of the Europeans – Christianity.

European religion

European people brought and practised their form of religion in the Caribbean too, namely Christianity, in its various denominational forms. How sad that this privilege is so often not extended to those they conquered and subjugated! This process began in the Caribbean with the imposition of Roman Catholicism upon the original Indian people by the Spanish in

the wake of Christopher Columbus' 'discovery' of the region
in 1492. According to Bisnauth, at that time before the
(European) Reformation, European people believed that they
belonged to a faith that was imbued with God-given worldwide authority, which they sought to extend beyond the
boundaries of Europe. Bisnauth states:

> As explorers, discoverers, *conquistadores* and traders sought
> to open up the region for economic exploitation, missionar-
> ies and priests sought to introduce what they considered to
> be the blessing of European civilisation to the indigenous
> people and to incorporate them into the fold of Catholicism
> – the religion of the *respublica christiana*.[52]

Believing that God had bequeathed the 'Indies' to the
Spanish, as God had given the Promised Land to the Jews, the
Spanish settlers, with the full authority of the king and queen
of Spain and the Pope, considered it their divine duty to
Christianize their new subjects. According to Bisnauth:

> In a series of five Papal Bulls, the Roman pontiff not only
> gave the Spanish Crown the exclusive privilege of Christ-
> ianising the natives, but he also gave the crown such exten-
> sive control over the Church in the Indies, that, for all
> practical purposes, the King functioned as the Pope's vicar
> in the New World.[53]

In so far as we are aware, Christianity was the first non-indige-
nous religion to come to the Caribbean. It was 'introduced' to
its captive audience with the cruel zeal of people whose view
of themselves and their faith was so lofty that any opposition
to them was opposition to God and God's will.

With the Reformation came a diversification, or denomin-
ationalization, of the church in Europe, based upon new
understanding of the nature and conduct of church, which
had a corresponding effect upon the religious life of the
Caribbean. Eventually, the representations of denominations
in the Caribbean mirrored the strength of those denominations in the European countries that had interests in the

Caribbean. As territories changed hands through conquest or deals, so the religious landscape became more complex, resulting in a Caribbean region where we can trace the presence of Catholics, Anglicans, Dutch Reformed Church, Lutherans, Quakers, Moravians and other churches. After the Methodist Church broke with the Church of England, they too beat a trail to the Caribbean, as did the Baptists, Presbyterians and others. Much of this was prompted and sustained by the work of the various British missionary societies, such as the Church Missionary Society and the Society for the Propagation of the Gospel.[54]

Later, during the nineteenth and twentieth centuries, American missionaries were to join in establishing churches and denominations throughout the Caribbean. As Davis puts it:

> After the virtual elimination of the (original) inhabitants by the Europeans, the Caribbean was peopled by Europeans, Africans, and most recently by Indians and Middle Easterners. At the various points of their survival, they brought their religions with them. Thus, it is technically correct to speak of religions (rather than religion) in the Caribbean; for, although the Caribbean has produced no great religion, it has absorbed several from outside: African traditional religions, Christianity, Islam, Hinduism, Judaism, North American cultism.[55]

The Caribbean, then, became imbued with a range of European Christian denominations, with their various interpretations of the gospel of Christ, all of which found followers. But the Caribbean is also the place where the religions of the indigenous people and those brought there by various means flourish and contend for space and priority. North American religious denominations, or 'cults', as Davis calls them, added to the religious landscape in the Caribbean. At the beginning of the twentieth century especially, Pentecostal denominations from the United States, such as the Church of God group of denominations, impacted on the Caribbean greatly.[56]

ETHNICITY AND CHRISTIANITY

The legacy of European Christian forms in the Caribbean can be seen in the manner in which these denominations, now indigenized, dominate the religious landscape. Nowhere is this more evident than in Jamaica, where, when people were asked in the 1991 Census which church they were associated with, they replied as follows:[57]

Anglican	127,331
Baptist	203,135
Brethren	26,243
Church of God	487,980
Jehovah's Witnesses	38,434
Methodist	62,208
Moravian	27,589
Pentecostal	175,235
Roman Catholic	93,401
Seventh Day Adventist	208,173
United Church	63,968
Other	197,686
None	554,546
Not Stated	33,718

While the newer American Pentecostal and Church of God constitute a block, as does 'None', the identifiable European initiated churches still represent a significant proportion of the Jamaican Church in 1991. Jamaica, from where the majority of Caribbean migrants to Britain have come, was in many ways typical of the Caribbean in terms of the penetration of Christian and other religious groups.

According to Knight and Palmer, by the mid nineteenth century the church presence in the Caribbean was deep and permanent, in both its Roman Catholic (mainly in the French Antilles, Trinidad, Saint Lucia, Grenada and Dominica) and its Protestant (mainly in Jamaica, Guyana and Barbados) manifestations.[58] In addition to the legacy of the original Indian people's faiths, European Christianity had become embedded into the life of Caribbean people, from which many British immigrants came. The story does not end there, however, because there was to be an even more populous religious presence upon the Caribbean landscape, that of the Africans held in slavery.

African religion

While the Europeans brought to the Caribbean their various brands of Christianity and supporting ecclesiastical structures, Alleyne argues that Africans brought a set of religious beliefs, individual and collective memory, and certain structures of religious behaviour and practice, which they were unable to engage in freely because of their slave status.[59] Others believe that some Africans managed to practise their religion almost unchanged.[60] The truth may be somewhere between these two opposing views. Clearly, Africans held in slavery and their faith would suffer restrictions of expression imposed upon them by their owners as part of the coercion required to keep them in their place of subjugation. Even then, as Stewart has identified, some of the social and cosmological traits of African traditional religions are identifiable in the Caribbean. They include, for example, use of the body and movements as key elements in religious practice, a belief in the supreme creator God, God as a distant entity, lesser deities operating the world so that fortune or misfortune rests with them, placatory 'worship', unity of the material and spiritual realities, veneration of ancestors and the earth, and life as a holistic phenomenon.[61] These religious traits, while not being exclusive to Africans, are certainly evident among them. Indeed, some are the same as those identified among the original Indian people of the Caribbean.

John Mbiti says these religious traditions emerge from an African world-view in which

Africans are notoriously religious, and each people has their own religious system with a set of beliefs and practices. Religion permeates into all departments of life so fully that it is not easy or possible always to isolate it.[62]

Such permeation is evident from the numerical extent of African religious following. Mbiti estimates that there were some 3,000 African people groups, each with their own religious system. This African cosmological view, that allows such proliferation of faiths and mass following, has led to misunderstandings and relational problems for outsiders, especially westerners, on two counts. First, for centuries westerners generally formed the view that African religious beliefs, including those taken to the Caribbean, were unsophisticated, primitive and therefore fit only for suppression. Second, westerners seem to have found it difficult to understand the African world-view sufficiently to have regard for it. Yet, with a little imagination on their part, and a commitment to freedom of expression of their fellow humans, co-existence and mutual learning could have resulted. In any case, the sheer numerical size of the African-descended population in the Caribbean has ensured that, notwithstanding the strictures placed upon them by their oppressors, the various African religious beliefs have survived and impacted significantly upon Caribbean religion. There is an evident presence in Black Christian practice in Britain today of African religious continuity based upon the tenacity of their faith.

Leonard Barrett points out that throughout the Caribbean, Africans seemed to have found ways to adapt their religious beliefs to their circumstances and practice, with the most identifiable expression being 'spirit possession'.[63] This went under different names in different parts of the Caribbean, depending upon the Africans who were transplanted there. For example, the Ashantis of Jamaica practised Kumina, the Dahomean of Haiti practised Vodum, the Nigerians of Trinidad practised Shango and a similar practice in Cuba was known as Santeria. Developments in Jamaica provide some useful insights into syncretistic developments involving Africans. It was African religious priests and priestesses held in slavery in Jamaica who led the way in the practice of 'ritual aggression' against the slave system, which became known as *obeah*. Derived from the Ashanti people, *obeah* means to take a child: *oba*, 'a child', *yi*, 'to take'. The threat to the enemy's, the European oppressor's, children is clear. The means of carrying out this practice against the enemy's children, or defending by exorcism some children against such threat, was orchestrated by the *myal* (the priest or priestess, minister). The *myal*-men or *myal*-women engaged in these rites while in a state of trance-like spirit possession. According to Bisnauth,

> Caribbean obeah derived its rationale from two strands of African belief and practice: that which was related to witch-craft, and that which was connected with magic. Witch-craft, in turn, involved a theory of causation that was concerned with the explanation of misfortune or evil. To the African mind, every evil occurrence demanded two explanations: how did it happen? And why did it happen?[64]

In Jamaica, Kumina describes the process within which this inquiry is conducted and executed, accompanied by drum-ming, dancing and alcoholic spirits, all of which lead the participant into a state of trance. In this state, the *myal* can communicate with the spirit that possesses him or her and receive instructions concerning the nature of the threat, or the solution to the problem. Barrett argues that in this state, the revelation

> may consist of the reason for the sickness or the death, sug-gest the cure for the illness, or warn of coming calamities. Under possession, the evil spirit that may have caused the person's illness may be captured. It might be a ghost sent by an *obeah*-man or woman to haunt the house. Under *Kumina* possession, the revelation is sometimes given in an unknown tongue, very often in an African language, now forgotten, but known to the possessed.[65]

To a casual observer, emphasis upon glossolalia, which occurs often at the height of rhythmic music and singing, 'inspirational' preaching and praying, the casting out of demons and trance-like spirit-possession, can look remark-ably like Kumina as described by Barrett and as I have observed it. Similar behaviour is evident also in the con-temporary practice among Caribbean British Christians of convening fasting services and all-night prayer meetings to confront adverse circumstances, similar to the practice of Kumina. These actions are not necessarily the same thing, but they do bear resonances.

According to Barrett, the mid to late nineteenth century ushered in what has become known as 'The Great Revival'.[66] This time allowed the African religions across the Caribbean, and particularly in Jamaica, to assert themselves, resulting in three distinct types of African religious expressions: Pukumina, mostly African in its rituals and beliefs; Revivalism, partly African and partly European Christian; and Revival Zion, mostly European Christian and a little African in its rituals and beliefs. We have to remember, however, that these religious manifestations were all the time operating, along with Caribbean original Indian religious practices, and alongside the European Christian denominations planted in the Caribbean. Also, there was the Asian expression of Hinduism and Islam operating as a syncretized form of Euro-Christian and African-centred religious practices. At no time did any one religious form enjoy the terrain to itself.

Another African-related religious form that has to be reckoned with, emerging initially from Jamaica but spreading to the rest of the Caribbean and, indeed, the African Caribbean Diaspora, is that of Rastafarianism. According to Barrett, this religion emerged as a direct result of the binary of 'domination and resistance'.[67] For Barrett, the genealogy of Rastafarianism is located in the resistance by freedom fighters, known as Maroons, against European-imposed servitude during slavery and colonialism in Jamaica and elsewhere. The uprising was led in the mid nineteenth century post-slavery period by the likes of Sam Sharpe, Paul Bogle and the Pan-African campaigner Marcus Garvey. The struggle culminated in a rejection of the 'European God' whom the oppressed slaves and their descendants believed had sided with their European oppressors. This led to the embracing of the Ethiopian Haile Selassie as the Black Messiah. Since the 1930s, the struggle both for self-identity for the African Caribbean and to identify the God of the African Caribbean have been engaged in by many, though not all, Caribbean

people who consider themselves African first. Not all accept
the notion of Selassie's deity, but most agree that the God
portrayed by European religiosity is not sufficiently Black to
be the God of the whole world. As Doreen Morrison points
out, Black Christians need a God who understands their
struggle and can bring healing to their troubled souls.[68] By
way of a wide range of faith expressions, Caribbean people
had come to know that God in the Caribbean prior to coming
to Britain.

Asian religions

According to L. L. Williams, and as alluded to above, the
Indians who migrated to the Caribbean as indentured labourers since 1838 brought with them their Muslim and Hindu
faiths, with the overwhelming majority embracing the latter.[69]
Although, according to Dayfoot, Christianity had reached the
periphery 'Malabar coast of India' by the fifth century and
maintained a minority status in what became a largely Hindu
and Muslim context, the indentured labourers who went to
the Caribbean in the nineteenth century were not from
among them in the main.[70] Dayfoot further states that the
Chinese who came to the Caribbean were largely Buddhists,
while people from the Middle East tended to be Maronite
Christians, a tradition that traces its origins to the time of the
Crusades. In this way, therefore, the main contribution of
Asians to the religious life of the Caribbean is to be found in
the practices of Hinduism, Islam and Buddhism, faiths they
embraced in their former homelands.

In the melting pot of Caribbean life and with the primacy of
Christianity as the religion of the European rulers, non-
Christian Asian and other religiosity soon became creolized in
the Caribbean. To begin with, East Indians who followed the
Hindu faith shared a number of beliefs with others, like
Africans, for example.[71] They believed in the existence of
ghosts, or *bhuts*, that were feared for their malevolent tendencies, in gods and in ancestors. They also came to believe in the
powers of the *obeah*-man of the Africans. Bisnauth says:

It was not long before they began to credit Brahmin priests, mahants and Muslim imams with the powers of the Negro obeah man, and to solicit from them charms, amulets and potions against the mischief of real and imaginary enemies.[72]

This creolization of the Indian went even deeper, since to many 'non-Indians' Hinduism and Islam were one and the same. The two ethnic groups were made to relate to each other across their religious lines in the interest of ethnic solidarity. While difficult to prove, we may surmise that through intermarriage further ethnic and religious syncretism occurred.

Various forms of religious syncretism occurred in the Caribbean as a result of the fusion of the intermingling of different religious expressions. Probably the most notable was the manner in which, when oppressed people were forced to adopt a foreign faith, they imbued the foreign icons and practices with familiar meanings. Bisnauth provides a good example of this and I quote him at length here.

> The practice of the Catholics of speaking of Jesus Christ as both God and the Son of God no doubt led to a vagueness in the understanding of the Indians as to the identity of Jesus, which was quite in keeping with the happy vagueness with which they had hitherto regarded the identity of Jocahuna. The Holy Spirit of Catholic teaching was quickly identified as Hurakan, the Mighty Wind, who blew with power whensoever and wheresoever he willed. There were times, however, when the Holy Spirit was identified as Guabancex. The Arawaks saw nothing incongruous in identifying the Holy Spirit with both Hurakan and Guabancex. In their understanding, the Mighty Spirit was free to assume whatever form he wanted. Equally, his worshippers were free to call him by whatever name they wished, since as either Hurakan or Guabancex he was one and the same spirit.[73]

Bisnauth states further that later on in the life of people in the Caribbean, during the nineteenth century in Guyana, for

example, the White Robed Army (Jordanite) Movement was
initiated in an alliance between an East Indian immigrant,
Bhagwan Das, and a young Grenadian, Joseph MacLaren.
The movement syncretized elements from Das' Hinduism
and MacLaren's Anglican Christianity. In one attempt to
convert Hindus to Christianity:

> The myth of the Nishkalanki Avatar (Spotless Incarna-
> tion), the use of bhajans (Hindu songs of praise) in which
> Yisu Masih (Jesus Christ) was lauded as Ishvari-ji (Lord)
> and Sri Bhagwan (God) – titles long ascribed to Vishnu or
> Brahma – the practice of Indian Christian preachers of
> using sections of the Bhagavad-Gita, the Hindu holy book,
> as the authority for their claim for Christ, helped to create
> the belief that Yisu Masih was the Spotless or Sinless
> Avatar. But, perhaps, no single factor helped create the
> belief more than the use made of the katha (chant) to
> propagate the Christian faith among Hindus.[74]

Here, the pattern of the traditional Hindu chant was sub-
verted by Christian catechists to tell the katha of Yisu Masih.
Turner tells also of other syncretistic movements across the
Caribbean, notably in Trinidad, where there is evidence of
'Hindu, Christian, and African religious forms, and in
Suriname [where] Indians have developed spirit cults that
supplant their original Islamic practice'.[75]

Summary

In this chapter I have sought to provide the ethnic and religious background of the antecedents of Caribbean British
Christians as an affirmation of their historic ethno-religious
roots. It is noted that Caribbean people are the descendants of
the interrelated ethnicities of the original Indian people,
Europeans, Africans and Asians. From this it is possible to
discern that few, if indeed any, Caribbeans can legitimately
claim to be ethnically or racially 'pure', given the complex
nature of Caribbean existence over the past 500 years. Over-

whelmingly, people are of mixed heritage to some degree. Also, Caribbean British Christians are the product of a context that has been influenced by the religious beliefs and practices of the different people. The faiths, including the dominant Christianity, that have emerged have been shaped from the beliefs and practices of the original Indian people, Europeans, Africans and Asians, as well as developing some expressions that are the product of the Caribbean. It is reasonable to assume elements of eclecticism and syncretism in these developments. These are the ethnic and religious formations, then, that constitute the foundations of the context of today's Caribbean British Christianity. Against this background of rich ethnic and religious diversity in the Caribbean, I now turn to their progressive expressions in Britain.

3

Ethnicity and Christianity in Britain

Introduction

Having argued in the previous chapter that a particular ethno-religious identity emerged in the Caribbean, this chapter analyses the progress of this group in Britain. My contention here is that the primary identity and definition of 'Caribbean Christians' in Britain cannot be understood apart from their roots in the Caribbean. What progress has been made in Britain is rooted in the Caribbean experience. This ethno-religious identity in Britain is analysed in this chapter in two main parts: first, the progression of an ethnic identity to Caribbean British, and second, the development of a Caribbean British Christian identity.

Black people in Britain

Although the main subjects of this study started arriving in this country from the late 1940s, Peter Fryer reminds us that there were Black people in Britain before the English arrived![1] He states that there were African soldiers in the Roman imperial army that occupied southern England during the third century AD. Little is known about the Black presence in Britain between the third and early sixteenth centuries. However, after the sixteenth century, the presence of both Africans and Asians is evident, and they were mainly but not exclusively slaves, servants and entertainers.[2] Fryer reminds us of three eighteenth-century notables among many.

First, Olaudah Equiano, a Nigerian who arrived in Britain in 1757, aged about 11; though in slavery, he became a journalist, author and anti-slavery campaigner. Writing of his experience, Equiano said:

> To kidnap our fellow creatures, however they may differ in complexion, to degrade them into beasts of burden, to deny them every right but those, and scarcely those we allow to a horse, to keep them in perpetual servitude, is a crime as unjustifiable as cruel . . . can any man be a Christian who asserts that one part of the human race were ordained to be in perpetual bondage to another?[3]

Second, Ottobah Cugoano, who was captured in Ghana and brought to Britain in 1772 at the age of about 13. Like Equiano, he was a writer and an outspoken anti-slavery campaigner, with a certain militancy mixed in. In the rhetoric of an Old Testament prophet or a modern-day Civil Rights campaigner Malcolm X, in a clear call for an uprising against slavery, Cugoano wrote:

> History affords us many examples of severe retaliations, revolutions and dreadful overthrows; and of many crying under the heavy yoke of subjection and oppression, seeking for deliverance. Yet, O Africa! Yet, poor slave! The day of thy watchmen cometh, and thy visitation draweth nigh. In that day the walls of deliverance are to be built, in that day shall the decree of slavery be far removed.[4]

Third, Fryer introduces us to Ignatious Sancho, who was born on a 'slave-ship' in the mid-Atlantic and brought by two English sisters to live in Greenwich at the age of two. Though brought up in slavery, Sancho dedicated himself to literature and music composition, excelling in both. One of his symphonies was even aired on BBC radio in 1958. Not an activist like the previous two examples, Sancho nonetheless exerted subtle pressure on the slave system by protesting to his literary contacts. Calling himself 'Africanus', 'Blackamoor', and his fellow Africans 'brother Negroes', Sancho wished 'health and peace to every religion and country throughout the ample range of God's creation'.[5]

An article in the *Independent* newspaper highlighted several Black people in Britain since the nineteenth century who have achieved well beyond the stereotypical servant and entertainer roles. These include a West Indian man who bought land in Brighton and built a terrace of grand sea-facing houses, now known as Royal Crescent.[6] The promotion of Black History Month has also had the effect of highlighting high achievers among Caribbean and other Black Britons over recent centuries, among them Mary Seacole, the nurse who worked alongside Florence Nightingale during the Crimean War. These are some of the many men and women who lived in Britain long before modern-day Caribbean people arrived. However, the defiance and determination to pursue the maximum they could humanly achieve, and their refusal to be defined by their circumstances, bear a striking similarity to today's Caribbean British Christians. Striking, too, is the God-centred view of life of many, if not all, of them.

Before the late 1940s, Black people lived throughout Britain, albeit in relatively small numbers and most evidently in areas supported by seaports, especially London. James Walvin states that during the era of European enslavement of Africans, London had a substantial number of 'exotic' Blacks.[7] These people – servants, footmen and coach drivers to the wealthy – were sometimes attired in the height of contemporary style, but the majority of them were poor, sometimes wretched. The Black presence in Britain, however, took on renewed impetus around the time of the mid twentieth century when Caribbean migrants, in search of economic gains, added to the relatively minor presence of Africans and Asians.

Caribbean migration

It is important that we know how and why Caribbean British people have come to be here. The troopship *Empire Windrush* has become a symbol of Caribbean migration in Britain since its arrival at Tilbury Docks in June 1948, bringing to the British shores the largest single passenger load of Caribbean travellers in modern times, some 500, mostly Jamaicans.[8]

This signalled the beginning of a major upsurge in migration activity into Britain, not just from the Caribbean but also from the rest of the New Commonwealth. As Colin Holmes points out, Caribbean migration was part of a wider economic migration pattern that saw similar people movement from Asia and Africa in response to Britain's industrial developmental needs and the demand for labour to assist in the reconstruction of the British economy.[9] This migration was due for the most part to what sociologists call 'push' and 'pull' factors, which took many forms. According to Frank Field and Patricia Haikin, social and economic privations at home in a post-imperialist, yet neo-colonialist New Commonwealth helped to 'push' people from places like the Caribbean, while Britain's post-war rebuilding programme and industrial boom created opportunities that helped to 'pull' people into Britain, in search of economic prosperity.[10] Such were the conditions in the Caribbean of the mid-1900s that Eric Williams described it as one of the most socially and economically unstable places in an unstable world.[11] Unsurprisingly, many Caribbean people sought to migrate, and although the majority were economic migrants, significant numbers fell into other categories too.

Some migrants were students, who preferred the option of studying in their adopted mother country to studying at home. According to Sheila Patterson, by 1961 Caribbean students constituted 19 per cent of the Black immigrant student population of around 36,000, larger than the Asian contingent of 13 per cent, the largest being West Africans at 33 per cent of the total.[12] There were, too, armed services personnel who chose to demobilize in Britain after World War Two. Patterson states that some servicemen who went home found the economic situation so discouraging that they soon returned to Britain, despite the poor employment situation that existed immediately after the war.[13] Another factor 'pushing' Caribbean migration towards Britain was the virtual closure of access to the United States to Caribbean people upon the passing of the McCarren Act of 1952, which severely restricted US immigration from the Caribbean.[14] This Act left Britain as the unchallenged 'window of opportunity' for Caribbean people seeking to migrate for economic and other reasons. Yet another line of Caribbean migration was the decision of many parents who themselves had already arrived in Britain to 'send for' their children to join them.[15] This writer arrived in Britain in exactly this circumstance, as did many known to me.

Significantly, in the context of this thesis, Philip Mohabir states that many Caribbean migrants were missionaries by intent, not simply part of the economic and other migrating factors.[16] Mohabir tells his own story about coming to Britain as a missionary in response to a divine call to do so. A similar story is told of D. A. Samson, a former national leader of the Wesleyan Holiness Church, who famously stated, 'Only one thing could carry me to England, the Gospel.'[17] These two men were not alone, but unlike the intimation of Mohabir, it would be misleading to suggest that 'many' rather than 'some' came to Britain on the mission pretext. The foregoing shows that the reasons for migration from the Caribbean to Britain were many and varied, as were the kinds of people who came. A Runnymede report emphasizes the changing migration situation:

> The growth in Britain's Black population is a post-war phenomenon. In 1951 there were 1.6 million people living in Britain who were born outside the UK, of whom only 0.2 million were born in the New Commonwealth. By 1971 there were 3.0 million people who were born outside the UK of whom 1.2 million were born in the New Commonwealth. The majority of these 1.2 million were Black workers attracted to Britain during the 1950s and 1960s by employment opportunities.[18]

Another report shows the increased momentum in Caribbean migration since the early 1950s.

> Movement to the United Kingdom from the West Indies never exceeded 1,000 a year before 1951, rose to 2,000 in 1952 and 1953, to 10,000 in 1954 and 12,000 in the first eight months of 1955. The majority of these are Jamaicans.[19]

This Jamaican majority is in keeping with a historic Jamaican tendency towards mobility in search of social and economic improvement and has a significant influence upon the ethnic balance of migrants in Britain. The factors for Jamaicans being a highly mobile people fall outside the scope of this research; I note the phenomenon as a matter of historical fact.

Field and Haikin state that Jamaicans represented the most populous Caribbean migrant group in Britain, while Trinidadians and Guyanese were among the lowest.[20] With the majority of Jamaicans being of African descent, while Trinidadians and Guyanese are of majority Asian descent, the high numbers of Jamaicans in Britain coupled with relatively low level Trinidadian and Guyanese migration has led to a significant majority of Caribbean people in Britain being of African Caribbean descent. Indeed the Caribbean church in Britain is largely a Jamaican church. However, these classifications are not as exclusive as they may appear, given the pluriform nature of Caribbean ethnicity, from whichever part of the Caribbean people come. Furthermore, in Britain Caribbean identity has steadily became subverted by being part of a milieu of ever-changing ethnicities.

Caribbean migration fed into this wider migration pattern, fuelling a significant increase in the number of 'Black' people in Britain, where Black now means African, Asian, Caribbean and others. Together, these have become known in Britain as ethnic minorities, or minority ethnic groups. By the time of the 1991 National Census, the total 'minority ethnic' population stood at just over 3 million, or 5.5 per cent of the total population of just under 55 million. Of this, 0.9 per cent, or 499,964, identified themselves as 'Black Caribbean'.[21] The 2001 Census shows a significant increase in the number of minority ethnic people, from 5.5 per cent to 7.9 per cent of the overall population. By this time, too, people in Britain of 'Caribbean' descent represented the second largest minority ethnic group, along with Pakistanis, also at 0.9 per cent. The largest minority was Indian, at 1.5 per cent. Observable here, therefore, is the phenomenon of Caribbean permeation of British society, initially through migration and then through indigenous biological increase, adding to the further complexity of Caribbean identity as well as helping to forge a new British Black identity. The mainly economic but multi-faceted Caribbean migration has had the effect of bringing thousands of new Black people into Britain.

Demographic settlements

When Caribbean people began arriving in Britain in the 1950s, they settled across Britain, mainly in England, in keeping with their reasons for being in Britain. Initially the main factor was employment. This led to a concentration of Caribbean and other minorities in the industrialized inner-city areas of the time such as London, Birmingham, Manchester and Sheffield.[22] Juliet Cheetham points out that these migrants were going in most cases to areas of expanding industry, but falling (White) population.[23] This led to minority ethnic people becoming en bloc a disproportionately higher minority in certain areas as compared with their presence overall in Britain: in the case of Birmingham, ethnic minorities added together are popularly expected to become a combined major-ity over the White population by the year 2020.

Industries such as steel and textiles in the north-west of England, and manufacturing in the West Midlands, were directly responsible for 'pulling' many Caribbean people into those areas during the 1950s and 1960s, according to Clive Harris.[24] Caribbean presence spread much wider, however, and Harris further states that the majority of those who came to Britain in the epoch-making *Windrush* landing found work in iron foundries, agriculture, railway and bricklaying in Scotland, Gloucester, the Midlands and South Wales. By the time of the 1991 National Census, Caribbean people were demographically widely dispersed with statistics showing that the greatest concentrations were in the South East, Yorkshire and Humberside, East and West Midlands, and Greater Manchester. Of the 3 million people of minority ethnic back-ground registered in the 1991 National Census, 96.5 per cent lived in England, 1.4 per cent in Wales and 2 per cent in Scotland.[25] According to the 1991 National Census the demographics of minority ethnic people in England break down in the following way: 1.2 per cent in the North (Tyne and Wear), 7 per cent in Yorkshire and Humberside, 6.1 per cent in the East Midlands, 1.4 per cent in East Anglia, 56.7 per cent in the South East, 2 per cent in the South West, 13 per cent in the West Midlands and 8 per cent in the North West.[26]

These statistics camouflage some other factors. First, Valerie Karn points out that because minority ethnic, and by implication Caribbean British people tend to reside in inner-city communities, from which well-to-do Whites and Blacks have retreated, they de facto live in relatively socio-economically deprived areas. Second, as a result, they are disproportionately represented as under-performing in key socio-economic indicators such as employment, health, education and housing.[27] Third, whereas Caribbean people lived in their different and disparate, mostly island countries in the Caribbean, they were to find themselves living closer together on one island, Britain, amid a people who hold little or no regard for them. If ethnicity meant little to them before, it now means a lot!

Towards a Caribbean British ethnic identity

As I have been discussing, ethnic identity in Britain carries with it major secular and religious implications. The first ethnic identity of Caribbean people in Britain, post-Windrush, was that of 'West Indians'. This designation was generally embraced and applied, both externally and internally. We see this, for example, in one of the first literary works produced from within the Caribbean British Churches where Ira Brooks uses the term 'West Indians' almost exclusively to describe people from the Caribbean.[28] The description, as has been pointed out above, was the legacy of Columbus' mistaken belief that he had landed in India, having sailed west from Europe to get there. Consequently, the area became known as the West Indies. In a similar vein, the people of the region became known as 'West Indians', a situation that prevailed at the time of the Windrush migration. In international cricket the side that represents the area is still known as the West Indies team. This identity was reinforced when, as West Indians, people suffered together the colour prejudice, rejection and racism that was perpetrated upon them corporately without regard to which island they came from, what ethnic mix constituted them, or to what faith or which Christian denomination they belonged.[29] However, the work of Asian Caribbean writer Philip Mohabir suggests that in Britain, the designation 'West Indian' was particularly embraced by Caribbean people of Asian/Indian heritage.[30] Although largely ignored, there always was something anomalous about describing as (West) 'Indians' those whose primary descendancy and features were apparently African.

A much greater problem loomed, however, because to continue to name these people, many of whom are British subjects, after where they have come from without reference to where they are, is to keep them in a permanent state of non-belonging, as 'foreigners'. An obvious shortcoming with Caribbean descended people in Britain being designated 'West Indian' is that this designation does not mention Britain; it therefore robs Caribbean persons in Britain of their British identity. This may have been fine for those whose intentions were a speedy return home, as indeed was the case with some West Indians. But this practice has become a means of 'othering' people who have settled and have taken on British citizenship, by disassociating their identity from a British one. This may also have served the intentions of some separatist 'Whites' and 'Blacks' in Britain. As Yasmin Alibhai-Brown demonstrates, right-wing political thinking has long held the view that Britishness is synonymous with Whiteness. This was particularly evident in Alibhai-Brown's encounter with Norman Tebbit on a Radio 4 *Today* programme.[31] For several reasons, then, West Indian as an ethnic designation slowly became a less used phrase for Caribbean heritage people in Britain.

West Indian gave way to 'Afro Caribbean' as a second ethnic identity of Caribbean people in Britain. This emerged in Britain in the wake of developments in the United States of the Black Consciousness Movement – which was an African-centric movement – during the 1960s, whereby Afro American became popular and spread throughout the African Diaspora.[32] That the African descended Caribbean majority in Britain became disaffected with their 'West Indian' ethnic designation was not surprising, given the Jamaican majority among Caribbean people in Britain, coupled with the African majority constitutive of that island's ethnic make-up. The initial reaction of many West Indians in Britain was to call themselves, and to accept being called, Afro Caribbean – a practice that at a stroke Africanized the Caribbean identity that had historically been 'Indianized' by the Columbus legacy. It rendered 'non' Africans invisible in Caribbean identity. No one was sure what 'Afro' meant, however, except that it had a pan-African resonance, which was probably sufficiently vague for a people who were somewhat distanced from Africa by 500 years of slave transplantation experience and ethnic fusion. There were during this time Afro hairdos, Afro art, and a range of Afro-centric iconography.

As alluded to above, the 'Africanization' of Caribbean British identity was largely the result of an over-reliance upon American Black ideology. There appears to have been the assumption of a direct correlation between the identities of Afro American and Afro Caribbean. Such an assumption did not take into full account the mongrelization of Caribbean identity in general, and geography. The difference between the two situations can best be seen by emphasizing that the 'Afro Americans' were situated in America, their parents having derived directly from Africa, while the 'Afro Caribbean' were situated in Britain, their parents having been twice removed, first from Africa, then from the Caribbean. There was, therefore, a significant contextual difference between the Afro American in America and the Afro Caribbean in Britain.

By the mid-1970s 'Afro' had given way to 'African' as a generic geo-ethnic description of Caribbean people in Britain. This did away with the ambiguity of 'Afro' and full-frontally laid the claim of Caribbean people to an African heritage. It was a further attempt to align British 'Africans' with American 'Africans', because as Afro Americans became African Americans, so 'Afro Caribbean' became 'African

Caribbean'. However, given that people in Britain of African Caribbean descent have historically shared little, if any, socio-political commonality with Africans in Britain of direct African descendancy, these identity developments were almost exclusively the making of the Caribbean Diaspora seeking to lay claim to their lost African identity, made more poignant by the struggle for 'racial' identity that is so manifest in Britain.[33] This was a 'Caribbean in Britain' identity crisis. As discussed above, the development in Britain of Africanizing Caribbean identity disenfranchises 'non' African descended Caribbean people, and it disinherits all Caribbean descended people in Britain of their British heritage, by making no reference to their being British. However, 'African Caribbean' held sway for quite some time. Probably the key to these developments was the element of self-naming, important to a minority people who had suffered centuries of being named by their overlords.

West Indians, Afro Caribbean, African Caribbean, et al have had to share their ethnic space with 'Black', which has come to be used as a socio-political, generic term for 'non-White' people in Britain. As Beckford describes it,

> The concept Black is a complex ethnic-political description. On the one hand it is a synonym for dark-skinned people, that is Africans, African Caribbean and Asians. On the other hand, it can encompass those who are not White or those engaging in resistance to domination, or what I call counter-hegemonic resistance.[34]

Caribbean identity has become submerged in a multiple and complex terminology. Black is so all-encompassing that according to Beckford it can be used generally for all people who are in solidarity against White hegemony, White power, or White supremacy. Adding to the complexity, another application that envelops Caribbean descended people in Britain is that of 'ethnic minorities'. This heterogeneous term implies a plurality of different ethnic groups, which are rarely defined and, therefore, frequently assume the meaning of 'non-White'.

This thesis argues that to be consistent with the history of Caribbean ethnicity, a terminology has to be found that legitimizes the ethnic complexity of Caribbean ethnic diversity as a result of the co-mingled existence of many people in the Caribbean, while simultaneously acknowledging their British identity. Acknowledging the reality that the term 'Caribbean' is a derivative from one of the original Indian people of the area, the Caribs, and is based upon the belief that these original Indian people were cannibals, it nevertheless commands universal acceptance among people from that area and outside. It is difficult to pluralize, but 'Caribbean' does not, like 'Indian', or 'African', side with any contemporary claimants of area identity. Negatively, it could be argued that like 'West Indian', 'Caribbean' was coined by the European colonizers. However, it remains a more neutral term and is better able than others to enjoy the acceptance of all the region's people.

This people, who have lived in the 'mother country' in significant numbers since the post-war era and who are now in their fourth generation in Britain, cannot continue to be known exclusively by where they came from. The overwhelming majority of Caribbean descended people in Britain were born here and almost all are now British citizens. Any current ethnic derivation must take account of this historic development, too. Hence, this thesis refers to Caribbean descended people in Britain as 'Caribbean British'. This accomplishes three significant feats. First, it avoids the wholesale Africanization of Caribbean identity, acknowledging Caribbean identity as being derived from original Indian people, Europeans, Africans and Asians in the Caribbean. Second, it embraces Caribbean heritage as a primary geo-ethnic identity. Third, it embraces British heritage, as the most recent addition to the development of the ethnicity of the people in Britain of Caribbean descent. Ethnic identity is important in the affirmation of any people as part of the diversity of God's creation of humanity.

Religious experience of Caribbean British people

Settling in Britain since the late 1940s, Caribbean British people brought their faiths with them too. Given the dominance of Christianity in its many forms in the Caribbean, inevitably Christianity now is the overwhelming expression of Caribbean British faith. Among minority faiths that were brought from the Caribbean, there are sprinklings of the presence of Pukkumina, Rastafarianism, Hinduism and Islam. In more recent times, there has been clear development of second and third generation Caribbean British gravitating towards the Black Islamic ideology of American Louis Farrakhan's 'Nation of Islam', a continuum of the Black Consciousness Movement that was evident in the United States in the recent past.

However, Christianity has been and remains the central and most followed faith expression of Caribbean British people. According to the 2001 Census, among minority ethnic (including Black African and Caribbean) people in England and Wales, 71 per cent were of Christian persuasion, with the remaining 29 per cent spread across a range of other faiths.[35] Understanding the Christian traditions followed by Caribbean British people requires a move away from the usual stereotyping of 'Black Christians equals Pentecostals', to a broader and more complex analysis of this people and their Christian belonging. As discussed above, the missionary activity that accompanied European expansionism meant that there was a very close approximation of Christian denominations in the Caribbean to those that operated in Europe and North America. This has meant that many Caribbean migrants have travelled to Britain as existing members of British denominations. Others came to Britain as members of denominations that did not exist here, which they sought to establish. All of this has resulted in a diverse denominational belonging of Caribbean British people.

One survey shows that there is a very considerable ethnic mixture in most church congregations and a near comprehensive presence of ethnic minorities across the British denominational spectrum.[36] The presence of Caribbean British

Christians is combined in the survey with those in Britain of direct African descent. However, Caribbean representation can be assessed based upon the 1991 National Census, which shows that Caribbean descended 'Black people' outnumber African descended 'Black people' by a ratio of two to one. This ratio changes in the 2001 Census, which shows Black Caribbean at 1 per cent and Black African at 0.8 per cent of the population. Applying the 1991 Census proportionality, Peter Brierley's research shows that of the 269,000 'Black' Christians attending churches in Britain in 1998, two-thirds, that is 180,000, or 4.8 per cent of the total churchgoing population in England of 3.7 million, were of Caribbean British ethnicity. This compares with their 0.9 per cent representation in the general population of Britain in the 1991 Census. By this reckoning, Caribbean Christians have a five times greater presence among British churchgoing than they do in the population at large. Brierley's statistics show also that 36 per cent of Caribbean British people are regular church attendees, compared with the 7 per cent of the British population as a whole. In terms of Caribbean British and African British presence in 'mainstream' denominations, Brierley's research shows that the Roman Catholic Church has 23 per cent of the total, just ahead of the Church of England, 22 per cent, followed by the Baptists with 8 per cent, the Methodists with 6 per cent, other denominations with 6 per cent, New churches with 4 per cent and Independent churches with 4 per cent.[37] Combined, Pentecostals accounted for just 27 per cent. Taken together, Brierley's statistics show that approximately 60 per cent of Black Christians attend the four 'mainstream' British churches. However, a recent Church of England report shows that as a percentage of the Church of England's overall membership, minority ethnic presence in England is only 3.1 per cent, as against the 9 per cent cited by Brierley. According to Brierley's survey, 22 per cent of the Black churchgoing population attend the Church of England, and that constitutes 9 per cent of the Church of England's overall attendance.[38] Although the Church of England's report measures committed membership and Brierley measures church attendance, the gap is significant and the truth of Caribbean British and other minority ethnic church affiliation probably lies some-where between these extremes.

While the overall picture of a pervasive Black and minority ethnic, and by implication Caribbean British, Christian presence across the denominational spectrum is clear, these statistics have to be tempered by the findings of the 2001 Census,[39] which shows significant changes in the numbers and distribution of minority ethnic people and their faiths in Britain. It shows that in England and Wales 75.69 per cent of the White population indicate they are Christians, which compares with 71.1 per cent of the Black population, 52.46 per cent of people of Mixed ethnicity, 27.18 per cent of Chinese and Others, and 4.06 per cent of Asians. Although the Census measures 'societal belonging', not official church membership or church attendance, this is quite striking as it has historically been assumed, and Brierley's research tended to support the notion, that a significantly higher proportion of the Black population are 'religious' as compared with the White population. By 'societal belonging' I mean that when people tick a box, as in the 2001 Census, they are stating generalized affiliation which requires no real commitment such as is required when one belongs to a church. The difference may be that Brierley measures church attendance in which Blacks may have a higher rate of adherence. Again, using the 2001 Census figures, it is possible to deduce that 38.7 per cent of the minority ethnic population of 4,635,296 are Christians. This means that whereas Brierley suggests a total of 440,100 minority ethnic Christian church attendees in 1998, there may in fact be 1.8 million minority ethnic Christians in Britain! A significant percentage of these will be of Caribbean British heritage.

The widespread presence of Caribbean British Christians exists in spite of the repeatedly stated historic rejection of Caribbean British and other minorities of colour who have attempted to engage with the mainstream denominations. Two possible reasons can be cited for this development: first, the problem of White rejection and exclusion of Black Christians has been exaggerated, and second, to the extent that Black British Christians were rejected, they have learned to rise above such rejection and have remained part of these denominations. There is evidence to support the notion that the matter is not as simple as is often suggested, for at a time when there has been a popular understanding that 'Black' people have been excluded from 'White' churches, Oliver Lyseight, the chief pioneer of the New Testament Church of God, now a leading 'Black-led' church in Britain, writes that his and other colleagues' experience in the early 1950s was one of being made to feel welcome and given opportunities to preach in both mainstream and White Pentecostal churches.[40] Lyseight recognizes that this was not the experience of everyone he knew, but his is as much part of Caribbean British experience as any other.

When I pastored a church in Sheffield, I was told about the minister of one local Methodist church in the Parkhill area who made strenuous efforts to welcome Caribbean British and other minority ethnic people into the local church. The story goes that he so fell in love with the early West Indians he met that in retirement he went to live in the Caribbean. This true story was told to me during research for my Masters degree. Apparently, the Victoria Methodist Church became a real place of welcome for early Caribbean Christians, and during my time in Sheffield (1989–96) meaningful relationships developed between that church and my own, particularly between the Caribbean British elements within both churches. Another person I met, a minister in the Elim Pentecostal Church, once took me to task concerning the claim of absolute White rejection of all Black Christians in Britain. He protested that he worked closely with several Black ministers over many years. While there was and is racism, this is not the whole story.

The complexity of the situation is further expressed in that some have pointed to the relational difficulties between Black British Christians in British mainline churches and their counterparts in the 'Black-led' churches. S. E. Arnold, former National Overseer of a Caribbean British-led denomination, has criticized some in mainstream churches for being guilty of patronizing their brothers and sisters in the Caribbean British-led churches, viewing them as theologically and liturgically

inferior 'clap-hand' churches.[41] This practice is a carryover
from the Caribbean, whereby those of a higher social standing
tended to belong to more conservative, literary-liturgical and
'state-like' churches, while those further down the social
ladder belonged to the more spontaneous, oral-liturgical,
'native' forms of church.

Black British Methodist Robinson Milwood, however,
describes some Black people as being refugees from White-led
mainstream churches.[42] These people, who were members but
left because they felt rejected by Whites in mainstream
churches, in his view did not have sufficient courage to fight
for their corner in their church. However, some 'refugees'
from mainstream churches, such as Io Smith[43] and Ira
Brooks,[44] believe they have found a better quality of religious
life outside of mainstream churches than they ever found
within them. Their brief experience of rejection in White-led
churches was quickly replaced by acceptance and nurture in
churches led by Caribbean British Christians. In spite of all
this, increasingly, the distinction between Black British
Christianity in churches led by Black British Christians and
that in churches led by White Christians is being blurred
gradually. This can be seen in the increased occasions of cross-
denominational participation in worship, forums, publications and social and political action. Several events testify to
this gradual integration. For example, the projects I have been
party to at the Centre for Black and White Christian Partnership, such as Black theology forums, publications and joint
learning initiatives, have all been done without discrimination
on the grounds of denominations, mainstream or Black-led.
None of this, however, can detract from the issues of discrimination in church and society, to which many testify.

That Caribbean British and other minorities have felt the
cold rejection of many at both institutional and personal
levels cannot be denied. This reality has been attested to by
too many for it to be qualified or explained away. Martin
Simmonds writes of his experience:

This sense of being frozen out of a fellowship from which
one had expected warmth and love, not only formed the hot

seedbed for spiritual alienation, but it reinforces the complexes of inferiority and superiority of one race over another, and it heightens the pain of social bereavement and cultural alienation.[45]

Another writer on these matters states:

> I can hardly forget the experience of our first visit to an English church. The pews were inscribed with people's names. I kept shuffling around in the hope of finding an unreserved spot where I could sit down. No one came to our rescue. Instead I could actually 'feel' the piercing effects of the glazed eyes of our hosts, who meticulously switched off their gaze in the event of our eyes meeting theirs![46]

These stories are among numerous written and verbally reported to me. Even allowing for a degree of over-reporting by repetition, the picture remains bleak concerning the treatment meted out to Caribbean British Christians since the Windrush. However, far from buckling under such rejection, Caribbean British Christianity has responded in two clear ways. First, some have left to join other churches that demonstrated a better understanding of God's love for their 'Black' humanity, while others simply have refused to be suppressed in the church of their choice or which has been theirs historically. The former is responsible for the burgeoning, fastest growing sector of British church life, the 'Black-led churches'. The latter is responsible for the current situation where more Caribbean British Christians are in attendance at 'mainstream' churches than in the ones led by Caribbean British and other minority leaders.[47] Milwood typifies this spirit of resistance.

Black-led agencies in mainstream churches

In response to the presence of Caribbean British and other minority ethnic Christians in the 'mainstream', White-led British churches, and coupled with the general acceptance that racism exists in the structures and people of these churches, the main denominations have acted by establishing Black caucuses within them. These national appointments are invariably replicated at regional or diocesan levels within these churches. In the Church of England the caucus is known as the Committee for Minority Ethnic Concerns. It was in the Church of England, too, that the Association of Black Clergy emerged and now seeks to be multi-denominational. Similar appointments have followed in the Methodist, Catholic, Baptist, Salvation Army and United Reformed churches.

There are signs of hope that these fledgling 'organizations' will become forces for unity both within and across cultural and denominational divides. One such sign is the coming together of leaders of these caucuses under the auspices of Churches Together in Britain and Ireland's Minority Ethnic Christian Affairs framework, of which I am Secretary. The Minority Ethnic Christian Affairs is a new department within Churches Together in Britain and Ireland. It has emerged from a predecessor department called Black Christian Concerns, and seeks to network and support minority ethnic Christians in Britain and Ireland.

In addition to these denominationally internal organs, other cross-denominational bodies have been established. Among them are the above-mentioned Centres for Black and White Christian Partnership in Birmingham, Oxford, and Leicester. Similar organizations went under different names, like Keyboard in Bristol, the Zebra Project in London, Christian Action for Racial Equality in Liverpool, CONTRAST in Nottingham and the Churches Commission for Racial Justice (CCRJ). These were attempts to collaborate across denominational and ethnic boundaries, and were nearly always formed at the behest of Caribbean British Christians. Some are no longer in existence, while new ones have arisen.[48] Although I have been referring to these as 'ecumenical' organizations, not all exist for this precise purpose; some, like CONTRAST, are educationally focused, others, like CCRJ, are focused on racial justice. In their own ways, they all offer hope for better intercultural Christian relations in the future.

Having examined the Caribbean and other Black presence in mainstream, I now turn to the Churches Caribbean British Christians initiated.

Black-led churches

If we are to hold the so-called 'Black-led' or 'Black majority' churches, significant numbers of which are led and peopled by Caribbean British Christians, in proper view, we must have a correct understanding of how they happen to come into being. Since the 1950s churches established by and in migrant communities have emerged in Britain with some frequency. And their growth and spread has been nothing short of phenomenal. As I demonstrate below, initially these churches were exclusively those to which Caribbean Christians belonged 'back home', but which they did not find operating upon their arrival in Britain. While many Caribbean Christians arrived in Britain already belonging to British mainstream denominations, many belonged to those denominations that were established in the Caribbean by American missionaries during the early twentieth century. Some of these Christians were Pentecostals, others were from the Holiness and other traditions. It was these people who began to meet in their homes for prayer and fellowship.

An example of a typical development is offered by Norma Thomas-Juggan in the establishing of the Church of God in Christ in Britain.[49] Typically, Christians arriving from the Caribbean would learn of one another and agree to meet for prayer and fellowship in a home, sometimes moving from house to house. The homes in which meetings were held invariably provided the necessary pastoral leadership. After a while the home would become too small, and a community, school or church hall would be booked. The next step was to purchase a building of their own as numbers grew, bringing a greater sense of stability, respectability and achievement. This was certainly the case in a number of churches I visited, and some I supervised as bishop, where owning a place of worship was of crucial and defining significance. In some cases, a handful of people would make massive financial sacrifices to purchase and maintain a property in their name. Often these were old and decaying buildings, owned previously by a mainstream denomination. A case in point is the Church of God of Prophecy in Dudley Hill, Bradford, where a membership of 15, mainly family, bought and tried to maintain a large property. It was clearly a struggle for so few people.

This phenomenon occurred against the background of the mixed, mostly hostile reception Caribbean British and other minorities received in church and wider society in Britain. This has fuelled the popularly held view that rejection was the main reason for these churches' existence. This view, made popular by White academics, has been largely imbibed by many Black people too. Even one of the very latest books to emerge from the Caribbean British sector still posits this popular myth about the *raison d'être* of those churches initiated by people from the Africa, Asia and the Caribbean. As Sturge puts it, 'Historically, both in the USA and in Britain, Black people were excluded from mainstream churches, thereby leading them to establish their own.'[50] Had this been the case, we might have expected to see several occurrences of mainstream churches being planted by migrant members who were rejected by those denominations to which they had belonged at home. This did not occur, however, because rejection was by no means the major reason for the establishing of non-mainstream churches led by Caribbean British Christians. Nor, as we shall see, were these churches established for reasons of ethnicity that might legitimize their being labelled 'Black', 'Black-led', 'Black majority', or even Caribbean British churches. Adrian Hastings rightly states that the new Black churches were not 'Black' in principle, but overwhelmingly so as regards membership.[51]

When referring to these churches, generic terms like 'African Caribbean Christianity', 'Black church', 'Black Pentecostal church',[52] 'Black Church Movement',[53] 'Black-led church', 'Black majority church', and 'Pentecostal-Holiness church'[54] are used to portray an ecclesiological homogeneity that does not truly exist among the community being described. Though only slightly different from 'Black-led', 'Black majority' is the most recently used phrase that appears to command near universal acceptance among 'Black Christians'. It has been pioneered by the African and Caribbean Evangelical Alliance, and therefore has a high degree of 'Black' ownership, unlike 'Black-led', which many felt was a White imposition. These terms camouflage the separate theological and denominationalized existence of the churches led by Caribbean British Christians. As Valentina Alexander shows, these denominations have different histories, worship styles and theologies.[55] Virginia Becher and Margaret Breiner point, on the other hand, to the historical/theological roots of the premier Christian organizations to which Caribbean British Christians belong. These roots and routes predate and are determinative of their expressions in Britain since the 1950s.[56] The three dominant theological-doctrinal streams – Pentecostalism, the Holiness Movement and Sabbatarianism – can all be traced to their American roots. Similarly, Roman Catholic and European/North American mainstream Protestant denominations also had pre-determinative influences upon Caribbean British Christianity. The central point that is made here is that Caribbean migrants brought their denominations with them to Britain and sought to set them up where they did not exist before.

Elaine Foster states that Black settlers from the Caribbean were deeply spiritual people who had a dynamic faith before they left their homes to journey to Britain.[57] Also, the records show that theirs was a deeply entrenched, denominationalized faith. Some have sought to deny this inherent denominationalism. Gerloff argues that the 'early mission' phase of the Black Church Movement in Britain was one in which the early Christian migrants had little or no interest in denominational affiliation or segregated Black congregations.[58] She further suggests, and this discussion agrees in part, that the migrating Black Christians had an inclusive ecclesiology within which evangelism occurred without regard to colour, culture, nationality and denomination, but which was subverted by the divide-and-rule tactics of outsiders. Gerloff says,

Large, partly White, American Pentecostal and Holiness headquarters [seized] the opportunity of gaining a foothold in Europe by gathering a great number of immigrants under their organisational wings and working towards administrative and economic centralisation.[59]

Here I take issue with Gerloff, because this portrayal of Black naivety and White American opportunism is not consistent with history as it has been researched and understood in this work. For example, Eric Pemberton et al state that the religious faith brought to Britain by Christians of the Pilgrim Holiness Church from the Caribbean formed the roots from which the Wesleyan Holiness Church of the British Isles would grow.[60] These authors point out also that while White reaction to the growing Black presence of the early migration era was mixed – some openly welcoming, others unable to accept and accommodate them – 'the desire to fellowship and worship with those of similar culture, colour and conviction burned long in the hearts of many'.[61] The rejection encountered by some Holiness Church adherents was, in this regard at least, merely incidental, not causal. We can reasonably state that the Black church in Britain is not the illegitimate child of rejection, but is born of the will of God!

We find that separate denominational development is not the result of American intervention; rather, it is the natural continuity of denominational identities that migrants brought with them to their new home in Britain. As Io Smith says, they came from various already existing denominations and they carried with them a vision and the burning desire of the faith of the Lord Jesus Christ, which they practised in the West Indies.[62] Philip Mohabir confirms this pattern when he says that Black churches have developed independently of each other.[63] This is sometimes true even within the same denomination. The development of this movement, therefore, is complex, but has at least three clear traits. First, it is denominational rather than non-denominational and usually has affiliation with a larger, often international, body. Second, it is ethnically defined, in that the overwhelming majority of its membership and leadership are from the Caribbean British, or some other Black or minority ethnic group. Third, it is self-impelling in response to missionary and evangelistic needs, rather than being driven by outside factors or interests.

Particularly because of the near univocal, if ill-informed, insistence that these churches are the by-product of rejection, I want to examine how some of the early ones got started. This review will illustrate the nature of their early development, making clear what the driving factors were, as told by the people themselves.

Church of God in Christ (CoGiC)

The authorized history of CoGiC has been written in recent times by Norma Thomas-Juggan[64] and provides the most authoritative documentation on the denomination. Thomas-Juggan shows that the denomination commenced operating in London in 1952, in the home of a migrant CoGiC member from Jamaica, Mrs (Mother) McLachlan. This makes it the first Caribbean British-led denomination to be established in Britain during the period under consideration. CoGiC is notably the largest Black North American Pentecostal body.[65] There is no evidence that McLachlan visited other British churches before starting prayer meetings in her home. Finding no CoGiC in England at that time, she started one with others. In its earliest days the Church's mission was one of providing a place of spirit-filled Pentecostal worship.[66] The denomination was formally recognized in the year of its initiation in England, 1952, by its Black-led international headquarters, based in the United States. Within a few months of starting, the fledgling fellowship was visited by the international Presiding Bishop, Charles Mason, while attending the World Pentecostal Conference at Westminster Central Hall in London. The international office moved quickly to provide support in the form of personnel for the work in England.

With support from America and with ever increasing numbers of migrants, CoGiC grew in number from its own migrating adherents and became a place of shelter for non-CoGiC

members who were unable to find their brand of Pentecostalism in the area. Thomas-Juggan says:

> Many of those who came to worship at Sussex Road came
> from various Pentecostal churches in the West Indies, i.e.
> New Testament Church of God, Church of God of
> Prophecy, Church of the First Born and others. They were
> drawn to the worship because it was the only church they
> knew where the worship was familiar. However, as soon as
> they were able to locate their own churches, they left and
> began to fellowship with their own.[67]

CoGiC was not established in Britain as a result of American
intervention, nor because of British oppression; rather, its
members from the Caribbean, not finding their denomination
in operation in their new British home, set it up. Assistance
from its parent body ensured its survival and its ability to provide a temporary home for those migrants that needed it.
CoGiC has remained a relatively small operation in Britain;
said to be the largest Black-led church in the world, its membership derives mainly from the United States,[68] and it has
not been able to translate its success in the United States and
other parts of the world to the UK. It is possible that a church
that started operating to provide worship space of a particular
sort for small numbers of people found it difficult to change
gear and discover a wider missiology.

Church of God of Prophecy (CoGoP)

A brief history of CoGoP in England can be found in my
Masters thesis of 1994.[69] Recognized as one of the more
respectable and progressive Black-led churches in Britain,
CoGoP was in fact first initiated in Bedford by a White
American missionary among White British people. Its first
National Overseer was an Englishman by the name of
England. C. T. Davidson, the Church's official international
historian, states:

The Church of God of Prophecy reached England in 1953, when Overseer Homer Rye organized the Church at 61 Victoria Road, Bedford, with thirteen members that included Herbert England, a minister with twenty-one years' experience. He was set forth for the ministry and chosen pastor of the new church.[70]

From early on, some Caribbean migrants joined Herbert England for worship, travelling from places as far away as Birmingham and London to Bedford, and there was no recognizable Caribbean-led Church of God of Prophecy congregation until after the mid-1950s. Not everyone travelled to Bedford, and those who did, did not do so consistently. Until 1955, CoGoP members in Birmingham were still sharing interdenominational Black Pentecostal worship with others. According to one of its founding fathers, T. A. McCalla,

> In 1955 a group of Christians from different denominations, including the Church of God of Prophecy, were worshipping at the Midlands Institute in the city of Birmingham for a period of time.[71]

The Church's American headquarters had launched its missionary activity in England as part of a world outreach evangelistic programme independent of Black migration. However, as increasing numbers of CoGoP members arrived from the Caribbean, new fellowships began and they were made aware of the presence of the denomination's national head in Bedford, and over time a national network was established.

CoGoP membership became mainly Black under the national leadership of Herbert England and the American headquarters. Three White majority congregations existed in Bedford, but as the number of new Black-led fellowships of CoGoP with members arriving from the Caribbean grew, alongside new converts, Caribbeans quickly outnumbered White English members. The commencement of this church's operations, then, clearly had little to do with the social conditions of Caribbean and other Black people, who having previously belonged to this denomination in their home countries then swelled its numbers and added to its growth in Britain.

New Testament Church of God (NTCoG)

According to historian Ira Brooks, the person who was to become the chief pioneer of NTCoG in Britain, Oliver Lyseight, left Jamaica in 1951 with the exhortation from a fellow minister in Jamaica to 'seek for members of the Church who [are] growing spiritually "cold" in Britain and have fellowship with them in prayer'.[72] Lyseight was already a NTCoG pastor by the time he left Jamaica for economic reasons. According to Lyseight in his autobiography, he with others attended and preached in British mainline and White-led Pentecostal churches soon after his arrival. In 1953 they responded to words of prophecies and their knowledge of the plight of many who fared less favourably than they in seeking places to worship and formed their own fellowship.[73] Although Lyseight's fellowship had non-NTCoG people in it, the work was established in the name of the denomination in which he was an ordained minister, although it took two years for the international office in America to recognize it officially. Lyseight points out that some members of CoGoP left NTCoG as they became aware of CoGoP's existence in Bedford.[74] However, the church quickly spread across England and Wales, overwhelmingly among Caribbean people. But this move to establish NTCoG churches was in recognition of a desire to replicate their particular church worship experience, enjoyed in the Caribbean prior to coming to Britain.

The desire to be part of a familiar worship setting is illustrated by Lyseight, who writes of arriving in Wolverhampton in 1951 as a 'Pentecostalist'. The first church he attended was the local White-led Methodist church.[75] There he received warm hospitality, and was taken home by a White family for lunch on his very first visit. Preferring a Pentecostal church in which to worship, Lyseight then found a White Pentecostal church where he worshipped for some time. However, he did not settle here either, leaving eventually to establish the denomination to which he originally belonged, the New Testament Church of God. It was Lyseight's personal initiative that led to the setting up of NTCoG and again it was not based upon rejection; quite the opposite, because from his own testimony he had been made to feel welcome by the White Christians he had lived among.

The seminal Wolverhampton branch of NTCoG started its life in the YMCA hall in September 1953, after Lyseight had managed to assemble a group of seven for worship. In 1955 two missions were organized as the first congregations of the New Testament Church of God in England.[76] That the official organization of the Church in England did not occur until 1955 is testimony to its allegiance to its US (White-led) headquarters, and it required a visit by the 'indefatigable executive secretary of world missions' to validate its authenticity as a Church in England.[77] According to Brooks,

> The work expanded in an unintentionally centrifugal manner: a new field would establish itself into the role of parent-body, send out workers who would concentrate on a radial course until the mission phased out.[78]

Brooks further points out that groups began to mushroom simultaneously in London and other cities where NTCoG members were arriving. He says:

> It is an interesting fact that while the organisation was developing in the Midlands and Northern England, similar operations in London, though simultaneous, were completely independent and totally unaware of their counterparts.[79]

Only after the installation of Lyseight as National Overseer by the international administration in Cleveland, Tennessee in 1956 did the New Testament Church of God in England become united under a centralized administration. Significantly, Brooks points out that at the time of the inception of the New Testament Church of God in Britain, the international polity of the 'Church of God', the parent organization, did not permit Blacks to be overseers.[80] It was not until

1958 that the General Assembly amended the constitutional ruling that prevented Black ministers from becoming Overseers.[81] Again, an examination of NTCoG's initiation shows it to be the result not of rejection by the host community, but of mission to provide for their members the church of their former Caribbean homeland. In the case of Lyseight, far from being rejected by the mainstream, he was embraced as a preacher and given ample opportunities to minister.

Bethel United Church of Jesus Christ (Apostolic) UK

The above pattern of Caribbean British migrants establishing their brand of denominations is a recurrent theme, and in 1955 Bethel United Church of Jesus Christ (Apostolic) UK was started.[82] Its founder, Sydney Dunn, arrived in Birmingham in early 1955 and states that he immediately searched for an Apostolic church. Finding none, he soon made contact with a few other Apostolic 'saints' and they commenced worshipping together in one of their homes, before acquiring a building of their own in 1959. The exclusive Pentecostal Oneness ecclesiology of Dunn and his compatriots meant that they were not interested in worshipping with any other 'pseudo' church. Again, the progress from arrival to establishing of their church did not allow for seeking to discover if they would have been welcome in a mainstream church.

Wesleyan Holiness Church

The Wesleyan Holiness Church started operating in the UK in 1958. Unlike the majority of churches led by Christians of Caribbean British descent, the Wesleyans' founder, D. A. Samson, hailed from Antigua, and was one of only a few Caribbean British national leaders who were not Jamaicans. The church used the name Pilgrim Holiness Church until 1980, when it adopted the title Wesleyan Holiness Church as a result of changes at its American headquarters.[83] While being historically very close to the Methodist Church, its

Caribbean members did not appear to consider joining upon arrival in Britain. Again, we observe the significance of denominational practice and ethnic familiarity to Caribbean British Christians.

Like the Church of God of Prophecy and the New Testament Church of God, this Church's White-led headquarters are in the United States and Samson came to Britain specifically to ensure that 'pilgrims' were provided with their own brand of church. This church is yet another good example of the manner in which churches led by Caribbean British Christians carved out denominationally separate lives. Samson left Antigua in 1957 specifically to gather and shepherd the scattered flock of 'pilgrims' known to be in Britain at that time. Once in England, he embarked upon a search and rescue mission for 'pilgrims'.[84] His vision was to establish a pilgrim work in Britain as part of the worldwide Pilgrim Holiness Church. He and others succeeded, spreading throughout the country. However, it was not until 1962 that the international headquarters in the United States recognized the work in Britain officially as a District, and this only after failed attempts had been made by them to align the fledgling Black-led work under Samson with existing White-led Holiness groups in Britain. These Caribbean British Christians demonstrate yet again their determination to continue to be part of their historic denomination, which provided the culturally sensitive Christian environment that they were accustomed to.

New Testament Assembly (NTA)

In similar fashion, the key two operators of the New Testament Assembly (NTA), Bernard and Powell, migrated from Jamaica to England and commenced operating here.[85] Their inaugural prayer meeting took place in the London home of one of their patrons at Fontenoy Road, Balham, London in 1961. According to these pioneers, they did not come to Britain with missionary intent to establish a church.[86] Although both pastored in Jamaica before arriving in

England, they insist that it was the call of God and the encouragement of others that impacted upon them 'shortly after
arriving' that caused them to consider establishing the church
they belonged to in Jamaica. NTA was a small national
church in Jamaica, compared with, say, the Church of God
of Prophecy or the New Testament Church of God. It continued in a similar vein in England as a small and quite
specifically London-based organization.

According to Brooks, NTA had broken with the New
Testament Church of God in Jamaica in 1954 over the issue
of the imposition of White national leadership upon the more
than 20,000 Black membership of the Jamaican church.[87]
Such radical anti-racist action is quite striking in the colonial
world of mid twentieth century Caribbean. This single-
minded approach to setting up NTA in Jamaica, based upon
the guarding of the integrity of their humanity and spirituality, meant that nothing less would do in Britain. By the time
of this denomination's inauguration in Britain, many other
Caribbean-led denominations had been in existence for
some time; however, no attempt at integration was made,
not even with other similar ethnic groups to themselves. In
this case, denominational affiliation held sway over ethnic
identity.

New churches: Rhema and Ruach

The churches led by Caribbean British Christians that were
set up from the 1950s to the 1980s were much the same as the
traditional Pentecostal and Holiness types. However, from
the 1980s onwards, a new kind of Charismatic/Pentecostal
church began to emerge among Caribbean British and other
minority ethnic groups. Rhema Christian Church is a contemporary expression of a modern Caribbean British-led
church.[88] The church started in 1991, with ten people led by
Mark Goodridge, who had been a leader in the Shiloh
Apostolic Churches of Christ, which he left to start Rhema.
According to its literature, it was formed in the last decade of
the twentieth century; it emphasizes its role as a prophetic

voice for the twenty-first century, being a family-oriented church offering quality worship, aggressive prayer, spiritual warfare, sound biblical teaching and practical Christian living. Its founder believes he is responding to a divine directive to establish new principles and minister to the entire Body of Christ.

Another church of a similar type is Ruach Ministries, with its motto 'Everybody is somebody'. Ruach represents another attempt to break the traditional denominational mould by embracing traditional vibrant Pentecostal worship but eschewing traditional prohibition regarding dress codes, and focusing upon street evangelism that targets the 'depressed housewife' to the 'suicidal businessman', and in particular drug abusers. Against this background, Ruach's numbers soon soared.[89]

Both Rhema and Ruach can be seen as responses to the disciplinarian, introspective and working class expression of the traditional Black Church. They are part of a plethora of new Black-led churches and fellowships in Britain that appear to be a contemporary response to a call for appropriate church and worship space for an emerging Black, still primarily Caribbean, British people, in similar fashion to that provided by the earlier churches. While many claim to be non-denominational, they may well have simply replaced the old ones. Again, whatever part racism and rejection may play in their existence, it certainly is not their main driver; something else is at work here that is much more profound than anything humans can devise. As previously stated, denominational allegiance and commitment to Christian mission expressed mostly as evangelism are to the fore of these operations.

Ecumenical organizations

Because of the proliferation of Caribbean British-led churches and the increasingly evident socio-political needs of the Caribbean British and other minority ethnic communities, the need for agencies that could harness the potential of these

churches became clear. Caribbean British and other Black-led
ecumenical agencies were needed. As I have pointed out elsewhere, for ecumenism to be relevant to these communities,
they have to hold the possibilities of providing answers to the
opportunities and challenges of their particular settings.[90]
This cannot be the ecumenism that is based on the existing
local and national models that were established in the post-
war era in Europe in 1948.

It has been correctly identified for some time that the work
of Caribbean British Christianity has tended towards an
other-worldly thinking, with insufficient emphasis upon the
social and political needs of the Caribbean British Christian,
other faiths and secular communities. It took some time, but
as Joel Edwards acknowledges these churches finally accepted
that 'God had called [them] to a prophetic ministry, to actually become involved in the fabric of society'.[91] By the 1970s,
social unrest brought about by an increasing awareness of and
opposition to racism and its resultant negative trends in education, employment and housing, highlighted the need for
Caribbean British Christians to act together. Edwards points
to some of the social ills of that time.[92] For example,
Caribbean British young people constituted up to 34 per cent
of some prison populations, featured disproportionately in
police stop and search and arrests, and were seriously dys-
functioning in British schools. Desmond Pemberton, the first
chairman of the Afro-Westindian (*sic*) United Council of
Churches (AWUCOC), argued that living in Britain placed
great social and political stress on West Indians and their
children. He believed that one thing above all else that the
Black Church could do was to offer spiritual and emotional
support to families and individuals under severe stress.[93] This
was a call for social action that demanded a response from
Caribbean British churches.

According to Edwards, these realities made Caribbean
British Christians respond with, 'Hey, something is going
wrong here.' Some concluded, he says, that God was calling
them to more than had been realized when establishing
churches for worship.

They began to see that the calling that God had put upon them as the people of the Diaspora was not to have a good time on Sunday and let the world go to waste on Monday. It was not just to come and celebrate on Sunday, have a great time and see our children drifting away, our senior people beginning to go into psychiatric wards, our children dying in police custody; but God had called us to a prophetic ministry, to actually become involved in the fabric of our society.[94]

Edwards further states that there was near universal realization that the social plight of the Caribbean British community could not be left to the authorities, but provisions needed to be made for the increasing number of senior citizens and for supplementary education for the young. Also, mediation was necessary on behalf of those suffering disproportionately at the hands of the police. Tellingly, Edwards says:

We must go down to the local police stations and talk about race relations. We must get involved in industry and business. We must go and talk to the local politicians and councillors and bring them into our churches, our conventions and say to them that there is a people of God here who believe in holiness but recognize that holiness and righteousness belong together.[95]

In response to these social and political conditions, several Caribbean British-led 'ecumenical' or umbrella organizations and agencies have arisen. I mention briefly some below.

International Ministerial Council of Great Britain (IMCGB)

Launched in 1968, IMCGB was the first ecumenical body to attempt to network the leaders of churches peopled by Caribbean British and other Black Christians.[96] Yet the ideals of its founder were much more grand. First, it was that IMCGB's membership was open to all Christian organizations. Second, the UK was not its only area of work; Africa, the Caribbean, Asia and wider Europe were within its scope of thinking too. However, in reality the majority of its members were and are from Pentecostal churches. The organization's stated aims are to bring about unity and recognition between the denominations; to provide authenticity to its member churches, their ministers and leadership; and to bring them into a line of unity, respect and understanding. IMCGB also provides training and licensure for all ranks of ministry for member denominations. Given that mainstream churches already enjoy many of these aims, the organization's main focus was, de facto, on the churches of the Black and minority ethnic communities. In fact, IMCGB's central purpose has seemed to be to ensure that the churches led by Black Christians enjoy the high esteem of their neighbours because of their competence.

If the aim was to attract a wide range of patronage, that failed to materialize, and IMCGB has enjoyed only limited success. 'Mainstream' churches that were not in need of the status on offer from IMCGB simply did not join. The organizations that accepted the cover of IMCGB have been the smaller independent fellowships and denominations, which benefit from the 'legitimacy' or authenticity that emanates from IMCGB membership. But independent churches overseas have also come under IMCGB's umbrella. This unifying organization has attempted to co-ordinate responses to social needs in education and in accommodation for worship, and has been most effective in their relationship with the national ecumenical bodies on behalf of their members. IMCGB is probably best understood, as its name suggests, as a ministerial council, not a council of churches, but its effectiveness has been hindered by its inability to engage ministers from the larger and more influential Caribbean British and other Black-led churches. Having survived the death of its founder Archbishop Desmond Douglas during the 1990s, IMCGB continues to prosper but has suffered a number of splits, resulting in other ecumenical organizations being formed. What was set up as an instrument of unity has itself become beset by disunity.

Afro-Westindian United Council of Churches (AWUCOC)

Virtually without acknowledgement of IMCGB, probably because of its lack of recognition among the main Black-led churches, AWUCOC was established in 1976 as a federation of those churches that had been initiated by West Indian Christians. Its declared aims were to promote a sense of unity without conformity, tackling social and educational issues but leaving doctrinal matters to member churches.[97] According to Wilfred Woods, two other issues were on AWUCOC's agenda: first, addressing racist White Christian attitude towards Black Christians and their religious institutions, and second, the tension between those who understand the gospel as personal salvation over against those who see it as an agent of social and political action. Writing in the same directory as Woods, Milwood makes an impassioned assertion that spirituality and politics are coterminous entities: all theology is political, he argues.[98] For him, to be indifferent to the political, economic and religious struggle for liberation of the poor and oppressed is to be anti-gospel and non-theological. This goes to the very heart of the matter when we consider the growing awareness of the need for Caribbean British Christianity to be involved not only in the spiritual but also in the social and political aspects of the lives of its members and in the affairs of society at large.

Brooks states that it was the threat of the disintegration of the Black community that brought the leading heads of Black-led churches together, which in turn led to the emergence of AWUCOC.[99] This was a tacit acknowledgement that IMCGB had not performed effectively as a unifying socio-political and religious organ. AWUCOC's constitution sought to respond to this by opening its membership to all churches in the United Kingdom with predominantly 'Afro Caribbean' congregations.[100] Its initial membership reflected the breadth of Holiness and Pentecostal traditions that were in operation at the time of its inception, as is clearly demonstrated by the roll call of churches in its first handbook.[101]

According to Brooks, the establishing of AWUCOC signals several things. First, it indicates a new willingness to put aside organizational differences in the interest of the welfare of their offspring. Second, it raises hope of the dawn of a new era of a mature Caribbean British Christian leadership committed to one another. Third, these leaders will now be able to speak with one voice, not doctrinally nor organizationally but politically, in the demand for equal distribution of both spiritual and material opportunities. Finally, Brooks identifies some symbolism in the fact that AWUCOC's first 'home' was in a building named 'Caribbean House'. The link between the new organization and people of Caribbean heritage is clear. Although constitutionally open to 'all churches in the UK with predominantly Afro Caribbean congregations', the reality is that AWUCOC's appeal was exclusively to Caribbean British Christians and their churches. Also, from the late 1960s there was an orientation towards Caribbean British churches collaborating for the general good. But they had to contend with a growing number of new ecumenical bodies trying to bring this about. The degree to which AWUCOC has or has not achieved its goals is not my main point; rather, what is demonstrated is the awareness of the issues and a willingness to tackle them.

African and Caribbean Evangelical Alliance (ACEA)

Yet another ecumenical organization focused on the Caribbean British churches is known today as ACEA. It began in 1984 as the West Indian Evangelical Alliance (WIEA). Its founder, Philip Mohabir, lists six aims of WIEA, which seem to resonate with those of other agencies:

1 To strengthen relationships within the West Indian community thereby giving it a corporate identity.
2 To build bridges between the West Indian and English communities.
3 To become a voice for the nation representing the West Indian churches on social and spiritual matters.

4 To encourage and equip leadership in the local church by conducting consultations and seminars.

5 To stimulate prayer and faith for revivals and restoration.

6 To mobilise the Church for evangelism.[102]

These visionary aims necessitated appropriate policies and an infrastructure to enable and ensure their execution; and the evolution of the organization suggests that its operators have been acutely aware of this. They needed to talk the talk and walk the walk.

Reflecting the changing attitudes to ethnic identity, in 1989 WIEA became known as the Afro Caribbean Evangelical Alliance. Then, in 1991, it experienced another name change and became known as the African Caribbean Evangelical Alliance. Finally, in 1993, in recognition of the need to articulate the difference between Africans who come to Britain directly from Africa and Caribbean people, the majority of whom are themselves of indirect African descent, its current name was adopted: African and Caribbean Evangelical Alliance.[103] Starting just eight years after AWUCOC, WIEA emerged as an offshoot of the Evangelical Alliance with a clear evangelical identity, which it has maintained throughout its evolution. Indeed, I argue that ACEA is much more aligned to evangelical identity of a European sort than it is to African and Caribbean identities.

Currently, ACEA views itself as, and indeed is, the premier ecumenical organization of what it calls Black majority churches. It is 'at the heart of Black Christian faith in Britain', according to its promotional literature. This is consistent with one part of the vision of its founder, who saw two issues as being at the heart of his rationale for starting the organization in 1984: first, reconciling the fragmentation among Black-led churches, and second, the polarization between Black and White Christian communities.[104]

Ironically, it was also in 1984 that AWUCOC held its launch of the ground-breaking *Handbook of Afro-Westindian Churches in Britain*. Three ecumenical organizations, IMCGB, AWUCOC and ACEA, were now vying for supremacy, for premier status and recognition as the main unification body for Black Christian churches. With hindsight it is possible to discern that one (IMCGB) had a focus on a council of ministers, another (AWUCOC) focused on West Indian churches, and the other (ACEA) focused on unity among evangelicals. From my conversations with individuals who were involved with these organizations, the perception seems to have been that AWUCOC was primarily concerned with Black/Black ecumenism, WIEA/ACEA's primary goal was Black/White ecumenism, and IMCGB was thought to be about ministerial accreditation, where it was recognized at all. There was also significant overlap in membership. Again, the recognition that Caribbean British Christians needed to set up organizations of their own to address the issues they understood to be present is what, for this study, is most significant.

Mohabir is responsible for initiating yet another ecumenical organization called Connections, with an international, inter-racial and interdenominational remit.[105] Connections views itself as an interdenominational, cross-cultural, multi-racial and multi-faceted ministry. Its intention is to network, promote self-help, train and equip leaders, engage in social action nationally and multi-denominationally. Connections offers still another ecumenical opportunity for Caribbean British and other churches.

Other ecumenical instruments have emerged since those discussed above, particularly local councils of Black-led churches with which I have personally been involved. Probably the only truly different one with a distinctly political premise is the Black Christian Civic Forum (BCCF), launched in 1996. It owes its origin to the issues arising from the Stephen Lawrence murder and subsequent inquiry, which was led by Judge William Macpherson. As yet, the BCCF has failed to take root and this raises questions about the capacity, willingness or resistance of Caribbean British Christianity to pursue an overt political agenda.

The outcomes of the foregoing ecumenical activities have been many and varied. However, as already stated, key to these ecumenical organizations is what they represent as attempts by Caribbean British Christianity to define and develop its identity as a people of faith which takes care of its own business. The degree to which this internal ecumenical development will extend itself beyond its immediate borders and reach out to influence wider society remains an unresolved matter. However, by their very presence, they offer hope internally and externally.

Minority faiths among Caribbean British people

Although the main focus of this work is Caribbean British Christianity, it is worth pointing out that the 2001 Census bears out that Caribbean British people are present in every recognized faith in Britain. This is indicative of the fact that several non-Christian faiths have been brought to Britain since the late 1940s and continue to exist today. For example, there is a range of Rastafarian organizations and groups in Britain, some forming a close alliance with the Ethiopian Orthodox Church.[106] This Caribbean religion has popularized itself into becoming for many much more of a socio-cultural identity than a religious faith. It is not uncommon to see, for example, Christians and sports people with dreadlocks, manifestly for style rather than substance.

Paul Weller notes how the British Hindu community has been swelled by migration from Trinidad, Guyana and other Caribbean Islands.[107] He also acknowledges that the British Muslim community includes some who historically are descended from the 'Indo-Pakistani subcontinent', arriving in Britain via the Caribbean.[108] And in recent times there has been a distinct movement of second and third generation Caribbean British people towards the Nation of Islam, a US variation of Islam found mainly among African Americans. This relatively new phenomenon in Britain is as yet scarcely written about, but recently, in 2001, I shared a platform at the University of Birmingham with a speaker from the Nation of Islam. And in due course I intend to conduct further research here.

The 2001 Census shows that people of Caribbean British and other minority ethnic identities are represented among Jews, Buddhist and other faiths in Britain. Rarely acknowledged in

academic studies but well known within the communities is
the existence of religious groups such as Pukkumina; other
more sinister ones like *obeah* are evident among Caribbean
British communities too. The religious identity of Caribbean
British people, though overwhelmingly Christian, is nonetheless complex.

Pragmatic identity and politics

The link between identity and political power of Caribbean
British Christianity is worth a brief examination. First, that
the churches and organizations of Caribbean British people
have become identified more by the ethnicity of their membership than by their history, tradition, doctrine and theology,
is testament more to the racialized context in which they
emerged and now exist than the intention of their pioneers
and members. As one of the first historians to emerge from
these churches puts it:

> We have come to be referred to by the term 'Black-led'.
> This is not the way we see ourselves. The term seems to
> separate White from Black Christians in one church.[109]

Yet it cannot be denied that a tendency to flock together along
ethnic lines is an identifiable trait among Caribbean British
Christians and other minority ethnic people in Britain. That
the pioneers did not view their work as ethnically determined
shows that this is an unwitting outcome from their missiological exploits. Many voices have been raised in protest at the
ethnicizing of what are ecclesiastical, theological and political
organizations. One such is that of Arlington Trotman, who
argues that this practice is inconsistent with the traditional
manner of identifying Christian denominations in Britain,
such as Methodist, Church of England, Roman Catholic,
Baptist and United Reformed.[110] To the extent that these new
denominations – led and membered by Caribbean British
people – can be grouped, Trotman argues that this should be
done on theological and historical grounds. This, he suggests,
would most helpfully render the majority of these churches as

'Holiness Pentecostal Churches', given that these churches now operating in Britain owe their roots to these two traditions in the main.

In recent times the African and Caribbean Evangelical Alliance (ACEA) has led a campaign to popularize the term 'Black majority church' (BMC) as the name for what used to be called 'Black-led church'. In his recent book, the former general director of ACEA, Mark Sturge, argues that any church that has 50 per cent or more of its members from Caribbean or African heritage should be known as a BMC. In rejecting 'Black-led church', Sturge calls 'Black majority church' a 'more excellent name'.[111] Apart from a difference in emphasis between leadership and membership, I struggle to see what is more excellent about Black majority church over Black-led church. My own assessment based upon this study is that the people who inhabit these churches (Sturge himself does not) prefer to be known by the names of their denominations rather than an externally imposed socio-political label that describes little other than the colour of their skin. As I have explained above, these churches comprise a wide variety of traditions. Churches peopled by Caribbean British Christians ought, I believe, to be paid the courtesy of being referred to by the names they give themselves. This, I believe, can be done even while acknowledging that the majority, or significant numbers, of their membership come from Caribbean British, Black and other minority ethnicity backgrounds.

Second, it is possible to identify this movement towards denominations. This denominationalism of Caribbean British churches can be viewed as fragmentation and schism. However, it can also be understood as an insistence upon establishing individual ecclesiastical identities, which is important in the quest to be known and recognized for what these really are; real people in real churches. It has been of significance to individual traditions that in the British context they did not become lost within the identity of others. Establishing their denomination became crucial.

However, for Caribbean British Christianity to become a political force in Britain, it has been acknowledged that it needs to be demonstrably more united and identifiable as not

just a spiritual body but a socio-political one as well. Here the
ability to say we speak for 500 Black majority organizations, or
3,000 Black majority congregations, carries with it significant
power. Tony Parry points out that were the various Black-led
denominations to unite, they would represent a significant
voice in our inner cities.[112] Joel Edwards complains that the
fragmented Black church constituency has exhibited little or
no community consciousness over and above their denominational structures.[113] This has changed with the passing of
time, however, because as Woods points out, by the 1970s,
some forward thinkers within the Black-led church movement recognized the necessity of these denominations working together.[114] Though this has not gone far enough, there
have been some noble attempts in addition to the work of the
ecumenical agencies described above.

One manifestation of the attempt to utilize ethnicity as a
political force was the 'Faith in the Future' event that was
staged by ACEA in 2000 as a celebration of Black majority
churches in the United Kingdom.[115] The conference was held
in Brighton from 5 to 8 July, and leaders and congregations
from the spectrum of the BMCs were invited to celebrate
their 'common faith'. In addition to the re-branding of the
Black-led church, this conference demonstrated the potential
political power of the BMCs by attracting both the Prime
Minister and Leader of the Opposition to address it. It failed,
however, to draw the attendance of a substantial number of
Black church leaders and members. I understand the reason
for this to be that Black Christians do not rally greatly around
blackness as an ideology, preferring instead to pledge their
allegiance to their denominations. In spite of this, some
important themes were addressed at the conference, including mission, human development and leadership. Serious
topics blended with Bible study, vibrant music and singing,
preaching and fellowship. It is noteworthy that the speakers
chosen for the set-piece 'main celebration' on each of the
four evenings were from the newer fellowships established
during the last decade of the twentieth century. 'Black
majority church' signifies a desire to coalesce ethnicity and
politics.

'Faith in the Future' was not the first attempt to broker a
new kind of Black, mostly Caribbean British Christian, identity through holding religio-political events. For example,
during the early part of the 1990s, ACEA sponsored the
annual Accord celebration, which was superseded by the
Highway Conference.[116] These events provided opportunities
for communal worship, dialogue and cross-denominational
solidarity on socio-political issues. In 1996 I led a regional
get-together of Caribbean British-led and other Black-led
churches in Sheffield called 'Together in Unity'. This event
was supported by the community of Sheffield, led by Black
Christians, and attracted approximately 2,000 attendees in
the City Hall. In the presence of the City's Lord Mayor, and
Black and White church and other civic leaders, the meeting
showcased the best in Black Gospel music and singing,
preaching and presentations. It represented a tangible result
of the meetings of the Sheffield Black Pastors Fraternal and
has become an annual event in that city. Together, these represent attempts to find ways for the self-expression of unity
along mainly ethnic lines for political purpose. This narrow
unity may be seen as a precursor to wider unity in and with
British Christianity.

There appears to be real tension concerning the true identity and function of Caribbean British-led churches and agencies. Are they to be recognized primarily as ethnically defined
religious groups, or as ecclesiastically defined groups, or
both? There are signs that the new *modus operandi* is one of
pragmatism; as one person has remarked to me, 'We are a
Black church when we apply for funding, but just church
when we worship.' It remains to be seen if the many
Caribbean British Christian denominations and church agencies will continue to build upon the start made with involvement in the social, political and economic aspects of British
life as the mediators for the betterment of Caribbean British
people and wider society. Without some form of ideological
and organizational alignment, this may not be as effective as it
could be. Such alignment would answer the repeated call
for unity and utterances against 'fragmentation', and signal
a new political vibrancy and willingness to engage with the

'principalities and powers'. 'Faith in the Future' may be seen, therefore, as symbolic of the kind of interest that will be shown in Caribbean British Christianity by the national power brokers when they sense that Caribbean British Christianity, probably aligned with like-minded others, is a united force for good. Who knows, maybe one day this Christian movement may even have its own political party and, certainly under proportional representation, the hope of an MP.

Summary

The foregoing survey of the development in Britain of the form of Christianity pioneered by people from the Caribbean demonstrates the complex multi-denominational and multi-agency context of this phenomenon. Its extent is exemplified by there being some 500 different Christian organizations established since the late 1940s.[117] The movement appears to be driven by the triage of ethnic affinity, denominational loyalty and a missiological (including social and political concerns) and evangelistic ideology.

4

Praxis: Some Acts of Caribbean British Christians

Introduction

As a means of gaining further insights into the ways of Caribbean British Christianity, in this chapter three specific areas of their activities are examined. First, I look at the interaction between Black – mainly Caribbean British – and White church leaders in Birmingham. Here I analyse the nature of this relationship as both groups sought to relate to the other better in the interest of Christian mission. Second, I analyse two events in the lives of a young Caribbean British couple of Christian backgrounds, but who no longer attend church. They remain people of faith, but express this differently from what one would expect to find in the churches they grew up in. Through the prism of the celebration of their marriage and the naming of their first child, I examine the way in which they seek to hold on to their expression of faith and to express thankfulness to God through imaginative rites of passage. There are lessons here for the Caribbean British-led churches if they hope to attract again people like these. Third, as a further means of listening to 'what the people say' I analyse a sample of literary works that have been produced by, in the main, Caribbean British Christian writers. While acknowledging that writing and publishing is a somewhat exclusive, even privileged form of information, it does provide a focus on the thinking of this community. These three object lessons are important because they provide snapshots of a people living out their faith within the context they find themselves as a consequence of their history. By looking at them, we can develop a deeper perspective of the understanding these people have of themselves and their God.

1 Black and White church leaders' meetings

According to James Cone, the Church is God's revolutionary activity in the world to change political, economic and social structures so that the distinctions between rich and poor, oppressed and oppressors, are no longer a reality among people.[1] But this cannot be achieved unless the different parts of the Church function together, recognize and appreciate each other; thereby bringing together the sum of their individual parts to greater effect than each is able to do on their own. However, Philip Mohabir points out that in his view, the Church in Britain has been split along racial lines, co-existing in separate religious silos, as doctrinally liberal, mainstream White, Black-led, conservative, fundamentalist, liberal, et al. Mohabir highlights this as an issue even between White evangelical churches and leaders and their Black evangelical counterparts. Commenting on the situation around the mid-1970s, he states:

> These two most dynamic groups of God's people in this country hardly mixed and seemed largely unaware of each other's existence. There was a quiet, subtle system of apartheid operating in Great Britain's churches.[2]

This experience of religious apartheid has led to the perspective among Black Christian leadership that they and their people have been slighted, ignored and neglected by the native religious community.[3] Elsewhere I have pointed to the historic ignorance that exists between 'Black and White' Christian communities as a direct consequence of this separate existence.[4] The Black and White church leaders' meetings were designed to explore the relationship between Black and White Christian leaders in Birmingham, both as a reflection on the past and as a pointer to the future.

Setting up the meetings

From late 1996 to 1998 a process began of bringing together, for discussion and possible action, Black and White Christian leaders in Birmingham. I had both academic and vocational interest in what could emerge. Academically, I was interested to have the opportunity to observe and analyse the nature of the relationship between Black and White Christian leaders. Vocationally, I was keen to see a framework develop that would outlast the experiment. I realized, as Norman Solomon points out in a discourse on Christian and Jewish relations, that dialogue cannot take place between abstractions, such as Christians and Jews, or Black and White, but only between people, and preferably between individuals.[5] An initial invitation to meet was extended by me to two local church leaders. One was a White charismatic leader of Together for Birmingham, and the other was a Black Pentecostal bishop. The first meeting occurred on 2 December 1996 at the Centre for Black and White Christian Partnership, in Selly Oak, Birmingham. The Centre for Black and White Christian Partnership was an established intercultural ecumenical centre for which I worked as director between August 1996 and July 2002. It is well known as a 'crossroads' or 'bridge' for helping Black and White Christians getting to know one another better.

At this meeting it was agreed that from our experience, Christian leadership in the city of Birmingham was racially divided. This division was not merely manifest in that there were Black-led and White-led churches, but more damningly that there was little if any meeting of the two. This failure to meet was probably due to what John Wilkinson refers to as the dialectical nature of the Black and White stories.[6] That is, because Black and White experiences have little in common, the two rarely, if ever, meet. However, we were clear that this state of affairs did not provide a suitable model for the unity or catholicity of the Church of God, whatever the reason. We needed to reflect upon the meaning of there being neither Jew nor Greek, bond nor free, male nor female, but one in Christ (Galatians 3.28). Or, as I prefer to say, 'There is both Jew and Greek, bond and free, male and female, all one in Christ.'

Division among leaders, we believed, sent the wrong signals
to lay members concerning the nature of the one body of
Christ of which all Christians were members. As Ivor Smith-
Cameron points out, good leaders have the ability to do more
than make people into followers, they transform followers
into new leaders.[7] Unless present leaders led others into
becoming reconcilers, the cycle of tangential disengagement
would continue. To church and non-church people alike, the
present state of affairs demonstrated that Christian leaders
did not practise the concept of one church. It was therefore up
to leaders to attempt to redress this.

We agreed that I would write on our behalf to selected
Christian leadership across the city, inviting them to attend a
mini consultation of approximately 20 individuals that would
be as representative as possible of the ethnicity and denominations of Birmingham's Christian community. This was
quite a challenge given that Birmingham has in excess of
500 churches and organizations.[8] We focused upon the five
mainstream churches and significant, particularly Black-led,
others. The provisional remit of the consultation, planned for
21 January 1997, was 'to address how, together, we might
improve relationships and work together better in the city of
Birmingham, for the building up of God's kingdom'.

In retrospect, the planning group was too narrow in terms
of denomination, ethnicity and gender. None of the three of
us represented mainstream Christianity. There was no Asian
representative, and there was not a woman among us. It is
quite amazing how easy it is to become unthinkingly exclusive
in our practice; a charge often levelled against Whites. For
example, Anthony Reddie asserts that many Black young
people are denied positive affirmations in British society
because they do not look British.[9] And as James Cone shows
in his polemical work in which he charges Whites with exclusion of African Americans, he too overlooked the special
needs of African American women and had to write a preface
correcting this wrong in a follow-up edition.[10] All fallible
humans we!

Looking ahead to the consultation, a problem that was
foreseen by the Black Pentecostal bishop and myself was the

challenge to get sufficient Black leaders to attend, given their
general reticence to attend ecumenical or consultation-type
meetings, particularly interracial ones. Tony Parry has
analysed this reluctance in West Yorkshire and locates it in
two causes. The first is Black church leaders' lack of time
owing to working secularly as well as for their church. The
second is the perception that such ecumenical working with
people who many Black church leaders do not regard as true
Christians may compromise their spiritual integrity. A basic
fear is that ecumenical 'union' will lead to the perception at
least of pernicious 'assimilation' with a brand of faith among
mainstream that is far removed from that which is practised
by Black Christianity. Added to this, the Alliance of Asian
Christians works with Christians of Asian background, many
of whom do not wish to be named publicly for fear of family
and religious reprisals. In an attempt to ensure an appropriate
Black presence, I agreed to invite 30 in the hope of attracting
ten to attend. We did not make any provision to ensure gender balance, which was a clear mistake, but we did ensure that
Asian Christians were invited through the involvement of the
Alliance of Asian Christians.

As a result of much continuing discussion and debate within and beyond the planning group, the theme was altered in
the run-up to the consultation. It became 'That Birmingham
may believe', based upon John 17.10, with the subtext, 'A
half-day for fellowship and consultation between Black and
White Christian leaders in Birmingham'. Four key objectives
emerged also, framed around the words 'fellowship, communication, relationship and oneness'. These were cited in the
consultation programme as:

1 To bring together for **fellowship** a nucleus of the multi-
  racial Christian leadership in Birmingham as a prelude to
  greater mission partnerships.
2 To facilitate the unambiguous **communication** of historical and current developments in Black-majority and
  White-majority churches.
3 To model Christian **relationship** building which is synonymous with the unity born of love, which will cause

our communities to belie ve that God sent Jesus to be
the saviour of the world, of which Birmingham is a part.

4 To develop and promote Christian principles and
actions which will affirm our oneness in Christ, across
racial and denominational boundaries.[11]

These objectives were recognized by the planning group as
having far-reaching implications, on which only a start was
envisaged at the consultation. Taken together, the objectives
sought to bring together a multi-denominational and multi-
ethnic leadership to learn of one another's historical and
contemporary contexts, thereby building and strengthening
relationships that both foster and epitomize Christian unity.
This perspective leant heavily upon the Pauline 'church as a
body'[12] concept, where diversity unites for the purpose of dis-
charging the duties the body exists to discharge; that is, to
convince an unbelieving world that Jesus Christ is the Saviour
of the world. However, in retrospect, the overall ethos of our
objectives remained overly non-conformist: Evangelical,
Pentecostal and Charismatic. Notwithstanding the stated
high ideals, insufficient attempt was made by the planning
group to ensure a proper breadth of denominational and
gender involvement in the planning and execution of the programme on the day. Our task was not an easy one, however.
Although church attendance in Britain is believed to be disproportionately 2:1 in favour of the female, the proportion of
female to male ministers across all denominations in
Birmingham is probably no greater than 10 per cent to 90 per
cent. Gelder and Escott show male/female ratios in churches
in England of 45 per cent/55 per cent in 1979, declining to 42
per cent/58 per cent in 1989.[13]

The consultation

On the day of the consultation, 33 Christian leaders attended,
all male (the only female in the room was my personal assistant) of which there were 17 Blacks, two Asians and 14
Whites.[14] Given the 2 to 1 Black/White ratio in the planning

team and probably because of the influence of the overt Black leadership, the consultation itself turned out to have a Black majority too, by 19 to 14. All except one of the Black leaders present were of Caribbean British origin, the other African British. The take-up of invitations by Black clergy surpassed our expectations, but in a city with an overwhelming overall White majority in the general and church population, the ethnic make-up of this meeting was anomalous. The 2001 Census bears this out markedly: 70 per cent of the population are White, the remaining 30 per cent being split between all minority ethnic groups, of which Caribbean British people are a minority.

Denominationally, there was a wide spread, with mainstream White-led and minority Black-led churches represented. However, the level of representation was problematic, given that neither the Anglican Bishop nor the Roman Catholic Archbishop for the area that includes Birmingham were present, a point made in a letter after the event by the Chairperson of Birmingham Churches Together.[15]

This brought into focus the question of who needed to be in the 'room' in order that a discussion may be considered legitimate. Here the words of Philip Potter, former General Secretary of the World Council of Churches, reminds us that one of the great merits of the Reformation was the discovery that the Church is a fellowship of participation in which everyone is a priest before God.[16] In a transcendent sense, it may appear to matter little, therefore, which of the 'priests' is present or absent, since the contribution of each is as valid as the other.

However, as Robert Beckford points out, this idealism is threatened by what he calls a particular type of White, patriarchal Englishness that seeks to dominate by locating itself within church management structures.[17] According to Beckford, this institutionalized White privilege is maintained, in part by conversations that take place when Black folks have 'left the room', as well as, I suggest, by frequent Black under-representation and unwillingness to engage. A challenge to this process seems to be to ensure that all appropriate participants attend and remain in the same 'room' for the duration of the consultation. A Black majority may be a use-ful corrective.

It had not been obvious when putting the programme together just how unrepresentative of the Birmingham church scene it was. From the minutes we note that of the eight named contributors on the day, five were Black; of the three White contributors, only one was from a mainstream church, and he an Evangelical Christian. The minutes of the con-sultation were taken by the only female in the room, my personal assistant. This further confirms the degree to which the consultation was dominated by Evangelicals, Black and White men. The leaders – two Caribbean British and one White British Christian – who had managed the process had designed the programme in our image. Although there were four main presenters, of which two were Caribbean British and two White British, the broad discussion demonstrated a Black hegemony. Yet there was an underlying theme that without a shared understanding of one another's history, experience and present concerns, expressive Christian unity was impossible. This consultation turned White liberal hegemony on its head, in favour of Black and Evangelical hegemony. This model finds resonance in the prophecy of the Old Testament prophet Joel of a time when justice for the oppressed would be achieved by God, empowering them to the point where the weak will say, 'I'm strong' (Joel 3.10).

The first speaker, the National Superintendent of the Wesleyan Holiness Church, was keen to highlight the pio-neering work of his two predecessors. They had established the Wesleyan Church in England in 1958 against many odds, based upon two key principles: a commitment to uphold biblical principles and to minister to 'every nationality'. This declared missiological remit was in contradistinction to the generally understood theories for the existence of churches like his, for example, rejection and the resulting psycho-therapeutic needs.[18] In pursuit of these objectives, he said his church was mindful to remain focused, thus avoiding the 'general pattern of churches to organize, formalize and para-lyse'. The sobering reality for the Wesleyan Church was that it remained small and overwhelmingly Black in Britain, in spite of its ambitious aspirations to appeal to every nationality. Caribbean British people continued to be its near exclusive membership.

A key weakness holding the Wesleyan Church back from achieving its goal, according to the superintendent, was the church's scant financial resources and inability to support full-time ministries. Indeed, according to Peter Brierley, this church had approximately 1,000 members nationally in 1989, which presents a real volume difficulty.[19] Looking further afield, he lamented the lack of co-operation between denominations generally and stressed that Black/White relationship had been 'affected by some unhelpful pronouncements from certain quarters', such as a reference to Black faith as a 'ghetto religion'. In plenary, another Black leader joked that White churches had 'helped to build' Black churches by their negative comments about Black people. This presentation highlighted the extent to which he felt that White Christianity has failed to understand the authentic nature of the Christian faith Caribbean Christians have embraced and practised.

While the superintendent was keen to encourage ecumenical relations, particularly between Black and White Christians, the second Black speaker, an area bishop for the New Testament Church of God, expressed concern over the 'strenuous efforts' that were being made, locally and nationally, to 'bring Black and White Christians together'. The bishop's concern was rooted in the issue of the basis upon which this coming together occurred. He argued that simply bringing people together in the same room was insufficient, unless it led to shared faith and shared understanding of the other. He cited two examples of the nature of his concern. First, there were some instances where Black people were members of committees, but were mere 'weak tokens' with little or nothing to contribute, because care had not been taken to ensure that the 'appropriate' Black people were selected. The charge of inappropriateness here seems one of pointing out that, apparently, at times in haste to ensure that a 'Black face' is in a group or committee, insufficient attention is given to the suitability for the task of the Black person asked or chosen. Second, he was aware of several 'Black and White occasions' when repentance and forgiveness were proffered and accepted, but he had yet to observe the fruit of these utterances in changed behaviours. The kind of 'fruit in keeping with repentance' (Matthew 3.8) that he had in mind included reparations for slavery and the purging of racism from the church and society. False and forced togetherness was unprofitable and ill-advised, he argued.

There was a tendency, the bishop argued, to return after public declarations to parochialism and minding our own business. This undercut the work that was being undertaken by agencies like Cross-Cultural Ministries, Evangelical Christians for Racial Justice, African and Caribbean Evangelical Alliance, Spectrum and the Centre for Black and White Christian Partnership. He believed that the main hindrance to a lived Christian unity was this rush to embrace one another's different humanity and Christian identities and what this means for reconciliation, before sufficient time and effort had been spent in facing with honesty the real issues of our different lives. 'Pushing Black and White too close', before resolving this central issue of identity, 'is not good,' he stated. Any reconciliation must enable people to have a clear answer to the question, 'Where is my identity in this melting pot?' Christian unity, he argued, should not be at the expense of compromising people's doctrinal, theological, cultural and individual distinctiveness. That is to say, Black/White ecumenism must have regard for the integrity of personal and denominational identities.

The bishop further argued that he believed that grass-roots Christians, lay members, were probably clearer about their identity and were therefore more united than ministers were. This was due to ministers being party to and upholders of 'organized religion', which meant that they were 'often the biggest obstacle to change' because they refuse to face up to difference. He cited the degree to which members of his organization, the New Testament Church of God, and those of the Church of God of Prophecy, both Black-led in Britain but White-led in their US headquarters, were now largely reconciled to one another, after years of animosity. However, this was not true to the same extent among ministers as it was for members of the two churches. Holding on to one's identity while being reconciled was the challenge and it was not resolved by leaders attempting to gate-keep: they needed to 'Free people to be!' According to him, there were some indications of this minister/laity dichotomy in that many Black young people had left the church to join the Black-affirming Nation of Islam, while others had even migrated to White-led churches. At the same time, the few Whites in Black-led churches were showing signs of migrating from Black leadership. For the bishop, these developments were signs of the untimely and ill thought out closeness of Black and White before a shared sense of identities has been achieved. The issue of religious/cultural identities and their relationship to Christian unity require further analysis, he thought.

The first of the two White speakers, a pastor of Riverside Church, an independent Charismatic fellowship in Birmingham, gave an overview of the history of his church and others of similar theological and cultural type. This history is remarkable in its resonance with that of Black-led churches, particularly the mission impulse in its *raison d'être*. His and other Evangelical and Charismatic White majority churches in Birmingham are the products of an absence of such churches in the city during the 1970s. Since that time, the inspiration of several individuals, along with several initiatives such as a 10,000-person event in Handsworth Park, Billy Graham's mission to England, Spring Harvest, Renewal meetings, a Rheinhard Bonke evangelistic crusade, and March for Jesus, has led to the existence of many such churches. He recalled one revival prayer meeting in the National Exhibition Centre that attracted 16,000 people, mainly White. The pastor admitted that all this meant that his church's contacts were mainly White and tended to associate with other White majority churches of similar history, culture and theology. A networking group has emerged among them, calling itself Together for Birmingham, and has declared that in Birmingham there is one church with many congregations and that the church's goal is that 'every man, woman and child needs to hear and understand the gospel of Christ'.

However, for this unity in the gospel to happen, he argued that congregations needed to pay the high price of sacrificing some of their independent ways of working. 'No unity without sacrifice' was his mantra. However, this was being stated from a position of being White and strong, relatively speaking, within the social-religious Birmingham context.

The second White speaker was an Evangelical Anglican priest, who argued that racism was endemic in White-led churches, which were resistant to social change. They often revert to 'square one' after appearing to improve. Self-interest and a preoccupation with 'trivia' were also hindrances to Black/White partnership, he said. For progress to occur, he argued, ethnically mixed congregations such as the one in which he is a minister, have to become unafraid to face up to and talk about significant issues like racism and its effects. Young Black people were especially ready to engage with contemporary issues that affect them, but they were unwilling to be patronized, even if as a consequence they suffered isolation. The priest advocated closer working at all levels as a way forward, including inviting each other to preach in their respective pulpits, joint Bible studies and a determination to refuse to go on without sharing with each other.

These talks and the plenary contributions highlighted a high degree of similarities in the concerns between Black and White leaders and the mainly Evangelical churches they represent. There was a fair mixture of enthusiasm and apprehension in both camps for and against closer working. There was also unanimity in the recognition that there was widespread ignorance of the other. Further exchanges simply served to highlight this, but surprisingly the divide was a multi-ethnic one; indeed, it became evident that the Black leaders present did not enjoy much, if any, greater partnership with and understanding about each other as against that between them and their White colleagues. The call for bridge-building was highlighted by one Black leader's reference to Winston Churchill's alleged remark that 'jaw jaw is better than war war'. He, the bishop of the First United Church of Jesus Christ Apostolic, believed it was right that the Churches were talking across ethnic and denominational lines rather than being at war with each other. Further discussion led to a 10-point Commitment.

1 The need for better personal contacts at local levels to get to know one another better, which will lead to change of mind, heart and action.

2 A commitment to co-operation in mission between individuals and churches in spite of doctrinal differences.

3 The need to realize that racism continues to exist among Christians and the corresponding need for repentance and reconciliation.

4 There can be no reconciliation without justice.

5 The need to join local council of churches.

6 A vision for Birmingham was needed that was neither exclusively Black or White, but a combination of both.

7 The need for a high profile Black-led 'convention' type event that would showcase Black talent but to which everybody would be invited.

8 The need for a Black Church Leaders Forum that would bring the Black leaders closer to one another.

9 A city-wide Black and White convention event to demonstrate intercultural Christian unity.

10 The contact details of all leaders present to be distributed to facilitate continued keeping in touch.

A letter subsequent to the consultation highlighted the necessity of a national or local directory of Black-led churches – a proposal already being worked on between the Centre for Black and White Christian Partnership and the African and Caribbean Evangelical Alliance.[20] This 10-point 'programme' reflected the corporate recognition of a lack of awareness among this group of Christian leaders about their context and showed a corresponding disposition towards changing this.

The consultation approved the continuation of an expanded working group to execute the agreed objectives. Several meetings of the working group followed and there were two further leaders' fellowships, on 15 May 1997 and 25 September 1997, both of which were poorly attended. In fact the meeting on 15 May 1997 was abandoned because of a near absence of Black leaders among the 12 in attendance. In spite of the declared good intention to meet, it was apparent that succeeding meetings were becoming increasingly difficult to fit into people's diaries. It soon became a case of willing spirits and weak flesh, or as noted by the second speaker, words but no action. The working group found it difficult to maintain momentum. However, due to this process, greater notice began to be taken of the Black Christian presence in Birmingham. For example, the chairperson of Birmingham Churches Together, upon receipt of the invitation to the second meeting, wrote:

> There was a meeting of 'main line' Church Leaders the other day. I reported on the first Fellowship and Consultation. Informally, I can let you know that they welcomed the initiative. They hope and pray that, together, the 'Objectives' will be realized. They expressed a desire to be at, or send personal representatives to the next half-day.[21]

Among other correspondences was a letter from the leader of the city-wide Prayer Breakfast, West Midlands Vision, who was keen to investigate how a greater level of Black participation could be achieved. These two letters were indicative of how greater visibility in the mainstream was being given to Black Christians in the city of Birmingham. The wider Christian community was showing a willingness to engage with Black Christian leaders, but it became clear that there was no cohesive critical mass of Black Christian leadership in the city. This was evident particularly in the near collapse of the Black presence in the second Black and White consultation and pointed to a serious flaw in this engagement strategy.

To deal with this, while the planning group of the Black and White Fellowship continued to meet and plan, I met with a few Black Christian leaders and put it to them that 'something needed to be done' to present a united front to others and to act as a unifying instrument among Black leaders. We agreed to establish a Black Church Leaders Fellowship. This was launched in the Council House in the presence of the Lord

Mayor of Birmingham and I chaired the Fellowship for some time afterwards, until it merged with a hitherto dormant Birmingham Council of Black-led Churches (CBLC), which is now represented at various levels within the city and recognized as the authoritative voice and point of contact for the Black-led churches in the city of Birmingham. For example, the chairman of the CBLC sits on the Birmingham church leaders' forum, representing Black Christians. The Council of Black-led Churches was nevertheless in the hands of a small political group from which it was problematic to wrest control. The strategy decided between other ministers and myself was that of strengthening the Black Church Leaders Fellowship (BCLF), thereby rendering the CBLC ineffectual, at which point the 'politicians' did not mind ceding control of it to the BCLF leadership.

Another Black and White consultation was convened on 25 September 1997, by which time the Black Church Leaders Fellowship had been launched. This event managed to attract a low turnout of 16, of whom six were Black, and represented a further deterioration in attendance at these set-piece meetings. In the attempt to press ahead with the agenda, the planning group continued to meet monthly and further Black and White church leaders' meetings took place on 19 March 1998 and 6 August 1998. During this time the planning group developed a revised charter of commitment, which read:

We are committed to:
1 Establishing a Birmingham-wide Black pastors and leaders Fellowship.
2 An annual multicultural Christian 'flag-ship' event.
3 The development of a communication framework for networking.
4 The encouragement of a leadership-based local cross-fertilization process.
5 Quarterly network meetings – alternating between wider group and planning group.
6 Supporting a planning group to resource quarterly meetings.

7 Weekends away.

8 The swapping of pulpits.

9 Recognition of the ongoing need for repentance.

10 Addressing the continuing existence of racism among Christians.

11 Striving for meaningful relationships despite doctrinal differences.

12 Addressing issues affecting young people.

13 Assurance that our fellowship and communication will lead to action.

14 Liberating grass-roots members to freely associate cross-denominationally and cross-culturally.

15 Recognition that there can be no reconciliation without justice.

16 A vision for Birmingham that is both Black and White.

17 Effective use of existing networks.

This second list of commitments was developed without due recourse to the one made earlier. It was as though the group developed organizational amnesia. The result was that there is a modicum of similarity to what went before, but no deliberate building upon it. One significant development was that we now clearly rejected the concept of a Birmingham in denial that was 'neither Black nor White' in favour of one that was self-aware and 'both Black and White'. From my experience, denying the existence of difference tends to result in the hegemony of the more powerful influence. In a 'neither Black nor White Birmingham', the sheer size of the White community suggests it would submerge the Black presence and lead to a monochrome society. Only a commitment to embracing difference can nurture the richness of variety.

One way of interpreting this list is that its implementation would facilitate the forging of meaningful and mutual relationships that would provide the basis of effective working together by Black and White churches to tackle social ills. However, for this to be fulfilled, consideration needed to be given to the necessary resources. This resourcing did not happen but this new aspirational list provided the inspiration for

the first major public Black and White event. The city-wide
event, planned for 3 October 1998, became the main focus of
the planning group, the nucleus of which remained as it had
begun. The meeting was convened under the heading, 'That
Birmingham May Believe' with approximately 300 people
attending, though many more were expected. The event had
Evangelical, charismatic and Pentecostal undercurrents and
provided further evidence that the project was not sufficiently
cross-denominational. It did, however, provide the opportunity to see Black and White leaders working together.

Following this event, I withdrew from hosting the planning
group for two reasons. First, I had seen enough of the intercultural and interdenominational workings between the two
groups, for my academic interest. Second, I needed to ascer-
tain whether the process had self-sufficiency to exist without
me, which would be necessary for its longevity as I would not
be able to stay with it indefinitely.

With my withdrawal, however, the group lost the appearance of neutrality it had had by meeting under the auspices of
the Centre for Black and White Christian Partnership. Since
then, the working group's denominational breadth diminished and its activities have gradually fizzled out so that it no
longer meets. There remains no co-ordinating centre for the
programme of work that had been developed. However, the
Council for Black-led Churches now champions the cause of
the Black Christian community and works alongside the
White-majority Birmingham Churches Together. Probably
the key outcome of the Black and White Christian leaders
project is the realization that a robust Black Christian relational framework is essential for Black and White Christian
dialogue, and such a council has been established. In such an
environment, Black and White Christians are able to relate on
the basis of mutual strength.

Summary

This engagement between Black, mostly Caribbean British,
and White Christian leaders, was typified by neither party

being beholden to the other. At no time was there any sense that Black leaders exhibited feelings of inferiority or that Whites acted in a superior way. Black leaders appeared to view their presence in Birmingham as normal and as much part of the Christian mission presence as other church communities. There was mutual learning, as people listened to each other's concerns, anxieties, hopes and aspirations. Once the framework for engagement was created, people of different ethnicity and denominational belonging engaged with Christian goodwill and mutuality. That the Black and White leadership fellowship did not survive the experiment probably means that there was no deeply felt need to construct 'mechanically' a Black and White framework for engagement. Indeed, it may indicate, too, that a more mature relationship is preferred whereby interactions happen spontaneously rather than when contrived, as was the case here. However, the framework began a dialogue that probably would not have developed otherwise, especially not spontaneously – it had not done so in the years previously. Now the ice has been broken and new things may happen spontaneously, or they may return to the easy status quo of segregation. Time will tell.

2a African British wedding ceremony

This particular piece of participant observation happened almost by accident. The couple involved, having become aware of my research in Caribbean British theology and having heard me speak and read my writings, asked me to officiate in the religious aspect of their wedding, and later in the 'naming' of their first child. According to Mbiti, the 'naming' of a child in African cultures is an integral part of human becoming.[22] The 'rhythm of nature' includes birth, naming, puberty, initiation rites and marriage. These two 'acts' offered this project the opportunity to observe at first hand a personal attempt by a Caribbean British couple to re-work aspects of their faith and spirituality. They wanted particularly to emphasize their African heritage in these rites.

I was interested in what lessons there might be for me in dealing with other young people in what this couple were doing in allowing me to experiment with culturally sensitive liturgy. I was interested, too, in what lessons there were for consideration by the Black-led churches as they attempt to retain and reach out to progressive young Black people in Britain.

These were two significant spiritual events in the lives of this young Caribbean British couple, both in their thirties. She was brought up partly Baptist, partly Roman Catholic, and is a professional counsellor. He was brought up as a Baptist, and is a computer expert and community educator. Like many of their age group, professional status and social consciousness, they were anxious to define their spirituality in ways that acknowledge their past, present and future. Despite both having typical Caribbean multi-ethnic heritages, they wished to embrace their African heritage. They also wanted to find ways of expressing their faith that demonstrate belief in God, not religious institutions, and to celebrate the lives of their families and friends, past and present.[23]

My role was that of 'minister' in both situations under review here. In the marriage ceremony, as in the naming ceremony, the couple, but mainly the woman, communicated their basic wishes and left the liturgical developments to me. The man summarized some areas that he wanted the blessing liturgy to cover. Their main request was that the services should be African-centred, yet appropriate for all people living in the African and Caribbean Diaspora. Having worked up a draft, I ensured that both had an opportunity to scrutinize it and offer suggestions. I was greatly assisted in my preparation and research by a senior lecturer in the University of Birmingham and the director of the African Self-Help Organization in Handsworth, Birmingham, who holds firm pan-Africanist views. Further insights were gained for this project from the works of John Mbiti[24] and Mervyn Alleyne.[25] A final source of contribution to the development of these liturgies was a former director of the African and Caribbean Evangelical Alliance, the Revd Ronald Nathan, under whose leadership ACEA pursued the African-centred approach mentioned above.

The rite of marriage

The couple were married in a registry office in the usual British manner. Then, at their home, I officiated in an African-centred blessing ceremony, the words and format of which, as described above, were worked out together between the couple and myself. The couple told me that they were not necessarily happy to have to engage in the civil part of their wedding ceremony performed in the usual British way, but did so to demonstrate their acknowledgement of themselves as part British and that their marriage would have validity in the eyes of the law of the land. That they wanted an African-centric blessing ceremony demonstrates their view of themselves as first and foremost people of African descent. Against this background, the ceremony proceeded.

The ceremony stated that this African-centred occasion was one of celebration to mark the marriage of the couple, for whom this was an ontological as well as a spiritual statement about their Africanness. The focus upon both their humanity and their spirituality was important because they, like millions of others living in the Diaspora, were at risk of losing the sense of their Africanness that is embedded in these two aspects of their existence. Worse still, some were ashamed of their African heritage, and as a consequence not only have they become westernized, but they have fallen *in* love with the West and *out* of love with Africa, the mother country. Therefore, the occasion served as a reminder to all African descended people of whom they really were and where they came from!

Of course, all attempts by its Diaspora to link up with African traditional practices have to reckon with the fact that Africa is a vast continent with many people, customs and practices. However, consistently across the continent, the African world-view concerning the rite of marriage was that it was not an isolated practice, but part of a wider whole. Marriage happened within a way of life that was considered cyclical and took its understanding from nature, the most noticeable feature being the seasons of spring, summer, autumn and winter, and day and night. At the helm of this cycle of life was God, and so the ceremony began with a focus on God. According to Mbiti:

> Expressed ontologically, God is the origin and sustenance of all things. He is 'older' than the Zamani period; He is outside and beyond His creation. On the other hand, He is personally involved in His creation, so that it is not outside of His reach. God is thus simultaneously transcendent and immanent.[26]

As the above extract demonstrates, long before the advents of Judaism, Christianity and Islam, traditional African religion and society had an exalted view of God as the Supernatural Being: Creator, Moulder and Constructor of everything. It is to the Supreme Being that Africans have always prayed. From a Christian perspective, God has self-disclosed in the incarnational person of Jesus Christ, in whose name we pray. While the figure of Jesus was not present in the traditional African world-view of God, many people of African heritage are now Christians or of Christian persuasion and therefore attempt to hold both their African and Christian heritages in creative tension. As a demonstration of that tension, I prayed for the couple 'in Jesus' name', the God–human bridge between humans and God. The next part of the ceremony focused upon the African view of humanity.

In traditional African view, humanity was central to God's creation. Human life had a natural rhythm which nothing and no one could destroy. This rhythm included birth, puberty, initiation, marriage, procreation, old age, death, entry into the community of the departed (the Sasa period), and finally into the company of the spirits (the Zamani period). This rhythm of nature meant that the traditional African view of life was holistic: it looked back, to the present, and to the future, and considered past, present and future as part of one life, which all shared together. Part of this sharing together was the imperative to remember those who were responsible for having brought us here, those from whom we have learned, and without whom we would not be here.

A primary means of remembering them was through the traditional pouring of water as libation on special occasions. We offered libation in the ceremony in remembrance of departed parents, grandparents, great-grandparents, brothers, sisters, or children. Each person was asked to recall someone from their past, call their names and pour some water. Several people wept as they did this. Libation in reference to the departed represented a symbol of family, continuity, contact, communion, fellowship and remembrance. This was also recognition of the mystical and transcendent ties that bound the living-dead to their surviving-living relatives. It acknowledged the unbreakable link between the visible and the invisible worlds. Everyone was exhorted never to forget their loved ones and to think of libation as one African-centred way by which to remember them. In this way, history is celebrated and learned from.

In the African view of life as holistic and cyclic, marriage constitutes a significant component of human existence. Getting married includes much more than the two people involved. It includes the two clans (families) of the marrying couple coming together in an act of interpersonal relationship. Unlike present-day European and North American concepts of the nuclear family, for African people family includes grandparents, parents, children, aunts, uncles, brothers, sisters who may have children of their own, and other relatives – anthropologists call this the extended family. Getting married signifies the couple's intention to continue the life cycle through procreation, ensuring the continuity of the family line. This is a sacred responsibility.

Historically, marriage was seen in African societies as accepting the obligation to bear children, and as a uniting link in the rhythm of life. It enabled the building of a family, establishing relationships between families and clans, and led to the existence of parents to be remembered after their death. During their lifetimes, marriage brought people together and gave them status in society; and at the end marriage enabled the regaining of a lost immortality at death. In African society, it was believed that everyone ought to marry and if possible have children. In fact, in some parts of Africa it was the understanding that the process of birth was only complete when you got married. To ensure marriage happened, some parents would arrange the marriage of their as yet unborn child. Getting married was important, and it was a spiritual event.

The concept of personal immortality helps us to understand the spiritual significance of marriage in traditional African societies. Unless someone had close relatives to remember them when they died, they were just nobodies who simply vanished out of human existence like a flame extinguished. Therefore it was a sacred, religious and ontological duty of every child to marry and have children to take forward the family's life. Marriage was seen therefore as a lifelong spiritual bond. Divorce was to be avoided. Marriage was not just about sex and physical bonding, it was crucially about a spiritual bonding for life of the living, the ancestors, and those yet to become alive (who dwell as it were in the 'loins' of their parents). At this point, prayer was made for spiritual bonding of the couple.

I reflected upon how it was that the journey of the African people included the Middle Passage, or the triangular slave trade route that went from Europe to Africa to the Americas, and accounted for the lives of millions of African ancestors. Those who survived it had to face lives that were often a worse fate than death. That anyone survived such genocide is testament to God's providence, their strength of character, their physical strength, and a belief in the dignity of their humanity. Since that time, the world has become a global village, with the ease with which we can all travel. So here, life has come together in the Diaspora where African descendants of slaves and Africans from Africa, along with Africans mixed with Asian and European blood, live together in Britain today.

For those from the Caribbean, our parents suffered overt racism in the years after the mass migration which started in the late 1940s. But this was no different from what Black people had suffered here in Britain over many centuries before. And as the report of the Stephen Lawrence inquiry and the Scarman Report before it demonstrated, Black people continue to suffer racism at the hands of a Euro-American White mindset that believes it is a superior race of humanity.

But guess what? We are here! And if we wish to stay, we will stay. This, as our parents before us knew, is God's earth, and we are part of God's human creation, made in God's image, and given the right and responsibility to be good stewards of it. No amount of White racism, xenophobia or fascism can ever change that. We are a people with a past, a present and a legacy.

Our legacy is simply this: Africa and its people share a rich spiritual heritage that binds us to each other, to the rest of humanity, and to God. And although this has taken a battering over the past 500 years, this spiritual heritage was given by God and we know that the gifts and calling of God are never taken back. And so I wished the couple all God's richest blessings in their marriage. I reminded them that their life together was not just to and for themselves, but that the rest of us were with them in spirit and prayers and were ready to help in whatever way we could. One way was to continually remind them of their legacy.

When our ancestors were taken into slavery, marriage was forbidden. Due to the tenacity of the indomitable African human spirit that refused to give up on their ideology of family, there developed a form of marriage ceremony, hid from their masters, known from the slave narratives as 'jumping the broom'. The following song is from such a ceremony:

> Dark an' stormy may come de wedder;
> I jines dis he-male an' dis she-male togedder,
> Let none, but Him dat makes de thunder,
> Put dis he-male and dis she-male assunder.
> I darefore 'nounce you befo de same.
> Be good, go 'long, an' keep up yo' name,
> De broomstick's jumped, de world not wide,
> She's now yo' own.
> Salute yo' bride!

I reminded the couple and those gathered that the same resolve to live out a commitment to marriage was needed today, because although there were no slave masters preventing us from getting married, the circumstances of western life and the attitude to marriage threatened in a similar way. At the conclusion of the ceremony, I said a prayer of dedication and blessing upon the couple for fruitfulness in every area of their lives.

Summary

This unusual liturgy for a marriage blessing fulfilled multiple purposes that together illustrate the complexities of Diaspora life. It served the need of education concerning African's history; celebrating what of that past is good, honouring those who have made it all possible, and authenticating what is now being done. For those who participated in it, the libation part of the ceremony, that allowed people to recall memories of their ancestors, moved many to tears as some for the first time found a way of connecting with their lost loved ones. It was clear to me that the Black church needs to connect with these people in a similar way.

To both the civic and the African-centred ceremonies of this wedding, the couple had invited their families, friends and neighbours. Significantly these included people of Black, White and mixed ethnic backgrounds. Judging from the comments made to me afterwards, no one was offended by the African-centred approach, which simply contrasted with and complemented the earlier focus on a western way of marrying in a register office. However, the couple themselves, having chosen not to marry or receive their 'blessing' in a church, were making their own statement about their non-belonging to the traditional Black church, which would scarcely, if ever, include these African elements in a wedding ceremony. Wedding ceremonies in the majority of Black British churches are based on the western Christian model with a veneer of blackness. Judging from this experience, the inclusion of libation as a time to remember deceased loved ones, for example, would be a useful addition to western marriage rituals when they are performed for people of African descent. Equally, adapting Asian religious-cultural practices for ceremonies of Christians of Asian descent would similarly resonate with them. A key message for Caribbean British Christianity is that

it needs to consider including other than Eurocentric elements in 'rites of passage' formulae, elements that resonate
with the instincts and experience of its constituency.

2b Child naming ceremony

Upon the birth of the first child born to this couple, I was
requested to conduct a naming ceremony for the new offspring. The process of developing the liturgy for the service
was conducted in the same manner as for the wedding ceremony and sought to include again words and symbols that
reflected their and their people's journey of life and hope for
the future. Below is a descriptive summary of the liturgy that
was specially developed and agreed with the couple, for which
I was the officiating minister. The term 'elder' was used in the
ceremony instead of 'minister' to better reflect African practice. Guests arriving were asked to present their gifts to the
child's parents and to greet them. Music by Ali Farka Toure
with Ry Cooder was played in the background, from the
album 'Talking Timbuktu'.

　　Proceedings began with a poem by Thomas Simmons.

　　One hundred years from now
　　It won't matter what car I drove
　　What kind of house I lived in
　　How much I had in my bank account
　　Nor what my clothes looked like
　　But the world may be a little better
　　Because I was important in the life of a child.

A formal welcome was extended to all present: family, friends,
elders, guests and the ancestors, who though absent in body
were acknowledged as present in spirit. Everyone was encouraged to greet one another with handshakes, hugs, kisses and
words of upliftment. In acknowledgement of the eternal bond
between the living and the departed, water was poured on to
the plant in a pot set aside for this purpose while the names of

living and/or deceased parents, grandparents, other relations and notable persons were called out.

At this point, a prayer was prayed by the officiating elder. It acknowledged God as Creator, and that we had gathered in that place for the express purpose of giving thanks and praises to God. Together we also acknowledged our indebtedness to God for his faithfulness to us as a people who had come through many tribulations and trials. We declared that it was God who had sustained, preserved and provided for us. To this the people said, 'Yes you have, Lord'. The officiating elder proceeded to lead the liturgy in remembrance of how God gave Africans knowledge of the mysteries of science and spiritualities that had sustained them since leaving the shores of Africa, through the difficult birth canal of the Middle Passage, the triangular slave trade route, and until this day. He recalled the co-mingled existence of life in the Caribbean where the ancestors survived hard labour, the whip, murder and the plantation. In the midst of their adversity God gave them a song, a hope and a future.

How they got over this, God alone knows. But having brought the African ancestors through such trouble, God now offered hope in the new context in Britain. And so, the officiating elder stressed that God had not left his people alone on British shores, but was present in the housing estates, the concrete jungles of urban life and the suburbia that was the reality of some of us. The people gathered were assured that God had not ignored the collective prayers of their ancestors and themselves, and was therefore with them in the midst of present challenges. To this the people responded, 'You have not ignored our prayers, Lord.' This faithfulness of God called for reciprocal commitment from the people.

The officiating elder led the people in pledging themselves to provide an environment where the child being named would be protected and provided for, and that they would ensure that he is raised up with knowledge of God, their history and legacy, with role models of integrity and dignity, to be a proud descendant of the African people. To this all the people said, 'Lord, we are committed to this work.' The officiating elder prayed that as God led Deborah the

Liberator, Esther the Defender, and Jesus Christ the Saviour, so he would lead the child into all truth. Again, the people responded, this time with, 'Lead this child, O Lord. Amen.'

The story of baby Samuel, his father Elkanah and mother Hannah from 1 Samuel 1.24—2.11 was read. This was followed by a New Testament reading about Jesus and little children from Matthew 18.1–14. A communal song had been chosen and was sung here.

> You're my brother you're my sister
> So take me by the hand
> Together we can work until he/she comes
> There's no foe that can defeat us
> When we're walking side by side
> As long as there is love we will stand.

The biblical texts and congregational song were a prelude to the official blessing and naming of the child by the officiating elder. This started with a prayer of thanksgiving to God for the male child he had blessed the family with. He was like a grain of corn planted into the soil. The officiating elder than led a commitment of all present in declaring themselves co-supporters in the care and development, watering, fertilizing and pruning of the child so that an abundance of fruit will result. God was invoked to shower down his blessings upon the child and his parents as they sought to grow the child from infancy to maturity. The prayer further asked God to develop the child spiritually, physically, mentally and socially. 'May his life journey afford him the knowledge of his predecessors, elders and peers; and the wisdom to contribute to the total fulfilment of his people.' To this the people said, 'Amen'.

The naming ceremony continued with the officiating elder asking the parents, 'What are the names of this child?' Once stated by the parents, the elder asked the parents what was the significance of the names. The parents explained each name and its meaning. One meant 'educator', another meant 'mighty', and the third meant 'placed in God's care'. Aspirationally, therefore, this boy child was being placed in

God's care and would one day be mighty and an educator. The officiating elder stated that Africa's historical experience was tied up in this child's name because it has always been in God's hand and care, even though that has not prevented atrocities. Through those adversities, Africa and its descendants were now stronger and able to teach others from their wealth of experience from their bitter journey. This child may have difficult times ahead but would emerge strong and able to teach others, provided that parents and guardians brought him up in God's tender care. With this exhortation, the child was named, with the officiating elder saying, 'I name you in the presence of God, the ancestors, present company of elders, family and friends. We welcome you into the human family. Amen.'

The people said together the Lord's Prayer in its traditional form:

Our Father, which art in heaven, Hallowed be thy name. Thy kingdom come. Thy will be done in earth, as it is in heaven. Give us this day our daily bread. And forgive our debts, as we forgive our debtors. And lead us not into temptation, but deliver us from evil: For thine is the kingdom, and the power, and the glory, for ever. Amen. (Matthew 6.9–13, KJV)

With this, the officiating elder invited those present to greet and congratulate the parents and child. The parents of the named child responded by dedicating the following poem, by Debon Panton, to their own parents:

Mama mi love you
Mi can't do without you
A you gi mi life
And teach mi what is right
You used to tek care of mi
Sen mi go to school,
Wash fi mi,
cook fi mi,
And gi mi mi food.

Although mi grow big,
Mi a still yuh likkle pickney,
Mama, Mama,
A love you yuh si.

When I was a child,
You did the best you could do,
Now as time go by,
Is my turn fi tek care of you.

Mama, mama,
You never let me down,
You gi mi everything that you did have,
Mi a go pay you back wid respect and all of mi love.

Papa
Papa mi know seh you love mi,
But yuh jus' neva seh it,
A love yuh tuh yuh si,
And wid your help mi wi mek it.
Everyday yuh get up gawn a work,
Sometime yuh nuh have nutt'n fi eat,
Sometime work jus a bus yuh shirt,
But day by day yuh still do it.
Papa, mi wah fi be jus like yuh,
Mi wah yuh fi andastan,
Fi mi time a go come tuh,
Mi wah fi be a real man.

They further said, 'If we by the grace of the Creator, are able to inspire such sentiments in our son, we will consider ourselves fortunate. Our thanks to all those who have made this day possible. We shall always remember the many kindnesses.'

Summary

In similar vein to the previous ceremony, of blessing the marriage, the naming ceremony sought to make sense of a historic complexity while embracing present realities. The combination of African, Caribbean and British thought included in the liturgy is representative of the different influences that bear upon this couple and their child in their life together. They were keen to live out this complexity in ways that attempted to make evident to onlookers who they really were and the values they embraced. Such living engenders knowledge and awareness in others and are seeds from which understanding grows. This rite contrasts with the kind of baby dedication that occurs in Black majority churches, which tend be cautiously Eurocentric. Here again, as in the wedding ceremony, libation was utilized to great effect to focus upon departed loved ones and the interwoven nature of life: past, present and future. The inclusion of African-centred elements in welcoming a child into the world and the family is symbolically important not least because of its notions of self-identity. Conducted in the presence of Whites and Blacks, this ceremony at the couple's home provided an opportunity for the affirmation of life.

This insight into the life of this couple provides an indication that many young, especially professional, Black people are ill at ease with Black Christianity, which they experience as insufficiently imbued with characteristics that are meaningful to them and not representative of the life journey upon which they are embarked. Caribbean British churches need to consider seriously how these critical rites of passage celebrations can better resonate with the whole humanity of its constituent members, and these second and succeeding generations of Caribbean British people, otherwise they will look elsewhere for fulfilment of these deeply felt spiritual and historical aspects of their lives.

3 Literary works

Having observed in the sections above some examples of Caribbean British Christianity working out its faith in Britain, here I add a third prism through which we gain further insights into the spiritual psyche of this community. This piece of research focuses upon identifying and analysing a sample of

the literary sources available in the Caribbean British
Christian genre. I have already pointed to Elaine Foster's
stress upon the need for authentic self-articulation, what she
calls 'whe dem sey' (that is, what is said by the people themselves).[27] This need to self-articulate is predicated upon a
deep-rooted desire to assure the accuracy and authenticity of
the information provided. Nobody can tell my story like I can,
since, as my mother used to say, 'Who feels it knows it'. In the
mid-1980s Ira Brooks said, 'It is essential that Black people
take initiatives in presenting their own awareness, through acting, films and writing.'[28] Norma Thomas-Juggan supports this
view by explaining that her reason for accepting the task of
writing the history of the Calvary Church of God in Christ was
that if it is not done now, the pioneering eyewitnesses will pass
on leaving no written legacy of this movement.[29]

Of course, writing is not the sole means by which a community can speak for itself. It may even be argued that writing
is a highly specialized art, not open to everyone. In recent
years we have experienced many communities finding creative ways to speak for themselves through art, video, websites,
public fora, to name but a few. All of these means are
deployed by the community under discussion. However, my
aim here is reasonably narrowly focused on a sample of books
written, in the main, by Caribbean British Christians in an
attempt to discover what concerns are being articulated by a
wide range of individuals. Their reasons for writing vary but
central to all is a near egotistic desire to tell their stories so that
a sceptical world can hear them 'from the horses' mouths'.
They are told in a manner that second-hand witnesses could
not do and it is possible to detect a slight angst against the
feeling that this has not always been the case. It's time to put
the record straight, so what are the people saying? I begin with
a review of some key anthology texts.

The editors of *A Time to Speak* demonstrate a growing
intolerance of Caribbean British Christians to others telling
their stories for them. They write:

'Black Christianity' in Britain has had many exponents and
apologists. Many have made their reputations and careers

from interpreting Black faith to indifferent intellectuals and earnest clerics. We, the victims of this spiritual coloniz-ation, have been observed and pronounced upon. We have read what has been written and said about us and have been provoked to various reactions. Some of us have been im-pressed that something has been learnt, but disappointed that that is where it usually stops. Others have been angered by the fact that yet again we have been the objects of exploitation for theses material, for street credibility or for conscience-salving. Over the years many of us have accepted this as the price we must pay for Christian unity. However, this colonization of our Black hearts is no longer acceptable to us: it's time to speak for ourselves.[30]

This determination to ensure the veracity of the information available concerning them is further evidence of the deter-mination to be understood that is at the heart of this thesis. This anthology presents the perspective of Caribbean British and other Black British Christians on many issues that hither-to were unavailable in print. These include, for the first time, an attempt to tell the Caribbean British story of 'Black-led' churches in Britain.[31] The work also explores themes such as how churches in inner-city areas are dealing with racism; the role of the Black minister; womanism; race relations; Christians in a plural society; learning from each other in a multifaith society; the Black American experience; and sig-nificantly, the imperative of telling one's own history. In this latter area, David Moore underscores the point with the poignant words of American Civil Rights campaigner Malcolm X, who states that a people without knowledge of their history are like a tree without roots.[32]

A Time to Speak is in many ways the antecedent of much of what exists today in that its cross-cutting themes ensure that Caribbean British Christian life cannot be seen as mundane or simplistic. It links inner-city life outside with inner-city life in the churches. It names important subjects like race, gender, self-affirmation and civil rights. All this is done while ensuring that the spirit of insularity is spoiled by a transatlantic reach, linking theology here in Britain with Black theology in the

United States. The corporate voice of these authors says in effect that God's people are a complex community that should not be reduced to a single issue community based on its lowest common denominator, this usually being race alone. The way to avoid this pitfall is to insist that the people in a given situation tell their stories as they have truly experienced them. Those stories are bound to be as diverse as their tellers' experiences. *A Time to Speak* demonstrates well the willingness of Caribbean British Christian authors to tackle a range of issues that affect or interest them, pulling no punches, and calling upon both the church and the secular community to work together for the betterment of all people.

Paul Grant and Raj Patel are also responsible for a second collection of essays, published under the title *A Time to Act: Kairos 1992*.[33] This publication explores the historical moment of 1992 with regard to Black life in Britain and Europe. The editors' explicit objective was to demonstrate how Black communities were resisting and showing a passion for justice, against 'everything that impoverishes and degrades'. For the editors, 1992 was above all a time for action. In my view, the essays do not quite match the editors' zeal and urgent call for action; instead, they patiently tell the stories and express the wishes of the individuals writing. The essays include the writings of a deceased community worker in Leeds under the title 'Redemption Song', that eerily depicts his experience of racism and God's power of redemption from such oppression. There is the testimonial of a campaigner against racism in the church; a speculative piece on 'if the Church was what it professed to be'; and a 'womanist bibliodrama' by a group using biblical characters like Hagar, Zipporah, Rahab, Orpah and Ruth that dramatizes Black women's challenges in society and in the church. Some contributors explore the link between dependence upon God through prayer, and self-reliance through work. Two re-evaluations of Columbus' 'discovery' of the Americas are offered, and the economic struggle between the poor southern hemisphere and the affluent north is examined, as is the human cost of immigration controls and the state of race relations in Europe. Finally this anthology explores the role of religion as the 'sigh' of oppressed people and as a possible tool for justice.

Another of the editors' intentions through this collection of essays was to

> inform the context in which Black Christians and others continue to do their Christian living and theologizing, rather than simply accepting the ways in which other people define our situation for us. It therefore enables self-theologizing through generating questions rather than by providing answers.[34]

These writers inform their context concerning the imbalance and injustice that persist in society. Importantly, they also demonstrate that an organized and determined church, utilizing human and other resources that are available to it, can make a significant difference by ushering in a sense of the kingdom of God among humankind. Some of these writers are concerned about life beyond narrow national boundaries. They want to see the rule of God within and beyond these boundaries. In both of the above anthologies, the editors speak the language of 'oppression/liberation' as a contemporary reality far more than their contributors do. It is probably to be expected that people with the drive to edit books of this nature are the politically activist type, inclined towards polemics. However, as the essay topics and contents suggest, the contributing writers appear more concerned with demonstrating their knowledge of subjects of particular interest to them in their situation than focusing on oppression and liberation. They do more than simply tell their personal stories, they reflect upon their context historically and contemporarily, socially, economically, politically and spiritually.

As part of my work as executive director of the Centre for Black and White Christian Partnership, three anthologies were published between 1998 and 2000. One of these focused on Caribbean British and other Black people's attitude and approach to prayer.[35] Another, *Preaching with Power*,[36] seeks to bring to a wider audience the style and content of Caribbean British and other Black British preaching. This project

meets head on the popular view that Black preachers adopt an
exclusively extemporaneous style and are therefore unsuitable
for written publication. That the anthology includes many
contributors from across the denominations is testimony to its
success in gaining broad appeal for a project that many people
told me was impossible: 'Black preachers are spontaneous
and oral, not literary', was the general sentiment expressed
to me.

Like in the Grant and Patel anthologies, it is notable how
wide a variety of topics these authors chose to write their
sermons on. Although a suggested list was offered, authors
were given total freedom to choose their topics, the result of
which are the following chapter titles: 'The way forward', 'A
new world', 'True worshippers', 'What do you want me to do
for you?', 'The church of God', 'Skin deep Christianity', 'Our
approach to God in prayer', 'From fear to forgiveness', 'The
power of the cross', 'The desired trinity', 'Is Jesus in your
boat?', 'Power and potential', 'Living out of vision', 'Double
for all your sins', 'Endings and new beginnings', 'Exalting the
Lord Jesus Christ', 'Arise and build', 'The spirit of life',
'Bringing a nightmare to an end', and 'A new and living way'.[37]

Preaching with Power exudes the Christocentricity that is at
the heart of Black Christianity in general and Caribbean
British Christianity in particular. It is often sung in these
churches that 'Jesus is the answer', and these written sermons
portray this in a significant way by focusing on the redemptive
nature of the cross of Christ and the changed life that results.
Those who do not frequent these churches may be unaware of
the degree to which this is so. A vindication of the strategy to
initiate the publishing of the work of these preachers, the
majority of whom had not published before, to a wider readership is evident in that 'Skin deep Christianity'[38] was entered
by the publishers into the Times Preacher of the Year Award,
1998 competition – and won! This brilliant young Seventh
Day Adventist preacher from Sheffield was unlikely to be read
in national newspapers, or heard on radio or television, apart
from this process.

The third anthology, *Sisters with Power*,[39] provided a literary
platform for Caribbean British and other Christian women to

publish, many for the first time. Again, topics were left totally
to the discretion of the authors. The subjects these women
chose to write on demonstrate a wide range of interests and
concerns. For example, they focus upon womanhood, single-
ness, insubordination, patriarchy, ministry, professionalism,
leadership, cultural recovery, the Bible, virtue and strength of
Black women. These women, who come from across the
denominational spectrum, demonstrate that their interests
are as wide as any group of human beings anywhere. Their
central theme, in so far as there is one, is power, or a critique
of how power works and what women can do to change the
male hegemony of power. These women's experience of male
power is not confined to Black men, as they also live in the
wider context where they deal with White men too.

Notwithstanding their experience of male hegemony, none
take the line that a God who is consistently referred to as male
is equally exploitative as the men in their religious and secular
lives. Instead, they argue that God's model is one in which
they have equal share of gifts and responsibility and that
contemporary men are acting ungodly in circumscribing their
roles and functions within the church. As though to prove
the point of female competence, several of the writers stress
the professional aspect of female life, and offer 'how to' tips
for others to follow. They proffer insubordination as a real
spiritual coping strategy and the Bible as resource tool-kit.
To the extent that liberation is a theme running through
this book, it is liberation from oppressive male ecclesiastical
structures.

All three of these books illustrate well the potential of
Caribbean British literary prowess, and it has been interesting
to observe, mainly through the internet, the way in which they
have been adapted by various mainstream compilers based on
their themes.

In 1992 the African and Caribbean Evangelical Alliance
published the results of a series of workshops that were conducted under the title 'Theology Study Group'.[40] The publication *Let's Praise Him Again* sought to present to a wider
readership what were the crucial elements of worship from an
'Afro Caribbean' perspective. In this publication, for the first

time, a coherent challenge is made to the use of terms like 'Black' and 'Black-led' as ecclesiological designations in Britain. Up to this point, any disquiet with the presumed White imposition of 'Black' as a prefix for the churches and organizations that are created by Caribbean British Christians had remained largely an orally expressed matter. Indeed, the term has been embraced and utilized by the people themselves. In *Let's Praise Him Again*, however, a challenge is mounted. The rest of the publication seeks to explore elements of worship to be found in the Caribbean British-led churches that are being established in Britain. It succeeds in throwing light upon the worship practice and theology of these churches. The popular use and regular appearance of Gospel choirs on television is but one expression of this kind of exposure.

Three other anthologies are worthy of mention here. First is *Catching Both Sides of the Wind*,[41] which is the initiative of a White writer interviewing Black people and then writing their stories 'for' them. While this model of working has been useful, even necessary, in the past, it is clearly more desirable for Black people to write about their own experiences – not have them written for them. This aside, the publication has provided these pastors from five different denominations the opportunity to express their concerns and thoughts about a wide range of social, political, economic, cultural, educational and religious matters. Second, in *Black Catholics Speak*,[42] Anthony Lobo brings together five Black Catholics living in Britain to reflect upon their lives and experiences as part of a commitment to 'telling and listening to our various stories'. Theirs is an attempt to stake their claim as Black Catholics to being an integral part of the Catholic Church. Third is a collection of essays, *Here to Stay*,[43] by 'women with West Indian roots'. It seeks to take readers into their situation to feel and understand their context. Using themes that revolve around memories and shadows, tangled lives, moments to care and a tear and a sigh, these women share with their readers what it is really like to live in Britain as Black women.

The above represent a sample only of the many anthologies written by Caribbean British authors, some of them being

written during the preparation of this book; consequently, it
goes without saying that there are many that are not mentioned here. This literary form has been utilized as a means
of Caribbean British and other minority ethnic Christians,
from a range of denominations, Black-led and mainstream,
expressing themselves on a range of social-religious issues. In
many cases, individuals were being published for the first
time. Writing therefore provides scope for self-expression, as
a tool of and sometimes for empowerment. People write not
just to cry for freedom, but because they are free to do so. The
topics covered demonstrate a wide range of interest among
Caribbean British Christians; they have done us all a service
by demonstrating this breadth both within the community as
well as to a wider audience.

Another means of literary communication is the journal
Black Theology in Britain. During my time as executive director of the Centre for Black and White Christian Partnership
we, together with colleagues, developed and launched this
communication tool, in 1998, published by Sheffield Academic Press. The idea of a journal emerged out of a concern
that there needed to be an academic, yet popular, literary tool
by which Black people in Britain could communicate their
theological thought to a wider audience. As the first editorial
demonstrates, the journal would have as its priority Black
'God-talk', or, as the articulation and expression of Black
faith experience within the context of Britain, a contribution
to global theological reflection.[44] This broad role of the journal displays an openness to both influence and be influenced
by the wider context. The approach has been rewarded by the
willingness of universities and church training colleges to
subscribe to the journal, thereby making it available to their
students and staff.

In November 2002 the journal was re-launched as *Black
Theology: An International Journal*, thereby removing the overt
British link. The publishers, Continuum – having taken over
Sheffield Academic Press – agreed with the board of the
journal that the international market was ready for a journal
of Black theology and that this one was best placed to cap-
ture that market. The change of name symbolized a further

extension of the reach of the journal, in terms of readership and contributors, by making it more appealing to the world market, especially in North America, Africa and the Caribbean. Caribbean British Christianity is therefore responsible for creating a literary tool that is destined to become the means by which they and other minority ethnic people reflect their context to a wider world community.

The journal is in a line of several attempts to articulate a British Black theology.[45] Several of these are unpublished theses which are located in two key centres, namely the Urban Theology Unit, whose higher degree programmes are validated by Sheffield University, and the Centre for Black Theology at the University of Birmingham. These attempts mostly followed the call by Gerloff for such developments.[46] Each proponent concludes that as the experience of minority ethnic people in Britain, including Caribbean British Christians, is one of pervasive oppression, the consequential nature of British Black theology has therefore to take on a liberationist perspective. As this book highlights the reality of racism historically and in contemporary Britain, however, there is another important phenomenon, that is the general attitude of Caribbean British Christians who refuse to adopt the status of 'the oppressed' or 'the victim' as their premier or defining identity. This defiant attitude is very evident in the various writings within the journal *Black Theology*. Its remit is the whole life experience of its writers and their context, which permits the development of literature that reflects on Black people's long pre- and post-slavery history, and their lives in various contextual settings.

While the journal under both titles has continued to address local and global theological issues from a Black perspective, a major deficit has been our failure to attract a strong readership among the churches of Caribbean British majority. From conversations with several people, there seems to be two main areas of concern. First, as discussed above, the very mention of the word 'theology' in many Pentecostal circles is problematic. The term is a synonym for liberal and weak doctrinal affiliation with scripture. A second area of difficulty for people concerning the journal is that they do not associate

their faith with 'Black'. For them, their faith is a denominational faith with Jesus Christ at the head of their church, so
while they may purchase Christian books or magazines that
are published by their denomination or written by some
renowned Christian author, they do not have the same affinity
with a product named Black. Naturally, then, when we put
together two problematic words, Black and theology, it may
not be surprising that we have difficulty selling the idea to the
Caribbean British Christian community. It may be that in
time we will need to modify the title again, even if the contents
remain similarly focused, if we hope to penetrate the popular
home market. Alternatively, we could decide that the main
audience for the journal is the academy, where such a title is
not problematic in the least.

Autobiographical works represent another means of Caribbean British Christianity telling their stories for themselves.
These adopt the familiar pattern of storytelling, with the subject being people's own lives. Four clear emphases can be dis-
cerned. First, these authors relate accounts of how they came
to leave their mother country. In the case of Philip Mohabir,
God called him to leave Guyana to become a missionary in
England.[47] Second, there is a description of settling down in a
new country, with the hardships and challenges of being in a
minority. According to Io Smith, this included facing colour
prejudice in Britain, sexism in the church and the opportunity
to rear a family and pursue a ministerial career.[48] Third, they
tell of accomplishments in Britain, which in the case of Oliver
Lyseight includes the notable achievement of pioneering and
establishing the now largest national Black-led church, the
New Testament Church of God.[49]

A fourth characteristic of these works looks both backwards
and forwards. Authors reflect upon what has been accomplished and what the future may hold. Ronald Hyatt uses
family and church photographs to depict his life journey in
Britain and speculates that the future is part of a divine cycle,
as the four seasons.[50] It is significant that these autobiog-
raphies are, in the main, by first generation Caribbean British
Christians. They project a holistic view of life experiences
as people for whom racism, for example, is but part of that

experience. Family, church and work are also integral to their lives. But given the general stereotype of that generation as being mainly under-educated, it follows that the majority of these works are not of the highest academic and intellectual standards. They tend to display plenty of zeal and commitment for the gospel and the people being served, but often lack academic and intellectual rigour. With succeeding generations we can realistically expect to see writing standards rise in the Caribbean British community.

Among the Churches that have been established in Britain by Caribbean British Christians, two have published their historical stories. These are the New Testament Church of God (NTCoG) and the Calvary Church of God in Christ (CCoGiC). Others, like the Church of God of Prophecy and the New Testament Assembly, have plans to do so. The New Testament Assembly originally planned to publish their history to coincide with their 40th anniversary in 2001, but plans did not materialize. The Church of God of Prophecy commissioned a history project in 2002 and I am a member of the project board. In *Where Do We Go From Here?*[51] Ira Brooks describes the missiological journey that has established NTCoG as the premier Black-led church in Britain. Prominent in this development is the role of Oliver Lyseight, the founder of NTCoG in Britain, alongside other 'missioners'. The theme of making heroes is evident also in the work of Norma Thomas-Juggan, who profiles the pioneers of CCoGiC.[52] It is probably unsurprising that a people brought up on biblical stories such as David and Goliath (1 Samuel 17) should want to make their own heroes who triumph over adversity to establish 'kingdoms'. Having established the exploits of the pioneers of their churches, these writers describe the accomplishments of these churches, before going on to speculate about the future.

Both Brooks and Thomas-Juggan portray their churches as discrete organizations with their own historical roots, significant present and concerned about their future. They are keen too to profile key individuals who are seeking to influence their context with what they understand as the true gospel. In an earlier work, Brooks speaks of the pioneers of NTCoG as a people 'bound by a mysterious chain in his most awkward environment in twentieth century Britain'.[53] Here, however, the chains do not signify being in bondage to fellow human beings but rather to God, who has called them under the guise of economic improvement only to set them to work preaching the gospel.

The purpose of these historical projects is clear; it is to make known internally and externally the facts concerning how these churches came into existence and the impact they have had upon society. They highlight to the outside world and internally who the heroes are who have led these churches to prominence and have left the legacies that endure. These works do not set out to be sociological and theological master-pieces, but it is reasonable to expect that future works in this field might lean in those directions.

Continuing the theme of explicating the Black-led churches in Britain, chiefly Caribbean British led and peopled, there have been two attempts to publish directories nationally. This is in addition to the directories published by churches them-selves. The first such directory was published in 1984 as *A Handbook of the Afro-Westindian United Council of Churches*.[54] This ground-breaking work went beyond listing churches; it added theological commentary and rationale for the legiti-macy of the existence of these churches. It recognized the need for these churches to play a political role in support of their constituency. In 2000, on behalf of the Centre for Black and White Christian partnership, I, with others, in particular the African and Caribbean Evangelical Alliance, published a new directory under the title *Black Majority Churches UK Directory 2000*.[55] The objective was again to provide a means of mapping the whereabouts of this growing community to facilitate net-working and mission. This directory, published at a time when other credible theological and historical literary material is readily available, satisfied itself with focusing upon technical contact details and some statistics about Black majority churches in Britain. Since their publication, these directories have begun to be used as tools of legitimacy for those Black-led churches that mainstream churches and organizations do not know well. However, realistically, the directories are not that kind of product, given that the churches listed had only to submit their details to be included – no church was vetted for suitability.

A final category of literary work that demonstrates Caribbean British Christians' preoccupation with explicating their faith, thereby engendering knowledge of themselves and of others, is that of theological works. I will look at a cross-section of theological works and some of the themes they deal with.

Robinson Milwood, in *Liberation and Mission*,[56] provides an exposition on life for a Black person in mainstream churches. His is a proactive approach that confronts the racism in the Methodist Church by asserting his right and that of other Caribbean British people to a full human existence in their church. Milwood pioneered a Black majority Methodist mission in London, putting in place the necessary supporting mechanisms for his ideology. The central point of his work is what we might call a theology of presence. That is, Methodists from Caribbean British and other minority ethnic backgrounds should not give any quarter in asserting their right to be part of the Methodist Church. And they should by their persistent presence and participation teach their racist fellow church members something of the freedom that comes from the grace of God equally given and received.

Philip Mohabir, in two works, *Pioneers or Settlers?*[57] and *Worlds Within Reach*,[58] utilizes the Old Testament story of the Exodus and elements of contemporary evangelism strategy to demonstrate that Caribbean British Christianity is interested in much more than its own survival. What is more, Mohabir espouses a passion for cross-cultural evangelism, demonstrating Caribbean British interest in reaching out beyond their ethnic borders. The man some have called 'God's little Guyanese giant' saw evangelization of the world as his primary mission, and not just to his fellow Caribbean British people. Mohabir's central theological tenet was that the sinful world needed to hear the gospel of Jesus Christ and that the church would spread that gospel more effectively if all parts of the catholic church worked together.

In similar fashion Joel Edwards, in *Lord Make Us One – But Not All the Same*,[59] uses his own background and experience as the basis for writing about 'seeking unity in diversity'. Staunchly evangelical, Edwards advances a strong argument for Christian unity based on sound biblical principles. This quest for unity in Edwards' case is essentially evangelical unity. We get from him a strong theological pull towards the centre of gravity from an evangelical point of view. However limited might be the aspiration in terms of the extent and nature of unity, it is evident that there is a sector within the Caribbean British-led church community that sees unity as a real goal. And as evangelicalism is a trademark of the community, it may be that unity between Black and White Christians may start with like-minded people from the evangelical centre. Edwards follows this work with an exposition on the salvific life of Jesus Christ in *The Cradle, the Cross and the Empty Tomb*.[60] In retelling the story of Jesus, Edwards shows that he is very much part of mainstream Christian faith, sharing a concern for orthodox Christian faith. The centrality of atonement in Edwards' work is quite in keeping with Caribbean British understanding of the work of Jesus Christ – he came among us as God incarnate as a babe, moved to the cross and the resurrection that left an empty tomb. These twin themes of unity and atonement are central to Edwards' thesis.

In the work of Ira Brooks, *Another Gentleman to the Ministry*,[61] we see a pioneering writer in the Caribbean British context who, albeit without the literary excellence of Edwards, demonstrates the inclination of the Caribbean British Christian community to focus upon the big picture. Brooks begins in autobiographical mode, moving on to social, cultural and political matters that attend British life in the religious and secular spheres. The work is full of self-confidence, acknowledging the need of and arguing for independence of his denomination from its US White-led headquarters. Brooks' theme is mature independence. This is exemplified by his own presence as a minister in Britain, having endured much hardship and perseverance to get along. Mature independence is exemplified also in Brooks' strenuous argument for NTCoG to consider standing alone from its US headquarters.

Anthony Reddie explores, as the title puts it, *Faith, Stories and the Experience of Black Elders*.[62] Presented as an offshoot of

Reddie's PhD research into the religious education of Black children in British mainstream churches, the writer examines the manner and effect of orally transmitting from one generation to another the wisdom gained from earlier generations. At the heart of these stories, according to Reddie, is a theological assumption concerning the humanity of all humankind under the reign of God. Reddie's work highlights both the need for and the willingness of Caribbean British elders to express and share their stories for their therapeutic self-worth and enhancement of the knowledge of 'the other'. It is noteworthy that in Reddie's work elders whose predecessors endured hundreds of years of slavery, colonialism, transplantation and the attempted imposed inferiorization, emerge with clear self-understanding as humans made in the image of God and the equal of other humans. Interestingly another of Reddie's works, *Nobodies to Somebodies*,[63] seems, at least in the title, to contradict the assumed humanity mentioned above. I do not agree with the notion that in the educational process of young people their starting point is as nobodies. Everybody is somebody as a starting point; it is possible from that point to become more fulfilled as a human being.

Challenging the notion that Caribbean British-led churches are preoccupied with their own survival are two other texts. First, Sidney Dunn's *Jehovah God in the Old Testament is Jesus Christ in the New*[64] singularly offers an apologetic for the Oneness perspective on the nature of God. This is significant because at a time when social, cultural and political issues appear to dominate, Dunn is more interested in delineating the doctrinal position of his denomination. No mention is made of his church, only its central doctrinal tenet, that is, that only those baptized in Jesus' name alone are 'saved'. This is not a belief I share, but this book models the passion Caribbean British Christians have for their church and theology. Second, answering the popular charge of being too heavenly minded and not sufficiently of earthly good, S. E. Arnold, in *From Scepticism to Hope*,[65] outlines a framework within which the New Testament Church of God, of which he was National Overseer at the time, can approach its social responsibility to its members and to wider society. Arnold acknowledges that there had existed an imbalance in the 'this world/other world' binary, but challenges his church to face up to the needs of their community in the here and now. In this work, Arnold demonstrates a self-awareness that might be expected to come about only through challenges from outside. Of course he, as national bishop of the largest Caribbean British-led church in Britain, is well aware of the ongoing debate concerning the need for the churches to address wider issues in addition to providing spiritual sustenance for members.

Arnold managed to secure a publisher for his work, but for many others their important reflections on their church's philosophy, history and doctrine remain stuck on the shelf. This is particularly so in the libraries of the Urban Theology Unit and the Centre for Black and White Christian Partnership, now taken over by the University of Birmingham, where there are serious collections of theses written by Caribbean British Christians. Too numerous to mention, these works are further signs of the seriousness with which this community takes the task of writing about and examining what others say about its faith.

Finally, I turn to the work of probably the most influential Black British theologian of our time, Robert Beckford, whose writings adopt a liberationist emphasis. Beckford's three major works, as with his contributions made elsewhere, begin from the assumption that Caribbean British, what he describes as 'African Caribbean' people, live in an oppressed, neo-colonial space and are in need of liberation. In *Jesus is Dread*,[66] Beckford posits Black theology and culture as the appropriate political tools for the overthrow of White power and oppression. By identifying Jesus as 'dread', a play on the dreadlocks and ideology of Rastafarianism as a symbol of Black resistance and empowerment, Beckford argues that the Black church should embrace the incarnate God in Jesus Christ as being at one with the Black struggle for liberation. Beckford succeeds in highlighting many of the social, cultural and political issues that affect Caribbean British people, and in this way assists the process of internally developed information provision, leading to greater self and other awareness. In his second work, *Dread and Pentecostalism*,[67] Beckford

further develops his thesis of liberation. It is, of course, the
traditional line in modern liberation theology to assert that all
people of colour who share their contextual space with White
people are unavoidably oppressed and in need of liberation.

Beckford therefore locks his philosophy exclusively within
an oppression/liberation model, and advocates 'a political
theology for the Black church in Britain' as its only remedy.
This strategy, as this study shows, is out of step with Caribbean British Christianity, because the community as a whole
does not understand its experience of oppression as the all-
encompassing and singularly most significant aspect of its
existence. While the reality of oppression remains a part of the
Black experience in Britain, it does not carry the overarching
prevalence suggested by Beckford's analysis. Such an analysis
and counter-strategy may have been applicable in a bygone
era, but it certainly does not hold centre stage in today's
Caribbean British Christianity. Beckford's analysis comes
under some criticism from Paul Grant in a review of one of
Beckford's works. While commending Beckford's political
morality and personal integrity, Grant says:

> One of the ironies of Robert's work is that it seems a little
> caught out of time. For all the post-modern cleverness that
> Robert uses to shape his arguments and make his points,
> Robert is most definitely a child of the 1970s.[68]

Beckford calls the Black church to become more politically
active, but uses the single motif of oppression and a corresponding single need for liberation to do so. For many whom
I speak to, their quest for political involvement has little or
nothing to do with being oppressed, and everything to do with
a sincere desire to participate in the political process as
citizens.

In Beckford's third book, *God of the Rahtid: Redeeming
Rage*,[69] he offers a theological strategy of redeeming the rage
that is, he argues, an ever-present companion of Black life in
Britain. By presenting wrath as yet another aspect of Carib-
bean British Christian life that needs liberation or redemption,
Beckford demonstrates the intractable nature of the oppres-

sion/liberation dialectic. In effect, this is a self-perpetuating philosophy that has the potential to have Blacks perpetually beholden to White benevolence, or, dependent upon their eventual overthrow.

The examples discussed here demonstrate that Caribbean British Christians are preoccupied with the entire scope of life in which racism is one, but by no means all, of their concerns. Fewer Black Christians now wish to live their lives in ways that suggest that a response to White mistreatment is the sole axis around which their entire existence revolves. A less polemical, more multi-faceted and holistic analysis of what the context of Caribbean British Christianity consists of, and therefore what tools are necessary to make progress, is needed. Within this, the philosophy of oppression and liberation would sit as an experiential component, not the whole of the context of Caribbean British Christianity. I believe this to be so because from my observation of many Caribbean British Christians, they do not now perceive oppression and a response to oppression as their definitive identity-former.

Summary

What this overview of literary texts demonstrates is that Caribbean British and other Black Christians have, since their entry into Britain from the late 1940s, moved beyond the single issue of liberation to a more complex one about human and Christian mutuality. These are not the words of people who believe themselves simply to be in bondage to White society; rather, they are declaring to White society that they are here, and that it would do well to recognize their presence and the contributions they are already making. These writings are not the desperate bleating of wandering 'lost sheep' but a declaration of what is, and sometimes a cry of 'Oh what a waste, because together we could accomplish so much more for the Kingdom of God.' Also, these writings make available to a wider audience authentic, self-articulated information about Caribbean British Christian praxis that has hitherto not been available. The community has taken corporate responsibility for the provision of information that facilitates the process of mutual knowing.

This chapter has examined three situations within the context of Caribbean British Christian existence: observing Caribbean British Christianity at work in relation to White Christian leaders, developing a theological understanding of what it means to be married and to bring children into the world, and recognizing the significance of adding literary skills to oral ones. What we observe is a confident, experimental, ethnically and religiously affirmative community. They appear sure of their humanity and their faith as rooted in God their creator and sustainer. Much of what they do can be interpreted as attempts to make known to the world the normalcy of Caribbean British Christianity. For them, their humanity and faith do not have novelty value, but are expressions of their God-created being. There remain areas of uncertainty and underdevelopment, but Caribbean British Christianity is confidently working out its 'salvation' as a people on a journey with the rest of British and global humanity.

5

Biblical Antecedent – The Incarnation

Introduction

One of the undertakings of the contextual model deployed in this study is to discover and posit a biblical theme that has been chosen for its antecedent qualities, or historical resonance with the contemporary experience of Caribbean British Christians. This chapter analyses such a biblical theme. My search for an appropriate biblical paradigm was guided by the discovery in this work of Caribbean British Christians as a people who have a complex historical and contemporary identity that takes on new forms in new contexts. This is a people who are misunderstood and sometimes rejected by the mainstream, yet remain triumphant.

In recent years, Liberation and Black theologies have used the popular biblical story of the Exodus, with its emphasis upon liberation from oppression, as an antecedent for the people they designate as poor and oppressed.[1] However, in my search for a biblical antecedent that is appropriate for the Caribbean British Christian context, I have concluded that a different theme is desirable. This is not to deny the continued existence of oppression in the experience of Caribbean British Christians and the wider Black British society, since this has been evident in this study; nor is it an effort to deny the need for liberation from all forms of oppression. Rather, the need for a different biblical antecedent from the traditional one of Exodus is signalled by the contextual theological praxis of Caribbean British Christians; a praxis defined more by what

they are 'for' than what they are 'against'. Liberation and
exodus bespeaks a negativity that if left unanswered con-
demns a people to a life of opposition and reaction. It is time
to be defined more in terms of reaching the Promised Land
than escaping Egypt.

This research shows that while Caribbean British Christians have suffered oppression in social, political, economic
and other spheres, they do not appear to have imbibed the
ideology that 'the oppressed' is their defining identity.
Instead, they insist on a self-identity as free people in God and
that such freedom extends to their human relationships. In
the words of an old song, 'I am free, praise the Lord I am free;
no longer bound, no more chains holding me'. It is a freedom
that begins conceptually and spiritually in the mind and
extends outwards to the rest of life. As Bob Marley would say,
'Emancipate yourself from mental slavery'. This liberated
attitude is demonstrable, for example, in the freedom with
which they set up and operate churches that are independent
of mainstream ones; the freedom with which they relate to
other Christian leaders on an equal basis; the freedom with
which they reinterpret their faith contextually; and the freedom with which they insist on telling their own stories,
instead of others patronizingly doing so on their behalf. These
people clearly understand their privilege to initiate and act
even in a strange land, and not just in response to adversity
but in answer to their missiological understanding of the need
to exemplify and share the Christian gospel with others. In
this way, being oppressed by others, though real, is context-
ualized as one of their realities, not the totality of the reality
faced by Caribbean British Christians. Exodus or liberation
from oppression then has been set aside as an overarching
or paradigmic theme and in its place comes a paradigm of
'Incarnation'. This represents a theology of realized liberty
rather than one in search of it.

Having embraced the incarnation as a paradigm for Caribbean British Christianity, I will explore how this resonates
with their past and present realities and their future aspirations. Some may find it unpalatable that I compare and contrast the Incarnation of Jesus with the existence of a particular

group of people. However, I do not find this strange, at least not when we recall that humans are made in the image and likeness of God. I do not seek here equality with God, but find resonance with God acceptable. I begin with a rendering of the Prologue of John's Gospel (1.1–18), which is used as the template for developing this thinking, because it provides the most succinct outline of the incarnation in scripture. Raymond Brown suggests that the Prologue may be best rendered in a four-strophe format:[2]

First strophe

1 In the beginning was the Word,
and the Word was with God,
and the Word was God.
2 He was in the beginning with God.

Second strophe

3 All things came into being through him,
and without him not one thing came into being.
4 What has come into being in him was life,
and the life was the light of all people.
5 The light shines in the darkness,
and the darkness did not overcome it.

6 There was a man sent from God, whose name was John. 7 He came as a witness to testify to the light, so that all might believe through him. 8 He himself was not the light, but he came to testify to the light. 9 The true light, which enlightens everyone, was coming into the world.

Third strophe

10 He was in the world,
and the world came into being through him;
yet the world did not know him.
11 He came to what was his own,
and his own people did not accept him.

12 But to all who received him,
who believed in his name,
he gave power to become children of God,
13 who were born, not of blood or of the will of the flesh
or of the will of man, but of God.

Fourth strophe

14 And the Word became flesh and lived among us,
and we have seen his glory,
the glory as of a father's only son,
full of grace and truth.

15 John testified to him and cried out, 'This was he of
whom I said, "He who comes after me ranks ahead of me
because he was before me."'

16 From his fullness
we have all received,
grace upon grace.

17 The law indeed was given through Moses; grace and
truth came through Jesus Christ. 18 No one has ever seen
God. It is God the only Son, who is close to the Father's
heart, who has made him known.

The above rendering of the Prologue suggests the manner in
which the original hymn may have been embellished at a later
date. However, for the purpose of this study, I take the
Prologue as a whole, including any embellishment on the
basis that the revised edition is what the writer wishes us to
relate to. The approach adopted in dealing with this text is,
first, to confine myself to it and attempt to (re)tell the story of
the incarnation as it may be 'heard' from within the context of
today's Caribbean British Christianity. As George Beasley-
Murray argues, the Gospel of John speaks according as
hearers and readers can receive it.[3] Second, I deal with four
key themes that emerge from this rendering of the incar-

nation; these are pre-incarnation, witness, incarnation and post-incarnation. I associate these with phases in the life of Caribbean British Christianity.

Pre-incarnation (1.1–5)

The pre-incarnation phase highlights some key issues that demonstrate resonance between *Logos* and Caribbean ancestors: 1) *Logos'* beginning in a time before now, 2) *Logos'* complex identity, 3) *Logos'* contributions to what is, and 4) *Logos'* light overcoming the darkness.

First, according to the Prologue, *Logos'* existence originates in a 'beginning' with God, before creation.[4] Brown says the 'beginning' occurs in the sphere of God, outside finite time, and is a designation that is more qualitative than temporal.[5] In other words, we are not dealing with a specific point in time; rather, with a concept outside of known time, the precise location of which is humanly unknown. Thomas Brodie suggests:

> In reading those three words (in the beginning), a public reader does well to lower the voice and pause momentarily – as one might in reading 'once upon a time . . .' For just as 'once upon a time' suggests a world that is wonderfully distant, so 'in the beginning' evokes a sense of something distant and awesome.[6]

What the Prologue is clear about, is that whenever that time was, *Logos* was there. The Prologue accords to *Logos* a sense of transcendent awe by locating its origin outside current time and even may be outside time as we know it.

As the Prologue espouses an existence for *Logos* that is rooted in the 'beginning' or in time before the present, so this study suggests that the existence of Caribbean British Christian ancestors is located in a distant past. The coming together in the Caribbean of Amerindian, European, African and Asian people as a new Caribbean ethnic identity was such a 'beginning'. Equally, the 'beginning' marks the initiation of a syncretized Christianity in the Caribbean, influenced by multiple denominational and other faith expressions. Syncreticism is generally viewed in a dim light, but in reality it is a trait of all expressions of the Christian faith, since none has been developed *nil initio*; all have learned from and have elements of others who belong to a different time, place and philosophy. As Jesus was declared by John to be rooted in a different time to those around him, so today's Caribbean British Christians can be understood to have their roots in an earlier time than now.

Second, the issue of the identity of *Logos* is instructive also, because, although in the English Bible it is routinely translated 'Word', Barrett points out that *Logos* has many meanings, most of which can be summarized under the two headings of inward thought, and outward expression of that thought in speech.[7] To understand *Logos* as word or speech, we must understand it first as the consciousness or thought that informs speech, as discussed in Chapter 1. Sanders and Mastin define *Logos* as divine wisdom, reason, or word,[8] and in attempting to convey that which the Prologue says was in the 'beginning', Adam Clarke argues that *Logos* is best left untranslated, for the same reason that the names Jesus and Christ are left untranslated: the unsuitability of alternatives.[9] The importance of retaining multi-faceted meaning applies also to Caribbean ancestors. As in the beginning *Logos* was inward thought and outward expression of wisdom, reason and word, so in a different beginning the ancestral Caribbean were identified by their multi-ethnicity and multi-denominationalism, descended and derived from the Aboriginal Indian people, Europeans, Africans and Asians. These nuances are easily lost by the tendency to simplify *Logos* as 'Word', or to commute Caribbean British people and their ancestors' complex geo-ethnic identities to terms like 'Black'.

Third, the Prologue highlights the crucial contribution of *Logos* to creation by stating that everything that was made was made through him. Indeed, according to the Prologue, nothing came into existence apart from through *Logos*.[10] The extent to which this is a role of 'creator' or participation in creation is unclear and does not need to concern us deeply here. However, in a brief examination of the argument,

Tasker refers to *Logos* as 'the world's Creator and Preserver', which seems to overstate the case for *Logos* somewhat, since the role of 'agent through whom creation happened' rather than 'sole creator' seems to be what is claimed by the Prologue.[11] I read the Prologue as depicting Logos as a co-creator with, or an instrument of, God in creation. In effect, the *Logos* as wisdom, reason and word can be said to have been God's active tool and agent in creation. The main resonance with Caribbean ancestors with regard to creative agency has to do with the role they played in helping to create what emerged as the British Empire, and from that the Britain of today. They participated in the creation of the world we know today through forced labour as slaves, indentured labourers, later as colonized people and a contemporary voluntary workforce. In addition to their economic contribution, missionary activities by British and other Europeans in the Caribbean and in Africa and Asia have meant that the ancestors have been integral to the development of the church also. Caribbean ancestors were undoubted co-agents of what Britain has become.

Fourth, there is evidence in the text of a tone of victory after a struggle, in that the light still shines, because the darkness did not overcome it. So, from the 'beginning' the *Logos*' life has been emitting light, and since creation that light has been shining in humanity's rebellious and unresponsive sinfulness; yet it shines on.[12] Dwight Moody Smith Jr points out that it is typical Johannine dualism to contrast light and dark, as he does in verse 5, which is reminiscent of a similar phenomenon in the Rule of the Community of the Dead Sea Scrolls.[13] However, with reference to the nature of Johannine theology, Sanders and Mastin argue that any understanding of dualism in John's Gospel cannot be other than 'ethical dualism', which is fully compatible with monotheism.[14] The battle between good and evil has been settled, even if its effects rumble on. Importantly, in the Prologue, good has overcome evil, the light has overcome the dark, or as J. H. Bernard puts it, the guiding thought is that the creation of light dissipates the darkness of chaos.[15] This is of course a basis of Christian hope, one rooted in the victory of Christ.

The principle of the darkness not overcoming the light of *Logos* resonates with Caribbean ancestral experience when we recall the sheer strength of character and resilience they showed in refusing to succumb to the difficult lives they lived under slavery. Their light of inner strength and self-understanding refused to be put out by the darkness of inhumanity. In spite of the struggle for survival through slavery, colonialism, indentured labour, religious and social subordination, all this and more failed to put out the light of Caribbean ancestors. Their indomitable spirit shined on, misunderstood by the opposing powers. The reason, wisdom, words and action of the *Logos*, like the complex ethnicity and faith of the ancestors of Caribbean British Christianity, have survived all attempts to suppress them.

Forerunner/witness (1.6–9)

These verses, which are among those assumed to have been inserted by John into the original hymn from which the Prologue is believed to have come, serve the purpose of introducing the character of John the Baptist as a witness to the coming of the enfleshed *Logos*. They indicate that God did not send a heavenly being to make this announcement, but another human being, 'one of us'. I want to posit the Caribbean Christians who arrived in Britain prior to and including the period of the establishing of Black churches in the 1950s as the witnesses and forerunners of those currently here. They are the generation that appeared before and sometimes overlaps with today's. That generation promised much of what could be, but was only a shadow of what is today. Three aspects of this role of witness/forerunner are explored here: 1) the sense in which this is perceived to be a role ordained by God, 2) the nature of the witness/forerunner, and 3) what the witness/forerunner tells of the potential of the coming incarnate one.

First, the Prologue announces the witness in grand style; as a man sent by God and who, at the appropriate time, appeared on the stage of history.[16] John's appearance is portrayed by the Prologue as no mere accident or coincidence; rather, this was a divinely ordained, historical figure, fulfilling a divine commission.[17] Barrett points out that this story resonates with the commissioning by God of Moses (Exodus 3.10–15) and the prophets (e.g. Isaiah 6.8).[18] Like them, John simply appears, out of what seems like nowhere, with little preparatory explanation, as the witness to the coming messianic epoch.[19] Forerunning therefore has a rich history. As discussed in Chapter 3, this is reminiscent of the understanding of many Caribbean Christians when coming to Britain; they believed themselves to be divinely commissioned by God for a spiritual work in an increasingly heathen nation. For some, the pretext was the search for material gain, a better life; but they now believe the real context was one in which God always had another agenda. They believe that God sent them here to take a stand for righteousness, repentance and faith.

Second, the nature of John's ministry is portrayed as that of a witness, attesting to the impending arrival of 'the light'. He was to do so with such conviction that the Jewish nation would believe that his witness was true. The significance of the witness is emphasized by Barrett, who points out that the concept of the witness or forerunner holds an important place in the thought of the Gospel as a means of attesting to truth.[20] Basically, truth does not attest to itself, and so even the divine light of God needed an announcer and that was John's role; to testify, to confess, to declare that by revelation he knew that 'the Light' of the world was coming soon. And this light was to be Jesus Christ, the mind of God fully revealed.[21] Such a mind of God would shine into the world's darkness. The forerunner will be ineffective if he or she cannot make a convincing case, full of passion, if not fact; and to do that they need to understand their role. As forerunners, Caribbean Christians had a particular light of God to shine in the British context. But they had a 'bushel' that was likely to cover their light; this was the fact that most of them came to live in Britain originally because of enslavement and later through economic necessity, with most of them intending to stay for 'just five years'. That mindset was soon replaced by greater permanence, however, and they focused on the work of putting in place the ideology and infrastructure that was to be used by those that came after them. These people were witnesses not only to who and what would come later, they were witnesses to the host community by their weight of presence and obvious determination to believe more fervently in God, and in the humanity and worth of Black people.

Third, Jesus as the illumination of God to humanity is said by John to be the genuine light for whom the Baptist's task was to bear witness.[22] No matter, therefore, who or what had come before, or the degree to which John's own light shone, his task was to point to the greater brightness of the coming light. There may even have been other great lights, including John's own self, but John's forerunning was not for them, it was for Jesus. As Barrett states, the Baptist might be supposed a light; indeed, in a sense he was a light, but he was not the light.[23] The true light was about to come to enlighten and to illuminate humanity. Previous lights, including John, were flickers of the truth, faint glimpses of reality.[24] Potential may be found in the witness, but the fulfilment of that potential can come only at the appropriate time in the coming of the promised light. The Caribbean Christians who were our forerunners pointed to a truly liberated generation, who are today's Caribbean British Christians, their light now undimmed by slavery, colonialism, servility, lack of education and other opportunities. Even if some of this has yet to be realized, the mentality exists and that will in time bring forth its fruit.

Incarnation (1.14)

Three clear lines of discourse emerge from this verse: 1) the congruent nature of the incarnate, 2) the significance of tabernacle, and 3) the 'glory' of the 'new' person. These are explored both from the perspective of Jesus and Caribbean British Christianity.

First, according to Bultmann, it is in this verse that we find in the Prologue the first clear assertion about the Incarnation of *Logos*.[25] The term 'incarnate' means, literally, 'in flesh'. [26]

The concept embraces the idea that a person or thing without changing its property, enters into a new condition, and becomes something that it was not before. The Prologue boldly states that *Logos* became flesh, that is, a human being. But Dennis Edwards warns against what he calls an inexact and exaggerated assumption that it is the human Jesus of Nazareth who pre-exists.[27] In this regard, the use of 'became' is misleading, because it suggests a metamorphism akin to a caterpillar becoming a butterfly. The point is, rather, that deity, the already existent *Logos*, remains so while becoming clothed with, or in, humanity. The divinity of Jesus can be understood within the context of John's clear indication that Jesus was also fully human. This proposition entails the idea of a unique kind of union by which God and human are together in one being or person.[28] By this, God is made more reachable and therefore better known, more specifically and more personally. Also, human nature in the person of Jesus is put into a new perspective in relation to the divine, who in Jesus has come among us as a particular man, without in any way ceasing to be the eternal and infinite *Logos*-God.[29] This is the ultimate terrestrial/celestial congruence.

This divine–human convergence or co-existence that creates something new yet retains both its individual parts may be compared with what has been brought about in Britain; namely, a new Caribbean British Christian identity. This group has emerged as a people who have kept hold of their Caribbean Christian identity, and have added another dimension to the old, thereby creating a new congruent identity. Today's Caribbean British Christians have emerged as the 'incarnate' Caribbean British Christians, embodying the ethnic-religious traditions of their antecedents, but also adopting many of the cultural and religious values of their contemporary British context. This explains, at least in part, why few Caribbean British people wish to be known simply as British, even less, English. Something new is added to what existed, but what existed does not cease to do so. In the case of Jesus, it is humanity added to divinity,[30] and in the case of Caribbean British Christians it is Caribbean ethno-Christianity added to British ethno-Christianity in a new setting.

Second, John further emphasizes that *Logos* not only put on human flesh, but that as that human being, Jesus tabernacled, that is, he lived for a while among us. The term 'tabernacle' is most appropriate here, for it emphasizes

> that the incarnate life of the Word was but a temporary sojourning. More probably, it means that the divine presence, which it was believed was especially located in the tabernacle and later in the temple, now came to dwell in the man Jesus.[31]

Likewise, Caribbean British Christians have taken up their abode among the people of Britain. They live in close proximity to and as one with contemporary society. However, they are not exactly like their predecessors, or their contemporaries. Part of their glory is their difference from those who have not developed in the same way, not travelled the same ethnic and religious road. As arguably Jesus was more integrated into society than his forerunner John, so Caribbean British Christians are more integrated within British society than their forerunners. They are different from their contemporaries by being Caribbean as well as British and Christian, but they live willingly among them.

Third, the Prologue proposes that the new person, derived from the pre-incarnate *Logos* and its newfound ally the human being, is full of glory. The meaning of the Greek *doxa*, translated 'glory', conveys dignity, honour, praise and worship.[32] These qualities were present in Jesus and observed by some. John generously affirms, 'we have seen his glory'. However, it is clear that not all of them saw his glory. It is interesting to ponder upon why some see while others do not. Is it because of deliberate blindness, or just lazy ignorance? Jeremy Begbie suggests that in order to discover, to discern and understand the qualities of the incarnate Jesus, it is necessary to 'get inside' of him. He suggests that in the modern world this might be done through art, literature, poetry, dance, icons, sculpture or music.[33] The people who are the subjects of my study here would argue that it is not possible to know Jesus other than through a personal relationship. Such a belief in a personal God leaves little room for knowing through the means suggested by Begbie, but these can surely assist in deepening one's knowledge of the divine. It is debatable whether it is possible via a third party to 'get inside' the person of Jesus and see his glory. Sometimes the inspiration of another person or thing opens up something that was hitherto unknown or misunderstood. However achieved, this inside knowledge of the glory of the incarnate Son of God, the 'infinite made finite', as Barbara C. Raw describes him, leads to a deeper understanding both of the divine and of humanity, since both are present in the person of Jesus.[34] The glory to which John refers, therefore, is not of *Logos* or humanity isolated from the other; it is the revelation of glory such as belongs to the God-man, according to Tasker.[35] And it is possible to behold the glory of his uniqueness.

A similar comment can be made about the 'glory', that is, the dignity and poise and honour of Caribbean British Christians. Their glory is of an individual and corporate identity that can only be known by getting close up or inside the community. This means that one needs to see inside their history, contemporary reality and aspirations. Such a beholding would lead to an awareness of the full or real 'glory' of Caribbean British Christian people. The incarnation, then, of that which is from a time before now, combined with that which is from this time, implies the coming together of spiritual elements from the past, 'in a beginning', with a contemporary literal expression in a new and glorious reality that can be seen if got close to, or inside of.

Post-incarnation (1.10–13, 15–18)

The most significant lessons from the post-incarnation section of the Prologue are three: 1) the coming of Jesus to his own who did not receive him, 2) the benefits of receiving and accepting, and 3) the price of rejection.

First, the invisible Creator, now appearing in the person of Jesus, found that when he came among those who should recognize and receive him, he was rejected instead. This is

hardly surprising given that he was not now recognizable as
the agent of creation, the invisible *Logos*, but was enshrouded
in humanity. Had he appeared as a strong wind or something
similar, people might have recognized him, but to show up as
a babe born in a stable to a virgin? Human imagination and
credulity was stretched to the limits. Barclay argues that in
order to recognize the 'creator' in Jesus, humanity needed to
perceive God's reason in action by looking 'outwards' at the
amazing order of the earth, 'upwards' at the wonder of the
universe, 'inwards' at our own complex constitution, and
'backwards' at the march of history.[36] He concludes that the
universe has always been such that, looked at in the right way,
it would lead men's minds to God. For this recognition to
occur, people needed to grasp that he who had the appearance of a thirsty and helpless traveller, in fact was the Son of
God who gives living water.[37] The non-recognition of the
identity of Jesus was due, therefore, to a lack of discernment,
the inability to interpret the life and works of Jesus in terms
of the manifestations of divinity. And so, according to the
Prologue, Jesus, by whom as *Logos*, the world came into existence, found himself unrecognized by his creation.

When *Logos* became flesh as a Jew in the land of Israel, he
was in a real sense coming home, but his own kinsmen gave
him no welcome, because of his complex identity.[38] According to John's Gospel, Jesus' not being received does not point
to 'innocent ignorance', but rather to considered rejection.[39]
That is, their rejection of the God-man Jesus is in light of the
experience of the forerunner and witness, John the Baptist,
and the evidence of the life of Jesus. The author of John seems
convinced that a people prepared has not fulfilled its calling.[40]
In spite of the announcement of the witness and forerunner,
the Jews did not accept the incarnate one.

This is similar to the manner in which mainstream Britain,
religious and secular, failed to recognize the value of the
Caribbean British Christians in their midst. They failed to
recognize people who belong to the same humanity as they,
who belong to the same churches as they, and the people
whose 'blood, sweat and tears' helped to create the British
Empire from which modern Britain has emerged. Instead of

being recognized as 'one of us', Caribbean British Christians were and are sometimes still seen as unwanted immigrants, even more than 50 years later. Caribbean British Christians find themselves rejected by their fellow human beings and fellow Christians, even by fellow members of the same denomination. This is after associating with and having first-hand knowledge of the humanity and faith of Caribbean British Christians and their forerunners before and since the 1950s. As in the first century, when 'he came to his own and his own received him not', so in the twenty-first century, 'they came to their own and their own received them not'.

Second, according to the Prologue, not everybody rejected Jesus, as Lightfoot points out:

> Some, however, in spite of the fact that they were 'in the world' (cf. 13.1, 17.11), did receive *Logos* (cf. 1.12, 13); they did not remain in the darkness and therefore had the light of life (cf. 8.12, 12.46); and to them was granted the 'right' or 'authority' of a new, divine birth, whereby they might become sons of the light (cf. 12.36), and thereby understand both their origin and its purpose.[41]

Of course, the drift of the Prologue discourse suggests that those who believed, like those who did not, did so not just in regards to *Logos*, but to *Logos/anthropos*, God-man, Jesus. Believing in the name, that is, all that he represents, implies believing in the God-man person. The Prologue insists that the right to the 'sonship' of God depends upon this belief in God and humanity. All people are the children of God in the sense that all humanity owes to God their creation and the preservation of their lives; but only some people become the children of God in the real depth and intimacy of the true 'father and child' relationship.[42] In other words, while by default all humans are passively children of God, those who are actively children of God are those who acknowledge the God-man relationship and co-existence. This is belonging taken to another level of divine existence.

Belief in the incarnate One grants a type of kinship that has its roots not in 'natural descent, nor of human decision' but in a supernatural belonging.[43] In other words, according to John, there is a belonging for people who believe in Jesus that is different from, and does not have its roots in, human will. To them,

> God's grace betokens his goodness and initiative in inaug-urating the salvation of all people. The reader of the New Testament will not be surprised to find that grace figures prominently, and appropriately, as Jesus Christ is named at the conclusion and culmination of the Prologue.[44]

Only through this God-man figure, Jesus, John argues, is this grace of God made available. The appearance of *Logos* in the form of humanity shows humans the way back to love; for each other and for the Creator God. What is more, whereas God had been invisible before the incarnation, the coming of Jesus now brought God to man in a manner that makes God known as one side by side with us. John conveys, too, that in Jesus *Logos* remained God, and that in a real way the imman-ence of God was revealed in the humanity of Jesus, who can, as a result of his two-natured being, reveal God to humans as never before experienced.

In the end it is the rejectionists who miss out, because Jesus had in himself, because of his divine origin, the gift to make others become children of God. The people's rejection of him did not make him any less who he really was. By analogy, rejection of Caribbean British Christians does not make them less who they truly are. It follows that those in Britain who accept Caribbean British Christians forge a new family that is multi-ethnic and diverse in other spiritual and cultural ways. It is interesting, for example, that many creative partnerships have been forged between Black and White Christian indi-viduals and groups in Britain, where people have been willing to get to know each other. And it is the case, as discussed in Chapter 3, that in inner cities in Britain it is the same 'rejected' ones who now constitute the majority of Christian worshippers. Indeed, those who accept the coming of Caribbean British Christianity and engage with it are blessed by the relationship.

Summary

The incarnation can be understood as the emergence of a new person who embodies the rich history of his or her ancestral past. It is the enfleshing of the eternal spirit in a manner that celebrates both old and new, past and present, invisible and visible. In so doing, the incarnation legitimizes an identity with its rootedness in the past and relevance in the present, even though the combination renders the new identity difficult to understand or accept. The God-man Jesus provides the template for incarnational God-talk on behalf of Caribbean British Christianity. The incarnation paradigm provides a framework for understanding and legitimizing their past and present experiences in light of a biblical story. It provides also further identity with the Jesus who is so much loved and worshipped among Caribbean British Christianity in Britain.

6

Towards a Theology of Respect

Introduction

In this final chapter, I offer a theological interpretation of the study of the Caribbean British Christian context that has been presented here. This is in line with my discussion in Chapter 1 concerning the formula of contextual theology. There I said that a thorough analysis of the context, coupled with reflection upon a biblical theme, would lead to a new theological premise. I have concluded that the new theology that emerges can best be described as 'a theology of respect'. Below I will explain what I mean by respect, but first let me explain how I have arrived at this conclusion.

Towards an understanding of 'Respect'

With particular emphasis on their ethnicity and faith, this study has tracked the development of Caribbean British Christians from their ancestral home in the Caribbean to the present time in Britain. It has highlighted the complex persona of a people who are sure of their identity and strong in their faith; not a people preoccupied with a longing to be free, but a people already free to be themselves. They are not held prisoner by their past, neither do they labour under the burden of inferiority, or a lack of identity. The key to engaging with this community is to understand them, their history, present setting and future aspirations. And in this chapter, I try to outline the framework that will assist this process and change the nature of the Black/White relationship from one of victim/victor, oppressed/oppressor, to one of equality in humanity and faith. In this new relational dynamic, the better each knows their self and the other, the better the quality of the relationship and the more mutually productive their future together.

While growing up in Jamaica and in England, I became accustomed to hearing the exhortation by parents and other adults to 'respect your elders'. This involved being first to greet them with 'good morning' or 'good evening', listening when they spoke, and treating them with deference at all times, based on the understanding that they were older and wiser. And in recent times, quite a common sight in Britain has been young Black men in particular touching clenched fist to clenched fist and uttering the single word, 'Respect'. It is often used as a form of greeting one another, as though to say, 'We know one another, we're safe'. The respect gesture can also be seen on sports fields, especially cricket when one player has performed a remarkable feat like hitting a boundary, or effecting a run-out or taken a catch to dismiss a batsman, and the players slap open palms in high-fives or touch fists. We see the touching of gloves after two boxers have come to the end of a fight. Having felt the power and experienced the skill of the opponent, respect is gained. The respect symbol shows appreciation for achievement by someone who knows how difficult what has just been done is to achieve.

Caribbean British Christians, coming from a complex ethno-faith background, having coped with all that life has used to challenge their ancestors, and they having flourished in the British context against the odds, and knowing assuredly that their human and Christian identity is God-ordained, now say in their context: 'Respect us'. American singer Aretha Franklin, in her classic song 'Respect', echoes what I believe is borne out in this study, that what people want most of all is respect.

What you want
Baby I got
What you need
You know I got it

All I'm asking
Is for a little respect.[1]

Franklin does not mind sharing what she has with someone
provided they respect her. However, as I have discovered,
respect is a much misunderstood word. A significant part of
my task here is to explain what respect is, how it works and
why it is a suitable theological motif for Caribbean British
Christianity. In Figure 1 I have devised a model for explaining
'respect', based on eight cornerstone principles: 1) information 2) relationship 3) ethnicity 4) faith 5) self 6) other
7) dis/regard 8) prophetic presence.

Figure 1: Respect axis

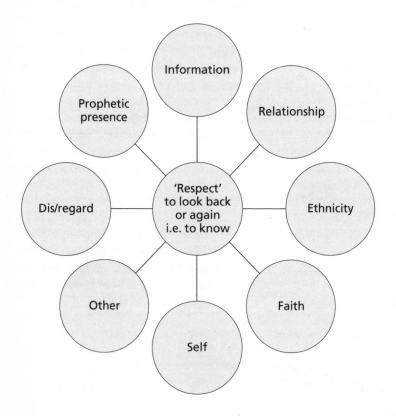

It was significant for me to discover that etymologically the word 'respect' is derived from the Latin *respicio*, literally, *re*, 'back', *specio*, 'look', or to 'look back', or to 'look again'.[2] The meaning implies further examination or exploration, which in turn connotes a deliberate act of taking an interest in knowing through spending time in the company of someone or something. Respect promotes relational depth over superficiality and knowledge over ignorance, as implied in my earlier argument in Chapter 1 about informed and sophisticated God-talk. This understanding of respect is consistent with the manner in which it is used in the Bible, where the term conveys meanings such as to consider or inspect (Genesis 4.4) and to look away from everything else (Hebrews 11.26).[3]

Respect is knowledge-based and inspired by a willingness to take the time to understand. Conversely, to disrespect is to be deliberately ignorant: to refuse to look back or again, to refuse to associate with and get to know. The incarnation offers an excellent example, and validation of the imperative, of knowing. Here, God makes known his self as the lover of humanity, displaying divine wisdom, reason and word in action. God does this by coming among humanity as one of us in the person of Jesus Christ. By tabernacling with us, God got into and under humanity's skin, and thereby spent time *in situ* experiencing and knowing. As the writer to the Hebrews puts it, 'For we have not an high priest which cannot be touched with the feeling of our infirmities; but was in all points tempted like as we are, yet without sin' (Hebrews 4.15). However, a lesson of the incarnation is that, though one of us, some rejected him: 'He came to what was his own, and his own people did not accept him' (John 1.11). They did not realize who he was because they did not take the time to look again at the claims made by their prophets, his heralder John, or the works Jesus did. In fact they disrespected him.

In order to respect Caribbean British Christians, the 'truth' about them must be sought, discovered and understood. As Cone says:

There is no truth for and about Black people that does not emerge out of the context of their experience. Truth in this sense is Black truth, a truth disclosed in the history and culture of Black people. This means that there can be no Black theology which does not take the Black experience as a source for its starting point. Black theology is a theology of and for Black people, an examination of their stories, tales and sayings. It is an investigation of the mind into the raw materials of our pilgrimage, telling the story of 'how I got over'.[4]

A form of respect therefore is the willingness to hear the voices of the people within the context and to treat their stories with the utmost seriousness. And this needs to replace the tendency for some to assume hegemony over or responsibility for them, rather as Adam assumed or was given responsibility to name Eve in the story of creation (Genesis 2). The forthright sentiments that are inherent in the anthology *A Time to Speak* cannot be overstated in terms of their poignant refusal to accept voicelessness as a normal state of affairs, whether externally imposed or self-imposed.[5] This work signals the end of an era when White 'exponents and academics' spoke and, equally inappropriately, wrote for Black Christians. As the creation of God, Caribbean British Christians assume equality with the rest of humanity and demand to be respected, not patronized or ruled over.

The significance of knowing the Caribbean British Christian community well is clearly illustrated in the following three examples. First, Walter Hollenweger, a White academic, states that Christians in Britain prayed for many years for revival and when it came they did not recognize it because it was Black.[6] Hollenweger takes some licence here since he offers no proof that such prayers were actually made. However, the message he conveys is clear, which is that the anti-Black colour prejudice of White Britons rendered them blind to the gifts Caribbean British Christian migrants brought to the British church context. Theirs was an act of disrespect in that they did not take the opportunity to get to know their new neighbours.

Second, Ron Brown, a former national bishop of one of the foremost Black-led churches in Britain, in his National

Overseer's Annual Address to the New Testament Church of God's national convention in July 2002, said:

> We Pentecostals were very unpopular, in fact, if you can find some of those books that were written 30 and 40 years ago, you will find that those that deal with religion usually classify Pentecostalism as a cult religion. *They did not understand it* [my emphasis]. Many were put out of the organized churches of the time because the Spirit of the Lord would come upon them and they would speak in tongues, or manifest under the unction of the Spirit of God. But today, the Church to which we belong is recognized. We now walk with kings and prime ministers, we now shake hands with governors, and lords.[7]

Brown is clear that the root of the problematic relationship between Black and White Christians in Britain was the ignorance of Whites concerning their Black Christian neighbours. As mainstream Christianity became more familiar with Black Pentecostals, acceptance and recognition resulted.

Third, Mark Sturge argues that it is 'not knowing' that is the root cause of prejudice, discrimination and intolerance.[8] Sturge points to the tendency to predicate one's view upon the 'old story' rather than the 'whole story' of a person's character for example. Utilizing the biblical story concerning Abraham and his nephew Lot, Sturge argues that the 'old story' glorifies Abraham as a virtuous man who was blessed because of his faith in God and vilifies Lot as an ungrateful individual who walked away from the protection of his uncle and ended up paying a high price. The 'whole story', according to Sturge, shows Abraham as a cheating, lying, deceiving and selfish individual upon whom God bestowed unmerited favour, while Lot became a tragic individual and a victim of circumstances. Sturge's point is that there is a human tendency to accept uncritically the 'old story', the traditional line, and too little inclination to reserve judgement on those matters about which we know insufficiently. Only after we have taken the opportunity to explore and familiarize ourselves are we able to make informed judgements.[9] Respect is based on the 'whole' not just the 'old' story.

Although the above writers do not use the term 'respect', they and many Caribbean British Christians express themselves in terms of knowing or not knowing when analysing or discussing their experience. For example, in Chapter 4, we find that the churches' attempts to record their histories is rooted in a need to provide information to dispel ignorance about these churches. It is the concept of knowledge that is applied here as the essence of respect and as the defining hermeneutical principle at the heart of Caribbean British Christianity's experience when thought of in theological terms.

Information

If respect is to be engendered fully, internally and externally, there needs to be quality information about Caribbean British Christianity. For quality to be assured, the source and substance of the information become crucial. Until the mid to late 1980s, practically the only source of information about Caribbean British Christianity was that provided by Whites, with the result that what was known represented White perceptions, not Black reality. A clear example of this is a chapter in *A Time to Speak* by Elaine Foster, which describes the development of 'Black-led' churches in Britain since the 1950s.[10] What she shows is that White writers held views about these churches that were at significant variance with reality. Whereas for Foster, the main reason for the rise of these churches was missionary zeal, White writers saw a different phenomenon at work. For them, Black-led churches were principally a response to racism in society and mainstream churches, social deprivation, economic frustration and a necessary psychosomatic guilt-reducing device. These factors were indeed at play; however, the emphasis depends upon what message one wishes to convey. For Caribbean British Christians, God was at work in them. For White reporters, Blacks were reacting to adversity. From within the community, Edwards depicts Caribbean British Christians as a people of pain and purpose, not just pain.[11] However, their purpose was not the product of their pain, and certainly rejection was not their only pain. These are a people with a divine purpose who suffer whatever pain comes in their line of duty.

The *Logos* brought to humans information about the nature of God in a manner that we did not know God before. God had sent prophets and other agents before, but only in the person of Jesus Christ does God become fully known to humans. So it is not just information that matters, the quality and authenticity of the information is equally significant. Historically very little has been written by Caribbean British Christians about themselves, but this has begun to change in recent times, as I described in Chapter 4. The Caribbean British Christian oral tradition has been added to by an increasing inclination to provide self-written data, which, added to that written by others from outside Caribbean British Christianity, provides a crucial basis for understanding this community. The determination to tell their true story is very real.

Another example of a factor concerning information is the manner in which the ethnicity of Caribbean British Christianity has been used to depict their religiosity. As is evidenced in Chapter 3, it is fair to say that Caribbean British Christians see themselves first as Catholics, Anglicans, Baptists, Methodists, Church of God of Prophecy, New Testament Church of God, New Testament Assembly, and so on. Outside observers, both Black and White, have tended to see them as Black Christians and Black-led churches. But as Ira Brooks insists, this is not the way we see ourselves.[12] Evidence of Caribbean British Christians' problem with information content and source is present in Arlington Trotman's challenge to the practice that began with White commentators of distinguishing the churches run by Caribbean British people by colour coding.[13] Like Brooks, Trotman insists that churches initiated by people from the Caribbean did not identify themselves by the pigmentation of their members; rather, they were set up and operated along the lines of the ecclesiology and theology of their parent organizations.

Trotman calls for these churches to be identified by their theology and history, if they must have a corporate identity

apart from the ones inherent in their particular histories. The
clear implication is that many observers looking on see a
Black mass of Christians without distinguishing denominational, historical and doctrinal marks, while the people
themselves are crystal clear that God has given them particular missions in different denominational camps. The focus
differs depending upon who writes the story. In a scathing
attack upon traditional western scholarship, Edward Scobie
argues that there is a long history of unflattering and pejora-
tive depiction of Black people.[14] He argues, for instance, that
although African civilization is more ancient than that of
Europe, its history has been distorted by half-truths, omis-
sions and outright lies by White historians. Scobie states that
it is a sacred duty of African scholars to rewrite their own
history and to find out the truth about their heritage.

Those involved in the project to produce the first journal of
Black Theology in Britain saw it as an act of information provision. Its editor, Emmanuel Lartey, declared that its aim is to
make known what Black Christians are thinking, feeling, saying and expressing about their experience of God.[15] He makes
clear that this written information would seek to highlight
developments in song, music, dance, drama and art work.
Lartey provides a round-up of written material that has been
produced since about the mid-1980s. It is a growing body
of 'Black literature'. The journal published its ninth issue
in November 2002, under the new title, *Black Theology:
An International Journal*,[16] edited by Anthony Reddie, and
continues to be a central resource of information for and
about the Caribbean British and other Black Christians. As I
have been arguing, the role of information is crucial in the
process of respect and when that information emanates from
the community itself, this provides not only greater possibilities of experiential accuracy, but it has for the community a
sense of self-satisfaction that it speaks for itself. Of course,
internal provision does not obviate the need for externally
developed information also. If Caribbean British and the rest
of British society are to get along as one yet diverse people
under God, information about both needs to exist and be
understood.

Relationship

Another principle of respect is relationship. To get to know others, we must get close enough to form a relationship. Relationship forming, formal and informal, has been a central feature of Caribbean British Christianity's existence, since the inception of this phenomenon, but it has not always been reciprocated. The significance of relationship for Caribbean British Christianity is evidenced in this book in at least three ways. There is the intertwining of ethnic and faith relations that are characteristic of Caribbean British Christianity. The imperative of relationship is evidenced also by the manner in which Caribbean British Christians have established frameworks for engagements and allowed others to happen since the 1950s, as presented in Chapter 3. Also, there has been an instinctive response to the need to know each other better and with practical outcomes, based on a Christian spirit of ecumenism. This, however, is based upon an ethno-religious model, not upon expectation of change in 'faith and order' terms, as I have previously emphasized.[17] I will examine some of these formal and informal 'structures' for relationship forming and their consequences.

Formal structures are evident both in Black-led and mainstream church sectors. The character of these has tended towards a mixture of ethnic and religious identity in such groups as the International Ministerial Council of Great Britain, the Afro-Westindian United Council of Churches, the West Indian Evangelical Alliance (now known as the African and Caribbean Evangelical Alliance, ACEA), and in recent times by a plethora of Black-led ecumenical agencies. These agencies include local and national councils of Black-led churches and associations that have proliferated around the country. They have not only been the vehicles for inter-Caribbean British and other Black relationships, but they have provided relational points between Black Christians and White Christians. The plural nature of Caribbean British Christianity means that its participants and operators do not necessarily have in-depth knowledge of each other and these constructs provide relational meeting points for mutual learning.

Within mainstream churches, formal structures of relationship have emerged in the form of Black-led internal organizations aimed at providing a focal point for and of Black and
minority ethnic Christian communities within the denominations. Today, mainstream churches like the Roman Catholic,
Church of England, Methodist, Baptist and United Reformed
all have Black or minority ethnic caucuses. Interestingly, the
mainstream churches that have not pursued this line of operation are the Charismatic and Pentecostal churches, like the
Assemblies of God and Elim Pentecostal Church. These
churches appear to have a colour-blind approach to these
matters, seeing no need for such constructs. The Black or
minority ethnic caucus organizations have provided relationship tools between the Black people within the denominations
and a meeting point between the Black people and their White
fellow members of the denomination.

The relationship between Black and White Christians has
been interesting to observe. Centres such as Keyboard,
Christian Action for Religious Education, the Centre for
Black and White Christian Partnership and a number of its
offshoots, and the Zebra Project are but a few of the formal
structures that have emerged to construct and support Black/
White relationship. In some cases, what has been learned is
that Blacks were unable to have any influence upon these
structures even where significant attempts were made to
ensure adequate representation of different ethnic groups.
Black/White relationship has been so lopsided as a historical
legacy that Whites still tend to want to control and Blacks
often let them. This was the subject of the Black and White
Leaders' Forum that was initiated by the Centre for Black and
White Christian Partnership and other organizations referred
to earlier in this book.

Informal relational structures are also evident in Black-led
and mainstream churches. For example, meeting places like
conventions, concerts, retreats and study courses have provided crucial spaces for Christians who did not truly know
each other to meet to learn about each other. At the Centre
for Black and White Christian Partnership, one of the characteristic traits was the opportunity for Black people from

different denominations to study together and discover the similarities that existed between their denominations and those of others. Often people found that their churches had similar roots, doctrines and practices, yet they had previously been taught that the differences were substantial and their faiths incompatible. At conventions and concerts, issues such as dress codes and music likes and dislikes came head to head. For example, in the New Testament Church of God, where hats were compulsory for the sisters, cross-fertilization with other Pentecostals where hat-wearing was not common practice has led to a change in behaviour; the ecclesiastical rule has not changed, but people's behaviour has. And in the case of the Church of God of Prophecy, the effects of these relationships have been dramatic in effecting changes that had not been bargained for. Jewellery wearing, including wedding rings, which had been banned, is now allowed.

The series of meetings between Black and White church leaders outlined in Chapter 4 has provided another example of relationship forming. Often uneasy and found to be largely unsustainable over time, this kind of engagement has nevertheless borne unexpected fruit. In this case, while the formal structures failed to persist, there are signs of informal, sometimes personal relationships enduring. These meetings provide a sound example of how Christians from different denominational and ethnic backgrounds can learn from and about each other. More so, they point to wider ranging meetings that embrace social, economic and political opportunities to interact with the other.

Relationship, then, is of major significance to Caribbean British Christianity as fellow children of God and citizens of the world. There is acknowledgement in this community that in Britain Christians should not exist on parallel lines; rather, they need to better understand each other, and that cannot be achieved without proper engagement. God's *ecumene* is relational, as in the metaphor of the body of Christ, interrelated and interconnected. In the ultimate relational act, God in Jesus shows how deep relationship can be, whereby the *Logos* continues to be *Logos* within a relationship in which *Logos* and *anthropos* co-existed in the one person of Jesus Christ. By their willingness to relate within and outside of their ethno-religious sphere, Caribbean British Christianity demonstrates the imperative of relationship, and along with information, this provides the basis upon which the act and process of knowing, or respect, happens.

Ethnicity

Being clear about who one is and being understood as that person, not some imaginary being in another's mind, is a further key to respect. Caribbean British Christians exhibit an attitude that essentially says, 'We are first and foremost human beings made in the image of God; and Christian members of the body of Christ. You need to get to know us.' In this book I have shown that there is a significant complexity and lack of knowledge about the ethnicity of Caribbean British Christians. It is evident also that ethnic affinity has been and continues to be a defining characteristic among this community. As in the Caribbean, demonstrated in Chapter 2, so later in Britain there has been a natural tendency to belong to one's people, clan, or community as ethnically defined (Chapter 3). This is made more poignant when communities become defensive because of perceived or real threats upon their existence or way of life. The West has tended towards a depiction of humanity as a hierarchy with White people at the top and Black people at the bottom. Black people in general, and Caribbean British Christians in particular, have become defensive as a consequence of this distortion of humanity and its interrelatedness. There has emerged, therefore, a determination to articulate a version of history that is more sympathetic to the people whose humanity has been distorted and questioned. Caribbean British Christianity has done this by appealing not to science but to the Bible and its teaching that all are made in the image and likeness of the one God. I have shown in earlier chapters how Caribbean British Christian and wider society have constructed their ethnic identity based on an understanding of their having been made in God's image.

From this study we gather that Caribbean British Christianity is emphatic in its assertion that there is but one humanity, made in the image of God, and that they are an integral part of that. However, any true knowledge of that one humanity has to take account of the diversity that is humanity's reality. Respect for humanity is predicated upon this appreciation that the diversity of humanity and its continual dynamic evolutionary progress that creates new identities is not a distortion but an essential part of what it means to be human. Knowledge of the particular ethnic identity of the Caribbean British Christian is essential, especially in view of the societal tendency to lump people together so that they lose their particularity. Caribbean British Christianity appears on the one hand to demand that there is recognition of the unity of humanity, but on the other that there is a determination to protect an ethnically defined identity based on their whole being: appearance, geography and historical belonging, as discussed in earlier chapters. Ethnicity is much more than the colour of one's skin, and yet skin colour is often the only consideration in relation to one's identity, character and abilities.

Faith

This study has discovered an inclination to camouflage and distort the identity of Caribbean British Christianity by grouping together an egalitarian denominational context under convenient headings. Against such a background, Caribbean British Christians appear determined that their faith, Christianity, is understood as universal and, therefore, not the prerogative of so-called 'established' churches. The setting up of Black-led and Black majority churches, described in Chapter 3, is clear evidence of a perspective that does not seek permission, but asserts its presence. The hegemony of established churches in British society means that Caribbean British Christians in Black-led churches have been perceived by some as a sort of pseudo-church, something exotic. On the contrary, Caribbean British Christians view themselves as bona fide Christians and have been engaged in the process of telling their own stories to this effect through history books, leaflets and oral tradition.

As with their understanding of humanity, Caribbean British Christians are keen to promote Christianity as the total creation of God. By this thinking, no one church or denomination has a divine right above any other to be regarded as 'church'. The church that is known among Caribbean British Christianity is a complex array of denominations and fellowships, all of which understand themselves as part of the Body of Christ. Simply referring to these churches as 'Black-led' and 'Black majority' infers that their main identifying characteristic is the pigmentation of their leaders and membership. Those who would truly know these churches by studying them will soon discover their plural identities: ethnically, denominationally, historically, doctrinally and theologically.

Greater knowledge of the Christian faith, as Caribbean British Christians have come to understand it, has led some to seek to move their practice of the faith away from its perceived Eurocentric form towards one that is more sensitive to Caribbean British Christianity's history and norm. For example, some have begun to experiment with syncretism between African and Caribbean cultural and religious practices and the western Christian form. This is the gist both of the Afro-centric wedding blessing and child-naming ceremony described in Chapter 4 and Valentina Alexander's writing in *Black Theology in Britain* on 'Afrocentric and Black Christian Consciousness: Towards an Honest Intersection'.[18] However, both the progressive and the traditional aspects of Caribbean British Christianity are now being represented in information forms like books, websites and art, and as more and more people from across the denominations relate to such information, respect is being engendered.

Self-respect

Respect for oneself means knowing oneself. The principle of self-respect as a trait of Caribbean British Christianity is self-evident. These people know themselves and like what they know. This is significant because 'self-respect' is a key principle in the theory and practice of respect. Self-respect is about self-knowledge – acquiring it and propagating it by all appropriate media. This is portrayed first by Caribbean British Christians' consistent efforts to make themselves known in all of their complexity through literary forms and other means including music and singing and art. The call from Caribbean British Christians to others is to look again at, or develop an informed perspective on, their entire being. One way to encourage this has been to develop a self-history that is reliable. For example, in his history of the New Testament Church of God, discussed in Chapter 4, Ira Brooks laments the fact that his was the first attempt to document the history of his or any other Black-led church in Britain. He states his 'passionate belief' that Black people, including the Black church, need to put their history on record.[19]

Brooks lauds other forms of recording history such as oral tradition and songs, but insists that the Caribbean British Christian history needs to be written down, because they live in a literary society. Equally, Thomas-Juggan cites the fact that many pioneers will die before long as one reason why we must hurry to record the history of the Black church in Britain, so that there is light to find our heritage in years to come.[20] In the Bible, in the book of Habakkuk, God instructs the prophet to write down his vision, David Baker suggests, for effective preservation and transmission.[21] To date, much has been accomplished, but little has been recorded by the people themselves. As the editors of *A Time to Speak* point out, it is not acceptable to have your story told only by others; Caribbean British Christianity must speak for itself.[22] This reflects a dictum that unless they write their own stories and histories, they continue to be at the mercy of the pens of well-meaning and sometimes hostile others.

Caribbean British Christian self-knowledge is a task made problematic by a history of denial and lack of information. Where information about Caribbean British Christianity has been available, it has tended to be unflattering, or written from an unsympathetic point of view, even when written by liberal Whites. Take, for example, the revisionist work of

Elaine Foster, who sought to correct the popular myth that Black-led churches in Britain had begun primarily because of racist rejection of Blacks by Whites in mainstream churches.[23] Foster shows and this current study confirms that missionary zeal was a far more influential factor than racism in giving rise to this 1950s phenomenon. To develop informed regard for self requires sound historical and contemporary information about self and a willingness to debunk false or outmoded self-concepts that have been imbibed over many years. As previously stated, this thinking was central in the minds of those of us who pioneered the journal *Black Theology in Britain*.[24]

Ethnically, Caribbean British Christianity respects itself by being clear about its history and contemporary existence. For instance, people of African descent have to tolerate the beginning of their history being made synonymous with the transatlantic slave trade, rather than beginning with the thousands of years that preceded the slave era. People of Asian extraction who are also from the Caribbean struggle to be acknowledged under the ethnic umbrella terms like 'Black' and 'African Caribbean'. Equally, respect for Caribbean British Christian ethnicity must acknowledge their British heritage. This is often overlooked in such terminology as 'African Caribbean' and a host of other terminologies that do not infer British heritage. The 2001 Census uses terms like Black British, Black African and Black Caribbean as a nod in this direction. I use the term Caribbean British precisely because of the need to embrace the whole ethnic identity to fulfil respect. As a model for other ethnic groups, and in recognition that every ethnic group is God-ordained, Caribbean British Christianity traces its roots to wherever they have come from, as discussed in Chapter 2. This is why I argue against those in Caribbean British Christianity who wish to superimpose an African identity upon Caribbean identity, ending up with African Caribbean as a universal identity for a diverse people of Caribbean descent.

Self-respect for ethnicity requires that Caribbean British people lay claim to and embrace their entire heritage – European, African, Asian, Caribbean and British – without unwittingly or deliberately excluding any. Knowing where one comes from, one's roots, is key to self-identity and the building of self-esteem. Denial is unhelpful; openness and honesty is likely to lead to greater self-knowledge and self-respect. A similar approach is required towards Caribbean British Christianity's brand of Christian faith. Caribbean British Christianity's operators should know their religious selves better than any outsider. This approach calls for each Black-led denomination to be self-aware and for there to be a corporate self-awareness of the diversity, strength and richness of Caribbean British Christianity. It is an old Caribbean saying that if you don't respect yourself, no one will respect you. Equally, if one does not know oneself, or one's faith, no one else can truly know you.

Other

Respect for the 'other' is synonymous with knowledge of the 'other'. And 'other' in the context of Caribbean British Christianity is nearly synonymous with Whites, both people and institutions. However, we do not begin from a point of equality of knowledge, we begin from a point whereby Caribbean British Christians have been taught to believe that their White Christian brothers and sisters are superior to them by being a better-quality humanity and having a better-quality faith. This is aptly demonstrated in earlier chapters where there was an assumed superiority of the Roman Catholic faith over that of the indigenous Caribs, or in my own example in Chapter 1 of an imported faith being deemed superior to the indigenous understanding of what pleases God. To achieve a level playing field, Caribbean British Christians have learned to challenge assumed superiority in personal and group relationships and to qualify what information is to hand, recognizing its sources and intent.

At a seminar in 1997 at Queen's College, Birmingham, the renowned American theologian James Cone argued passionately for Black people to start studying White people. He argued that Whites had studied Blacks for years and that the way forward is for there now to be a body of literature about

Whites as perceived by Blacks. I believe Cone's proposal has merit. In this way, 'Black studies' could be run alongside 'White studies'. However it is to be achieved, respect – knowledge of the other – has to be seen as an imperative in the process. The amount and type of information available about White people has tended to make Black people develop a perverse regard for Whites, based upon hegemonic information that has located Whiteness in the realm of good and Blackness as evil. The Christ image, for instance, has been used to portray the incarnated *Logos* as a European. This White image needs to be demythologized. If we are to truly know each other, we cannot simply accept what is handed down about the other, we need to engage in our own study of the other, as is apparent in the church leaders' meetings in Chapter 4.

Dis/regard

This study of Caribbean British Christianity shows that for them, respect is a non-negotiable requisite for mutual co-existence as Christians and as humans. However, there is a significant difference between respect and regard. Respect stops short of a requirement to like, regard, esteem, or show deference to someone: their ethnicity, faith or anything else about them. The main demand that respect makes is that it commits us to forming the relationship necessary for knowledge. Failure to stop and look again, or look back long enough to know is failure to respect; it is disrespect. One interpretation of the intention behind Sturge's philosophy of 'don't dis me if you don't know me' is that if after 'knowing me' you decide to 'dis' me, then that is bearable because you know what you are 'dissing', you have paid the respect of knowing. 'Dis' in this context has a variety of similes, among them disrespect, disassociate, disregard and dismiss. Having respected one's Christian affiliation, for example, it may become clear that religious tastes are different in ways that require separation.

Where this position is reached based upon knowledge, there remains the possibility of continued association, even after the decision not to 'live in the same house', as it were. A similar position may be reached in familiarization with ethnic groups. Understanding the other person's ethnic group does not compel admiration or esteem; it could lead to a position of disregard. For example, some within Caribbean British Christianity have grown in their dislike for western culture the more they have studied it. For them, admiration has given way to dislike as their awareness of what is meant by 'European culture' has increased. As more impartial information has become available, respect results in disregard.

Caribbean British Christianity, then, by moving away from respect as automatic regard, is vulnerable to the possibility of not being regarded after being respected. This, however, is no more than God allows. Humanity is invited to get to know God (respect) but not compelled to esteem God. Of course, there is a price for non-regard. The incarnation story, as discussed in Chapter 5, states that those who receive Jesus are given power to benefit from divine sonship. So that while we are not compelled to regard, disregard has its consequences, and while respect brings us into a place of knowing, disrespect denies us the benefits derived from a relationship.

At a personal level, for some, once they truly know their self and faith, they may discover elements that they do not regard. Take, for instance, the discovery that a Black-led Pentecostal church in Britain has racist, deep-south American roots, as in Chapter 3. Such a revelation is the result of showing respect, getting to know, but it leads to non-esteem and disregard. Or take the discovery that an African-looking person has European roots; they may prefer to disregard their European heritage in preference to a clear African identity. Or the example of the couple described in Chapter 4 who wish to progress in the practice of their faith from a purely western Christian model by emphasizing their African ethnic and faith identities. Learning about, or respecting oneself, or the other, is powerful in and of itself and holds out possibilities for progress. Knowledge, the saying goes, is power. We might suppose that the utopia of respect whether in our relationship with God or with other humans is 'informed regard'. This is where we know the other and hold them in esteem or regard.

Prophetic presence

The foundation upon which all of the foregoing stands is what I call the prophetic presence of Caribbean British Christianity. A prophet is 'one who speaks forth openly, or is the proclaimer of, a divine message'.[25] Prophetic behaviour is that which persists in the face of adversity to proclaim the message they believe God has given them to deliver and to live how and where God has directed them. One of the ways in which Caribbean British Christianity demands and emphasizes respect is by their prophetic presence. They refuse to be silenced or sidelined even while the tide of intolerance in mainstream churches and society and the difficulty of operating Black-led churches continues to militate against them. As in the story of the incarnation, they live in a public domain that neither understands them nor welcomes them, yet they continue to minister. Within the remit of this study it is possible to locate prophetic presence in three contexts: mainstream churches, Black-led churches and the wider community.

It is reasonable to ask why Caribbean British Christians remain in mainstream churches, which tend to be White-run and peopled, given the racism that is said to exist there. Beckford puts it in polemical terms: 'What kind of freed slaves worship in the slave master's house?'[26] He says:

House Negroes were those living in the master's house, eating his food and serving his interest; by contrast, Field Negroes ate discarded food, sought to escape and prayed for the master's death.[27]

For him, Black Christians in White churches are little different from the House Negroes during the era of African enslavement by Europeans. Beckford does acknowledge, however, that modern-day 'House Negroes', like their predecessors, engage in different forms of 'resistance'. One mitigating reason why it may be acceptable for Caribbean British Christians to belong to mainstream churches is when such belonging provides a strategic position of empowerment from which to work resistance.[28]

My problem with Beckford's analysis is that its *raison d'être* is exclusively tied to the oppression/liberation dialectic, as though the only expression that Black people have is in response to White behaviour. His argument suggests that the only legitimate reason Black people can have for belonging to White-led churches is in order that they may engage in resistance. Sultan Muhammed makes the point that religion itself may be described as the 'sigh of the oppressed', and this would be an obvious case in point.[29] He argues that, particularly in the Third World, religion has been used as an inspirational and liberating factor for many people in their struggles for independence and freedom from western domination. While this may be said of religion in general, it does not fully explain why, following Beckford's reasoning, Black people in Britain would choose to belong to White churches in order to work out their liberation. It is just possible that Black Christians belong to British mainstream churches because they believe in the doctrines, faith and mission they espouse, not because they see such places as the battleground of resistance.

David Moore provides another reason why Caribbean British and other Black Christians belong to mainstream churches in Britain. Quite simply, their parents, families and friends belonged to these denominations from their places of origin in the Caribbean.[30] It is a historic belonging, which seems to have come under extreme stress in Britain, so much so that he compares the existence of Black people in the Church of England with the story of the dry bones of Ezekiel 37. He believes that as spiritual life returns to these bones, Black Christians in mainstream churches will discover their true historic contribution and contemporary relevance in the church. This Black belonging to White churches has its price.

A further example of mainstream belonging is provided by Robinson Milwood, who reminds us of the indelible psychological, cultural and spiritual mark that rejection has left upon Caribbean British Christians who thought they were coming to the mother country in the 1950s.[31] For him, the racism inflicted upon Black Christians by a White system insensitive to their needs has meant that Black Christians have had no choice but to engage with the liberation struggle in mainstream churches. They did not go there with that intention, but it has been thrust upon them as a price they have had to pay to belong. Charles Amjad-Ali says that the quest for justice is, in fact, part of the prophetic heritage of the monotheistic traditions.[32] It is a pity, therefore, that whereas the mission of the Church is the liberation of all people, because of the racism internal to the church Black Christians in mainstream churches have to spend time fighting their own battles of liberation rather than engaging fully in the struggle for liberation in the wider world.[33] This struggle has, however, to be viewed as part of their experience and activity, not as an all-encompassing occupation.

Clearly, if they choose to, Caribbean British Christians can leave mainstream churches; but, as some argue, why should they leave their historic church because some do not wish them to be there? Also, if God has brought you into contact with a Christian community that happens to be White, why should you not be able to worship there? Lorraine Dixon insists that as a baptized member of the body of Christ in the Church of England, she is as entitled to belong as anyone else.[34] By remaining in the mainstream churches, Black Christians provide a challenge to the racism of some of their White brothers and sisters, thereby providing opportunities for respect, and informed regard, to be engendered. Given the intractable nature of racism, Caribbean British Christians in the mainstream need to answer the question, to what extent is their presence prophetic or pathetic?[35] Can it be right that Caribbean British Christians remain in White churches to engage in internal liberation struggles simply to co-exist, rather than engage in liberation mission in the world? Is it possible to do both? Or should Caribbean British Christians leave mainstream churches altogether in order to engage in wider liberation for justice in the world? In coming to a decision, Dixon expresses well what Caribbean British Christians have to contend with:

Finding one's place as a person in one of the mainstream churches in Britain can be a difficult process. The structures that continue to make us invisible in our own churches are the result of history and White supremacist practices that promote Black inferiority. It is against this sort of background that minority ethnic communities in Britain have to struggle for identity, self-confidence and self-esteem.[36]

In the face of such 'othering' and alienation within their own church, Black Christians have engaged in elaborate liberation struggles just to protect their own survival.

In recent times, Anthony Reddie has produced work that seeks to promote liberation through learning new ways of educating Methodist children and young people. In *Nobodies to Somebodies*[37] he presents practical ways of using theology for education and liberation. Here again, however, it appears that what is being done is preparing Black Methodists for the battle they face within the Methodist Church, rather than being prepared for mission in and to the world. I believe we have to do both, but must avoid a preoccupation with self-preservation as a way of life. The conclusion drawn from this study is that Caribbean British Christians in mainstream churches do not simply exist there to struggle for their survival, but are there out of choice and remain there because their lives of mission consist of much more than the issues relating to racism.

A second aspect of prophetic presence in Caribbean British Christianity is to be found in its operation of Black-led and Black majority churches in Britain. This prophetic presence is evident in many ways. I have already described how some believe themselves called to the work they do and as a consequence, they stand firm in the face of adversity. For example, Black-led churches represent a profound concept of Black space in which Black power reigns supreme. James Cone defines Black power as Black freedom, Black self-determination, wherein Black people no longer view themselves as without human dignity but as human beings with the ability to carve out their own destiny.[38] In mainstream churches and society at large, Whites generally hold leadership positions, but within Black-led churches the entire power structure is peopled by Blacks. Black people determine the times and contents of services, Black preachers preach, and Blacks as human beings and as Christians determine their own ecclesiastical destiny.

In this 'Black space', Black Christians can be themselves without being self-conscious about colour and ethnicity as they seem to be in mainstream churches and wider society. In Black-led churches, Black people practise to fulfil God's commission to have dominion (Genesis 1.28) and in this affirmation of the essential worth of Blackness, infer to those looking on, 'get used to me'.[39] Janet Johnson describes her experience of growing up in a White church context that showed her nothing of who she was as a Black young person. This changed when she attended a Black-led church and heard a Black preacher in a dialect she readily identified with; there and then it clicked, she says.[40] Here, the Black-led church functions as a source of learning not only for Blacks, but for Whites also. The challenge for them is to discover how similar Black resonance can be provided in White church spaces.

Prophetic presence is evident also in the response to their being called by God to minister in the British context. The Black-led churches do not rely on the whim of the system to access funding, for example. Rather, they depend on God to provide through their hard work in raising funds, and acquiring property and other facilities for their churches. S. E. Arnold describes how the New Testament Church of God embraced a programme of social responsibility in response to the growing awareness of the social needs of their community.[41] He calls it the gospel in action. However, this social programme goes beyond the acquisition of property to a demonstration of the liberating effect of the gospel in terms of a national community action programme in education, training and service provision for youth, elderly and persons with other social, economic and spiritual needs. The sense of independence among Caribbean British Christianity provides a level of dignity based on having achieved the creation of their new world; they create as God created. Angela Sarkis puts this in terms of being a professional.[42] She argues that it is the duty of the Christian to develop a plan for one's life that leads to independence even while recognizing that others play a significant part in one's life.

Another feature of Caribbean British Christianity's prophetic presence, particularly evident in Black-led churches, is their propensity to create their own heroes. Usually these are the pioneering grandees of the churches in Britain. Brooks does this to great effect in spotlighting Oliver Lyseight, founder of the New Testament Church of God in Britain.[43] Skilfully, he describes how Lyseight rose from humble beginnings in the Caribbean to become the national leader of 'a mighty army' of saints in Britain. Norma Thomas-Juggan similarly creates heroes out of several characters of the Calvary Church of God in Christ.[44] She celebrates lay people and bishops alike, past and present, as akin to Old and New Testament biblical patriarchal and matriarchal figures in their contribution to the church. Prophetic presence is important for 'respect' because it insists that one who is made in the image of God and is a part of the church has equal privilege to share in the things of God with others. By such presence, the true character of Caribbean British Christianity is made visible as one of integrity and independence.

The prophetic presence of Caribbean British Christianity is also evident in the community. As mentioned in Chapter 3, it became clear to church leaders in the community that they needed to engage with the secular powers in order to help change the social and political condition of their people in schools, prisons and other public services. Today, through the presence and work of instruments like councils of Black-led churches in Britain, Black Christians and what they stand for simply cannot be ignored. From the top of government to local operators, Black Christianity, in which Caribbean British Christians are prominent, is taken seriously and consulted regarding their views on the issues that affect both their communities and society at large. These people who were once noted just for their fancy clothes are recognized for the godly principles for which they stand: justice, equality, fair play, righteousness and unity in diversity. By being present in mainstream and Black-led churches and in society at large, refusing to melt into the background, Caribbean British and other Black Christians elicit respect. Prophetic presence models itself on the incarnational approach evident in Chapter 5

and resonates with the apostle Paul's words to the Corinthians in which he describes them as a letter written not with ink
but with the Spirit of the living God, to be known and read by
all (2 Corinthians 3.1–4).

Conclusion

What this study has discovered is the extent to which Caribbean British Christianity has been utilizing the principle of
'respect' in carving out an identity that is mediated not
through other people's perceptions and actions, but through
their own. The basis of this identity is rooted in their own self-
perception that they are God-ordained to live incarnationally
in the world as human beings and as followers of Jesus Christ.
They have implicitly been calling upon a misinformed White
British church and society to get to know them for who and
what they really are. They have shown that it is possible to co-
exist with adversity, yet thrive, and not be negatively defined
by it. In the words of Aretha Franklin, what Caribbean British
Christianity is asking for is a little respect! Because knowledge
can lead to disregard, the ideal outcome for the respect
philosophy is 'informed regard'. They may not characterize it
as respect *per se*; this is my own perception of what has been
accomplished and what is needed as a way forward. I am here
proposing that, based on Caribbean British Christianity's
history and current situation, a theology based on respect,
that is, knowing one another and living out that knowledge, is
the way forward that will bear productive fruit as theology
translated into action. Because knowledge is power, a theology of respect represents a dynamic resource within any and
all contexts.

Notes

Chapter 1

1 L. Morris, *Luke*, Tyndale New Testament Commentaries, revised edn, Leicester, Inter-Varsity Press, 1995, p. 15.

2 C. Selltiz, M. Jahoda, M. Deutsch and S. W. Cook, *Research Methods in Social Relations*, London, Methuen, 1965, 1977, p. 2.

3 T. May, *Social Research: Issues, Methods and Process*, Philadelphia, Open University Press, 1993, p. 111.

4 J. Vincent, 'Developing Contextual Theologies', in I. K. Duffield, C. Jones and J. Vincent, eds, *Crucibles: Creating Theology at UTU*, Sheffield, Urban Theology Unit, 2000, pp. 23–32.

5 M. Bulmer, ed., *Social Research Ethics*, New York, Holmes & Meier, 1982.

6 M. Sturge, 'Don't Dis Me If You Don't Know Me: Rereading the Abraham–Lot Narrative', *Black Theology in Britain: A Journal of Contextual Praxis*, Vol. 4 No. 1, 2001, pp. 62–77.

7 E. Foster, 'Out of this World: A Consideration of the Development and Nature of the Black-led Churches in Britain', in P. Grant and R. Patel, eds, *A Time to Speak: Perspectives of Black Christians in Britain*, Birmingham, CRRU/ECRJ, 1990, pp. 57–70.

8 Grant and Patel, eds, *A Time to Speak*.

9 S. E. Arnold, *From Scepticism to Hope: One Black-led Church's Response to Social Responsibility*, Nottingham, Grove Books, 1992, p. 55.

10 J. Edwards, ed., *Let's Praise Him Again: An African Caribbean Perspective on Worship*, Eastbourne, Kingsway, 1992, p. 54.

11 J. D. Aldred and G. Parris, 'The Bible and the Black Church', in C. Rowlands and J. Vincent, eds, *Bible and Practice: British Liberation Theology – 4*, Sheffield, Urban Theology Unit, 2001, pp. 50–67.

12 'Onward Christian Soldiers', words by Sabine Baring-Gould (1834–1924).

13 E. Lartey, 'Editorial', *Black Theology in Britain: A Journal of Contextual Praxis*, No. 1, 1998, pp. 5–7.

14 R. Patterson and J. Dougall, eds, *Virtue's English Dictionary, Encyclopaedia Edition*, London, Virtue, 1977.

15 R. Petersen, 'Theological and Religious Pluralism', in J. W. de Gruchy and C. Villa-Vincencio, eds, *Doing Theology in Context: South African Perspectives*, Maryknoll, Orbis Books, 1994, pp. 219–28.

16 D. Hayes, 'Emerging Voices, Emerging Challenges', in D. G. Schultenover, ed., *Theology Toward the Third Millennium: Theological Issues for the Twenty-first Century*, Lampeter, Edwin Mellen Press, 1991, pp. 41–60.

17 C. T. Nelson, 'The Churches, Racism and the Inner Cities', in Grant and Patel, eds, *A Time to Speak*, pp. 3–10.

18 M. W. Dube and J. L. Staley, eds, *John and Postcolonialism: Travel, Space and Power*, London, Sheffield Academic Press, 2002, p. 9.

19 *Black Theology in Britain: A Journal of Contextual Praxis*, No. 1, 1998, pp. 7–9.

20 M. Phillips and T. Phillips, *Windrush: The Irresistible Rise of Multi-Racial Britain*, London, HarperCollins, 1998.

21 C. Boff, 'Methodology of the Theology of Liberation', in J. Sobrino and I. Ellacuria, eds, *Systematic Theology: Perspectives from Liberation Theology*, London, SCM Press, 1996, pp. 1–21.

22 D. Morrison, 'Resisting Racism – By Celebrating "our" Blackness', *Black Theology: An International Journal*, Vol. 1 No. 2, 2003, pp. 209–23.

23 E. Pemberton, 'African Slave Religions in the Caribbean', *Black Theology in Britain*, No. 2, 1999, pp. 90–116.

24 A. T. Browder, *Nile Valley Contributions to Civilization*, Washington, DC, Institute of Karmic Guidance, 1996, p. 41.

25 I. S. Bhogal, *On the Hoof: Theology in Transit*, Sheffield, Penistone Publications, 2001, p. 7.

26 J. H. Cone, *Black Theology and Black Power*, Twentieth Anniversary Edition, San Francisco, Harper and Row, 1989, p. 125.

27 Cone, *Black Theology and Black Power*, p. 126.

28 Arnold, *From Scepticism to Hope*, p. 65.

29 V. Karn, ed., *Ethnicity in the 1991 Census, Vol. 4, Employment, Education and Housing Among the Ethnic Minority Population of Britain*, London, The Stationery Office, 1997.

30 P. Fryer, *Staying Power: The History of Black People in Britain*, London, Pluto Press, 1984, p. 373.

31 R. I. H. Gerloff, *A Plea for British Black Theologies: The Black Church Movement in its Transatlantic Cultural and Theological Interaction*, Frankfurt am Main, Peter Lang, 1992, p. 55.

32 M. Howell-Baker and T. Bolton, *Am I My Brother's and Sister's Keeper: Black Majority Churches and Development*, London, Christian Aid/Centre for Black Theology, 2003.

33 E. Williams, *From Columbus to Castro: The History of the Caribbean, 1492–1969*, London, Andre Deutsch, 1970.

34 Fryer, *Staying Power*, p. 373.

35 Edwards, ed., *Let's Praise Him Again*.

36 I. Hannaford, *Race: The History of an Idea in the West*, Maryland, Johns Hopkins University Press, 1996.

37 T. Tschuy, *Ethnic Conflict and Religion*, Geneva, WCC, 1997, p. xi.

38 I. Wallerstein, 'The Construction of Peoplehood: Racism, Nationalism, Ethnicity', in E. Balibar and I. Wallerstein, eds, *Race, Nation, Class: Ambiguous Identities*, London, Verso, 1991, pp. 69–85.

39 P. Gilroy, *There Ain't No Black in the Union Jack*, London: Routledge, 1987, p. 217.

40 R. Sondhi, 'Diversity and Equality', *Connections*, Spring 1998, pp. 10–11.

41 S. Small, *Racialised Barriers: The Black Experience in the United States and England in the 1980s*, London: Routledge, 1994, p. 29.

42 Karn, ed., *Ethnicity in the 1991 Census, Vol. 4*.

43 R. W. Birchfield, ed., *The New Fowler's Modern English Usage*, 3rd edn, Oxford: Clarendon Press, 1996, p. 266.

44 *Partnership News*, Winter 1999, p. 6.

45 V. Alexander, *Breaking Every Fetter: To What Extent has the Black Led Church in Britain Developed a Theology of Liberation?*, unpublished PhD Thesis, University of Warwick, 1996.

46 J. Aldred, ed., *Sisters with Power*, London: Continuum, 2000.

47 J. Grant, *White Woman's Christ and Black Woman's Jesus: Feminist Christology and Womanist Response*, Atlanta: Scholars Press, 1989, p. 9.

48 R. Beckford, *Jesus is Dread: Black Theology and Black Culture in Britain*, London: Darton, Longman and Todd, 1998.

49 'Advice to Members', in *Minutes of 89th General Assembly of the Church of God of Prophecy*, Cleveland, TN, White Wing Publishing, 1996, pp. 164–5.

50 A. G. Reddie, *Faith, Stories and the Experience of Black Elders: Singing the Lord's Song in a Strange Land*, London, Jessica Kingsley, 2001.

51 R. Nathan, 'Caribbean Youth Identity in the United Kingdom', *Black Theology in Britain*, No. 1, 1998, pp. 19–34.

52 A. E. McGrath, *Christian Theology: An Introduction*, Oxford, Blackwell, 1995, p. 117.

53 S. B. Ferguson and D. F. Wright, eds, *New Dictionary of Theology*, Leicester, Inter-Varsity Press, 1988, p. 680.

54 McGrath, *Christian Theology*, p. 118.

55 McGrath, *Christian Theology*, p. 119.

56 J. W. de Gruchy, 'The Nature, Necessity and Task of Theology', in de Gruchy and Villa-Vincencio, eds, *Doing Theology in Context*, pp. 2–14.

57 S. B. Bevans, *Models of Contextual Theology: Faith and Culture*, New York, Orbis Books, 1992, p. 2.

58 W. A. Elwell, ed., *Evangelical Dictionary of Theology*, Carlisle, Paternoster Press, 1984, p. 271.

59 Vincent, 'Developing Contextual Theologies'.

60 Vincent, 'Developing Contextual Theologies'.

61 D. F. Ford, ed., *The Modern Theologians: An Introduction to Christian Theology in the Twentieth Century*, Oxford, Blackwell, 1997, p. 13.

62 Ford, ed., *The Modern Theologians*, p. 12.

63 Lartey, *Black Theology in Britain*, No. 1, 1998, pp. 7–9.

64 D. J. Hesselgrave and E. Rommen, *Contextualization: Meanings, Methods and Models*, Leicester, Apollos/Inter-Varsity Press, 1989, p. xi.

65 Boff, 'Methodology of the Theology of Liberation'.

66 Wang Hsien-Chih, 'Some Perspectives on Homeland Theology in the Taiwanese Context', in R. S. Sugirtharajah, ed., *Frontiers in Asian Christian Theology: Emerging Trends*, Maryknoll, Orbis Books, 1994, pp. 185–95.

67 Vincent, 'Developing Contextual Theologies'.

68 Beckford, *Jesus is Dread*, p. 1.

69 J. H. Cone, *For My People: Black Theology and the Black Church*, Maryknoll, Orbis Books, 1992, pp. 28–9.

70 Beckford, *Jesus is Dread*, p. 45.

71 Cone, *For My People*, p. 7.

72 Vincent, 'Developing Contextual Theologies'.

73 Lartey, *Black Theology in Britain*, No. 1, 1998, pp. 7–9.

74 R. Beckford, *Dread and Pentecostalism: A Political Theology for the Black Church in Britain*, London, SPCK, 2000.

75 B. Burke, 1999, 'Antonio Gramsci and informal education', the encyclopaedia of informal education, http:www.infed.org/

thinkers/et-gram.htm

76 Cone, *For My People*, pp. 105–6.

77 M. Manley, *Jamaica: Struggle in the Periphery*, London, Writers and Readers Publishing Co-operative Society Ltd, 1982, p. 11.

78 Y. Alibhai-Brown, *Who Do We Think We Are? Imagining a New Britain*, London, Penguin, 2001, p. 45.

79 Alibhai-Brown, *Who Do We Think We Are?*, p. 13.

80 D. T. Smith, *Lives of Service: Obeying God's Call*, Cleveland, TN, White Wing Publishing, 1996.

81 C. T. Davidson, *Upon This Rock*, Vol. 1, Cleveland, TN, White Wing Publishing, 1973.

82 Ferguson and Wright, eds, *New Dictionary of Theology*, pp. 502–3.

83 'Advice to Members', *Church of God of Prophecy*, pp. 164–5.

84 L. L. Williams, *Caribbean Theology*, New York, Peter Lang, 1994, p. 3.

85 D. Lamont, 'Deconstructing Patriarchy', in Aldred, ed., *Sisters with Power*, pp. 36–49.

86 Cone, *Black Theology and Black Power*, p. 155.

87 Elwell, ed., *Evangelical Dictionary of Theology*, p. 157.

88 A. Boesak, *Black and Reformed: Apartheid, Liberation and the Calvinist Tradition*, Maryknoll, Orbis Books, 1986.

89 M. Kinnamon and B. E. Cope, eds, *The Ecumenical Movement: An Anthology of Key Texts and Voices*, Geneva, WCC, 1997, p. 79.

90 Phillips and Phillips, *Windrush*, p. 98.

Chapter 2

1 F. R. Augier, S. C. Gordon, D. G. Hall and M. Beckford, *The Making of the West Indies*, Essex, Longman, 1994, p. 3.

2 P. M. Sherlock, *West Indian Nations: A New History*, Kingston, Jamaica Publishing House, 1973, p. 1.

3 C. V. Black, *History of Jamaica*, Kingston, Carlong Publishers Caribbean, 1983, p. 10.

4 D. Bisnauth, *History of Religions in the Caribbean*, Kingston, Kingston Publishers, 1989, p. 1.

5 R. J. Stewart, 'Religion in the Anglophone Caribbean: Historical Overview', in J. W. Pulis, ed., *Religion, Diaspora and Cultural Identity: A Reader in the Anglophone Caribbean*, Amsterdam, Gordon and Breach, 1999, pp. 13–36.

6 K. Davis, *Emancipation Still Comin': Explorations in Caribbean*

Emancipatory Theology, Maryknoll, Orbis Books, 1990, p. 5.

7 E. Williams, *From Columbus to Castro: The History of the Caribbean, 1492–1969*, London, Andre Deutsch, 1970.

8 L. Boff and V. Elizondo, *The Voices of the Victims, 1492–1992*, London, SCM Press, 1991, p. 59.

9 Augier et al, *The Making of the West Indies*, p. 3.

10 Black, *History of Jamaica*, p. 10.

11 F. W. Knight and C. A. Palmer, eds, *The Modern Caribbean*, London, University of North Carolina Press, 1989, p. 1.

12 Davis, *Emancipation Still Comin'*, p. 5.

13 Boff and Elizondo, *The Voices of the Victims*, p. 59.

14 M. Jagessar, 'Pan Recipe: Philip Potter and Theology in the Caribbean', *Black Theology in Britain: A Journal of Contextual Praxis*, No. 5, 2000, pp. 68–89.

15 www.cricket.org/link_to_database/ARCHIVE/CRICKET_NEWS/2002/COT/0789

16 Knight and Palmer, eds, *The Modern Caribbean*, p. 1.

17 Williams, *From Columbus to Castro*, p. 18.

18 G. K. Lewis, *The Growth of the Modern West Indies*, New York, Monthly Review Press, 1968, p. 47.

19 Augier et al, *The Making of the West Indies*, p. 12.

20 Knight and Palmer, eds, *The Modern Caribbean*, p. 20.

21 Sherlock, *West Indian Nations*, p. 241.

22 Williams, *From Columbus to Castro*, pp. 9–10.

23 Williams, *From Columbus to Castro*, pp. 43–5.

24 Williams, *From Columbus to Castro*, pp. 43–5.

25 H. Thomas, *The Slave Trade: The History of the Atlantic Slave Trade 1440–1870*, London, Macmillan, 1997, p. 11.

26 Augier et al, *The Making of the West Indies*, p. 67.

27 E. Pemberton, 'African Slave Religion in the Caribbean', *Black Theology in Britain*, No. 2, 1999, pp. 90–116.

28 Thomas, *The Trade in Slavery*, p. 235.

29 C. L. R. James, *The Black Jacobins: Toussaint L'Ouverture and the San Domingo Revolution*, Reading, Cox and Wyman, 1980, p. 6.

30 Bisnauth, *History of Religions in the Caribbean*, pp. 81–2.

31 M. Alleyne, *Roots of Jamaican Culture*, London, Pluto Press, 1988, p. 70.

32 Williams, *From Columbus to Castro*, p. 45.

33 J. M. Roberts, *A History of Europe*, Oxford, Helicon, 1996, p. 381.

34 Augier et al, *The Making of the West Indies*, p. 199.

35 Williams, *From Columbus to Castro*, pp. 349–50.

36 Bisnauth, *History of Religions in the Caribbean*, p. 140.

37 *The Hutchinson Almanac 2000*, Oxford, Helicon, 1999, pp. 216–17.

38 Sherlock, *West Indian Nations*, pp. 241–2.

39 B. Brereton, 'The British and French West Indies', in Knight and Palmer, eds, *The Modern Caribbean*, pp. 85–110.

40 Sherlock, *West Indian Nations*, p. 241.

41 R. Nettleford, *Jamaica in Independence: Essays on the Early Years*, London, James Currey, 1989, p. 1.

42 R. Beckford, *God of the Rahtid: Redeeming Rage*, London, Darton, Longman and Todd, 2001, p. 89.

43 M. Phillips and T. Phillips, *Windrush: The Irresistible Rise of Multi-Racial Britain*, London, HarperCollins, 1998, p. 11.

44 H. Beckles, 'Columbus and the Contemporary Dispensation Within the Caribbean', in P. Grant and R. Patel, eds, *A Time to Act: Kairos 1992*, Birmingham, Black and Third World Theology Working Group/ECRJ, 1992, pp. 41–50.

45 E. Foster, 'Out of this World: A Consideration of the Development and Nature of the Black-led Churches in Britain', in P. Grant and R. Patel, eds, *A Time to Speak: Perspectives of Black Christians in Britain*, Birmingham, CRRU/ECRJ, 1990, pp. 57–70.

46 E. Thomas-Hope, 'The Patterns of Caribbean Religions', in B. Gates, ed., *Afro-Caribbean Religions*, London, Ward Lock Educational, 1980, pp. 4–16.

47 Stewart, 'Religion in the Anglophone Caribbean'.

48 Bisnauth, *History of Religions*, p. 7.

49 Stewart, 'Religion in the Anglophone Caribbean'.

50 Stewart, 'Religion in the Anglophone Caribbean'.

51 Bisnauth, *History of Religions*, p. 10.

52 Bisnauth, *History of Religions*, p. 12.

53 Bisnauth, *History of Religions*, p. 14.

54 Bisnauth, *History of Religions*, p. 201.

55 Davis, *Emancipation Still Comin'*, p. 51.

56 Gates, ed., *Afro-Caribbean Religions*, p. 52.

57 *Population Census 1991*, Vol. 1 Pt 14, Statistical Institute of Jamaica, 97b Church Street, Kingston, Jamaica, 1996, p. 12.

58 Knight and Palmer, eds, *The Modern Caribbean*, p. 104.

59 Alleyne, *Roots of Jamaican Culture*, p. 77.

60 Knight and Palmer, eds, *The Modern Caribbean*, p. 104.

61 Stewart, 'Religion in the Anglophone Caribbean'.

62 J. S. Mbiti, *African Religions and Philosophy*, Oxford, Heinemann Educational, 1990, p. 1.

63 L. E. Barrett, *The Rastafarians*, Edinburgh, Sangsters Book Stores, 1977, p. 17.

64 Bisnauth, *History of Religions*, p. 91.

65 Barrett, *The Rastafarians*, p. 19.

66 Barrett, *The Rastafarians*, p. 21.

67 Barrett, *The Rastafarians*, p. 29.

68 D. Morrison, 'Resisting Racism – By Celebrating "our" Blackness', *Black Theology: An International Journal*, Vol. 1 No. 2, 2003, pp. 209–23.

69 L. L. Williams, *Caribbean Theology*, New York, Peter Lang, 1994, p. 76.

70 A. C. Dayfoot, *The Shaping of the West Indian Church*, Florida, University Press, 1998, p. 13.

71 Bisnauth, *History of Religions in the Caribbean*, p. 154.

72 Bisnauth, *History of Religions in the Caribbean*, p. 155.

73 Bisnauth, *History of Religions in the Caribbean*, p. 29.

74 Bisnauth, *History of Religions in the Caribbean*, pp. 212–13.

75 H. Turner, 'New Religious Movements in the Caribbean', in Gates, ed., *Afro-Caribbean Religions*, pp. 49–57.

Chapter 3

1 P. Fryer, *Staying Power: The History of Black People in Britain*, London, Pluto Press, 1984, p. 1.

2 Fryer, *Staying Power*, p. 79.

3 Fryer, *Staying Power*, p. 109.

4 Fryer, *Staying Power*, p. 100.

5 Fryer, *Staying Power*, p. 97.

6 D. Adebayo, 'Revealed: Our Hidden History', *Independent*, 23 July 2003.

7 J. Walvin, *Black Ivory: A History of British Slavery*, London, Fontana, 1993, p. 11.

8 M. Phillips and T. Phillips, *Windrush: The Irresistible Rise of Multi-Racial Britain*, London, HarperCollins, 1998, p. 152.

9 C. Holmes, *John Bull's Island: Immigration and British Society, 1871–1971*, Basingstoke, Macmillan, 1988, p. 15.

10 F. Field and P. Haikin, eds, *Black Britons*, London, Oxford University Press, 1971, p. 90.

11 E. Williams, *From Columbus to Castro: The History of the Caribbean, 1492–1969*, London, Andre Deutsch, 1970, p. 498.

12 S. Patterson, *Dark Strangers: A Study of West Indians in London*, Middlesex, Penguin, 1963, p. 45.

13 Patterson, *Dark Strangers*, p. 45.

14 Patterson, *Dark Strangers*, p. 45.

15 A. Haynes, *The State of Black Britain*, Antigua, Root Publishing, 1983, p. 15.

16 P. Mohabir, *Building Bridges*, London, Hodder and Stoughton, 1988, p. 119.

17 P. Pemberton, E. Pemberton and J. R. Maxwell-Hughes, eds, *History of the Wesleyan Church in the British Isles*, Birmingham, The Wesleyan Holiness Church, 1983, p. 6.

18 Runnymede Trust and the Radical Statistics Race Group, *Britain's Black Population*, London, Heinemann Educational, 1980, p. 1.

19 Royal Institute of International Affairs: Board of Studies on Race Relations, *Report on Jamaican Migration to Great Britain*, London, Chatham House, 1956.

20 Field and Haikin, eds, *Black Britons*, p. 6.

21 V. Karn, ed., *Ethnicity in the 1991 Census, Vol. 4, Employment, Education and Housing Among the Ethnic Minority Population of Britain*, London, The Stationery Office, 1997, p. xx.

22 Runnymede Trust and the Radical Statistics Race Group, *Britain's Black Population*, p. 5.

23 J. Cheetham, 'Immigration', in A. H. Halsey, ed., *Trends in British Society since 1900*, London, Macmillan, 1972, pp. 451–508.

24 C. Harris, 'Post-War Migration', in C. Harris and W. James, *Inside Babylon: The Caribbean Diaspora in Britain*, London, Verso, 1993, pp. 9–54.

25 Cheetham, 'Immigration'.

26 *Census Report for Great Britain*, Vol. 1, London, HMSO, 1991.

27 Karn, ed., *Ethnicity in the 1991 Census, Vol 4*.

28 I. V. Brooks, *In Chains They Shall Come Over*, Birmingham, New Testament Church of God, c. 1970.

29 R. L. Hyatt, *Walking with God in this Troubled World*, London, Minerva Press, 1999.

30 Mohabir, *Building Bridges*.

31 Y. Alibhai-Brown, *Who Do We Think We Are? Imagining a New Britain*, London, Penguin, 2001, p. xvi.

32 See M. E. Dyson, *Making Malcolm: The Myth and the Meaning of Malcolm X*, New York, Oxford University Press, 1995, and J. H. Cone, *Martin & Malcolm & America*, London, HarperCollins, 1993.

33 P. Gilroy, 'Steppin' Out of Babylon – Race, Class and Autonomy', in the Centre for Contemporary Studies, *The Empire Strikes Back: Race and Racism in 70s Britain*, London, Hutchinson Education, 1982, pp. 276–314.

34 R. Beckford, *Dread and Pentecostalism: A Political Theology for the Black Church in Britain*, London, SPCK, 2000, p. 2.

35 See 2001 Census results: www.statistics.govuk/census2001/profiles/uk.asp

36 P. Brierley, *The Tide is Running Out: What the English Church Attendance Survey Reveals*, London, Christian Research, 2000, p. 143.

37 Brierley, *The Tide is Running Out*, p. 136.

38 *The Collection of 2002 Statistics of Ethnic Origin: Report by the Research and Statistics Department of the Archbishops' Council*.

39 2001 Census results: www.statistics.govuk/census2001/profiles/uk.asp

40 O. A. Lyseight, *Forward March: An Autobiography*, Wolverhampton, George Garwood, 1995, p. 34.

41 S. E. Arnold, *From Scepticism to Hope: One Black-led Church's Response to Social Responsibility*, Nottingham, Grove Books, 1992, p. 7.

42 R. Milwood, in A. Jackson, ed., *Catching Both Sides of the Wind: Conversations with Five Black Pastors*, London, British Council of Churches, 1985, pp. 31–64.

43 I. Smith with W. Green, *An Ebony Cross: Being a Black Woman in Britain Today*, London, Marshall, Morgan and Scott, 1989.

44 I. V. Brooks, *Another Gentleman to the Ministry*, Birmingham, Compeer Press, c. 1985.

45 M. H. Simmonds, *A Portrayal of Identity: A Study of the Life and Worship of the First United Church of Jesus Christ, (Apostolic) UK*, unpublished Thesis, Department of Theology, University of Birmingham, 1988, p. 31.

46 Brooks, *Another Gentleman to the Ministry*, p. 15.

47 Brierley, *The Tide is Running Out*, p. 135.

48 J. D. Aldred and M. Sturge, eds, *Black Majority Churches UK Directory 2003/4*, London, ACEA/CTBI, 2003, pp. 149–56.

49 N. Thomas-Juggan, *Story of the Calvary Church of God in Christ*, Enfield, Norma Thomas-Juggan, 2000.

50 M. Sturge, *Look What the Lord Has Done: An Exploration of Black Christian Faith in Britain*, Bletchley, Scripture Union, 2005, p. 42.

51 A. Hastings, *A History of English Christianity 1920–1990*, London, SCM Press, 1991, p. 621.

52 Beckford, *Dread and Pentecostalism*, pp. 2–3.

53 R. I. H. Gerloff, *A Plea for British Black Theologies: The Black Church Movement in its Transatlantic Cultural and Theological Interaction*, Frankfurt am Main, Peter Lang, 1992.

54 A. Trotman, 'Black, Black-led or What?', in J. Edwards, ed.,

Let's Praise Him Again: An African Caribbean Perspective on Worship, Eastbourne, Kingsway, 1992, pp. 12–35.

55 V. Alexander, *Breaking Every Fetter: To What Extent has the Black Led Church in Britain Developed a Theology of Liberation?*, unpublished PhD Thesis, University of Warwick, 1996.

56 V. Becher and M. Breiner, *Black Christians: Black Church Traditions in Britain*, Birmingham, Centre for Black and White Christian Partnership and Westhill RE Centre, 1995, pp. 13–15.

57 E. Foster, 'Out of this World: A Consideration of the Development and Nature of Black-led Churches in Britain', in P. Grant and R. Patel, eds, *A Time to Speak: Perspectives of Black Christians in Britain*, Birmingham, CRRU/ECRJ, 1990, pp. 57–70.

58 Gerloff, *A Plea for British Black Theologies*, p. 55.

59 Gerloff, *A Plea for British Black Theologies*, p. 55.

60 See Pemberton, Pemberton and Maxwell-Hughes, eds, *History of the Wesleyan Holiness Church*.

61 Pemberton, Pemberton and Maxwell-Hughes, eds, *History of the Wesleyan Holiness Church*, p. 5.

62 Smith with Green, *An Ebony Cross*, p. 42.

63 Mohabir, *Building Bridges*, p. 193.

64 Thomas-Juggan, *Story of the Calvary Church of God in Christ*, p. 34.

65 See S. M. Burgess and G. B. McGee, eds, *Dictionary of Pentecostal and Charismatic Movements*, Michigan, Zondervan, 1988.

66 Thomas-Juggan, *Story of the Calvary Church of God in Christ*, p. 37.

67 Thomas-Juggan, *Story of the Calvary Church of God in Christ*, p. 35.

68 See Burgess and McGee, eds, *Dictionary of Pentecostal and Charismatic Movements*.

69 J. D. Aldred, *A Black Majority Church's Future*, unpublished Masters Thesis, University of Sheffield, 1994.

70 C. T. Davidson, *Upon This Rock*, Vol. 1, Cleveland, TN, White Wing Publishing, 1973, p. 696.

71 Bishop T. A. McCalla, regional bishop in the West Midlands, in a face-to-face interview/conversation with the author for research towards a publication on the history of the Church of God of Prophecy in the UK (unpublished).

72 I. V. Brooks, *Where Do We Go From Here? A History of 25 Years of the New Testament Church of God in the United Kingdom – 1955–1980*, London, Charles Raper, 1982, p. 12.

73 Lyseight, *Forward March*, p. 36.

74 Lyseight, *Forward March*, p. 37.

75 Lyseight, *Forward March*, p. 31.

76 Charles W. Conn, *Like a Mighty Army: A History of the Church of God 1886–1976*, Cleveland, TN, Pathway Press, 1977, p. 297.

77 Conn, *Like a Mighty Army*, p. 297.

78 Brooks, *Where Do We Go From Here?*, p. 15.

79 Brooks, *Where Do We Go From Here?*, p. 15.

80 Brooks, *Where Do We Go From Here?*, p. 16.

81 Brooks, *Where Do We Go From Here?*, p. 8.

82 'Welcome' booklet, Bethel United Church of Jesus Christ (Apostolic) UK.

83 Pemberton, Pemberton and Maxwell-Hughes, eds, *History of the Wesleyan Holiness Church*.

84 Pemberton, Pemberton and Maxwell-Hughes, eds, *History of the Wesleyan Holiness Church*, p. 6.

85 New Testament Assembly Handbook, 2nd edn, p. 2.

86 Becher and Breiner, *Black Christians*, p. 22.

87 Brooks, *Another Gentleman to the Ministry*, p. 104.

88 Rhema Christian Church Information Pack, 2000.

89 'History of the Church', Ruach Ministries, Brixton, London.

90 J. D. Aldred, 'The Black Church in Britain and their Relations with the Ecumenical Movement', in *Pfingstkirchen und Okumene in Bewegung*, Frankfurt am Main, Verlag Otto Lembeck, 2001, pp. 181–98.

91 J. Edwards, *The Jamaican Diaspora: A People of Pain and Purpose*, Kingston, Morgan Ministries International, 1998, p. 9.

92 Edwards, *The Jamaican Diaspora*, p. 9.

93 D. Pemberton, 'Foreword', in *A Handbook of the Afro-Westindian United Council of Churches*, 1984 edition, London, Centre for Caribbean Studies, 1984, p. 4.

94 Edwards, *The Jamaican Diaspora*, p. 9.

95 Edwards, *The Jamaican Diaspora*, p. 10.

96 See D. Douglas, *The Handbook of the International Ministerial Council of Great Britain*, Watford, IMCGB Publications, 1990.

97 W. Woods, 'The Black Church Movement in Britain', in *A Handbook of the Afro-Westindian United Council of Churches*, 1984 edition, London, Centre for Caribbean Studies, 1984, pp. 7–10.

98 R. Milwood, 'How is Theology Political?', in *A Handbook of the Afro-Westindian United Council of Churches*, pp. 14–15.

99 Brooks, *Another Gentleman to the Ministry*, p. 107.

100 'Constitution', Afro-Westindian United Council of Churches.

101 Woods, 'The Black Church Movement in Britain'.

102 Mohabir, *Building Bridges*, pp. 195–6.

103 'A Snap Shot', African and Caribbean Evangelical Alliance leaflet.

104 Mohabir, *Building Bridges*, p. 194.

105 'Linking the Nations, Serving Christians Overseas', Connections information pack.

106 P. Weller, ed., *Religions in the UK: A Multi-Faith Directory*, Derby, University of Derby/Interfaith Network for the United Kingdom, 1997, p. 676.

107 Weller, ed., *Religions in the UK*, p. 289.

108 Weller, ed., *Religions in the UK*, p. 450.

109 Brooks, *Where Do We Go From Here?*, p. ix.

110 Trotman, 'Black, Black-led or What?'.

111 Sturge, *Look What the Lord Has Done*, p. 31.

112 T. Parry, *Black-led Churches in West Yorkshire*, Leeds, Churches and Neighbourhood Action Project, 1993, p. 5.

113 Alexander, *Breaking Every Fetter*, p. 286.

114 Woods, 'The Black Church Movement in Britain'.

115 'Faith in the Future' souvenir programme.

116 Alexander, *Breaking Every Fetter*, pp. 284–5.

117 J. D. Aldred and M. Sturge, eds, *Black Majority Churches UK Directory 2000*, London, ADP Services, 2000; see also Aldred and Sturge, eds, *Black Majority Churches UK Directory 2003/4*.

Chapter 4

1 J. H. Cone, *God of the Oppressed*, San Francisco: Harper San Francisco, 1975, p. 238.

2 P. Mohabir, *Building Bridges*, London, Hodder and Stoughton, 1988, p. 190.

3 M. Goodridge, 'In Our Churches All Are Welcomed', in *A Handbook of the Afro-Westindian United Council of Churches*, London, Centre for Caribbean Studies, 1984, p. 19.

4 J. D. Aldred, ed., *Preaching with Power: Sermons by Black Preachers*, London, Cassell, 1998, p. vii.

5 N. Solomon, 'The Third Presence: Reflections on the Dialogue', in T. Byfield and M. Braybrooke, eds, *Dialogue with a Difference*, London, SCM Press, 1992, pp. 147–62.

6 J. L. Wilkinson, *Church in Black and White*, Edinburgh, Saint Andrew Press, 1993, p. 4.

7 I. Smith-Cameron, *The Church of Many Colours*, London, Jeyaram Press, 1998, p. 155.

220 RESPECT

8 *Christian Life Across the City: The Birmingham Christian Directory, 1997*, Birmingham, Birmingham Christian Media Services, 1997.

9 A. G. Reddie, 'Peace and Justice Through Black Christian Education', *Black Theology in Britain: A Journal of Contextual Praxis*, No. 6, 2001, pp. 73–85.

10 J. H. Cone, *Black Theology and Black Power: Twentieth Anniversary Edition*, San Francisco, Harper and Row, 1989.

11 From the programme of 'That Birmingham May Believe' Consultation, 21 January 1997.

12 D. Guthrie, *New Testament Theology*, Leicester, Inter-Varsity Press, 1981, p. 744.

13 A. Gelder and P. Escott, eds, *Church in Life: A Snapshot of Church Life in Britain at the Beginning of the Twenty-first Century*, London, Churches Information for Mission, 2001, p. 9. See also P. Brierley, *Christian England: What the Church Census Reveals*, London, MARC Europe, 1991, p. 79.

14 Minutes of the meeting, 21 January 1997, Centre for Black and White Christian Partnership archive.

15 Letter from the Revd J. Nicholas Latham, Chairperson of Birmingham Churches Together, 22 January 1997.

16 P. Potter, 'Report of the General Secretary: Sixth Assembly of the WCC, Vancouver, 1983', in M. Kinnamon and B. E. Cope, eds, *The Ecumenical Movement: An Anthology of Key Texts*, Geneva, WCC, 1997, pp. 52–60.

17 R. Beckford, *Macpherson and the White Church*, talk given to the Christian Network for Racial Justice Conference at the Centre for Black and White Christian Partnership, December 2001.

18 R. I. H. Gerloff, *A Plea for British Black Theologies: The Black Church Movement in its Transatlantic Cultural and Theological Interaction*, Frankfurt am Main, Peter Lang, 1992, p. 18.

19 Brierley, *Christian England*, p. 41.

20 Letter from the Revd J. Nicholas Latham, 22 January 1997.

21 Letter from the Revd J. Nicholas Latham, 13 February 1997.

22 J. Mbiti, *African Religions and Philosophy*, Oxford, Heinemann Educational, 1990, p. 24.

23 V. Alexander, 'Afrocentric and Black Christian Consciousness: Towards an Honest Intersection', *Black Theology in Britain*, No. 1, 1998, pp. 11–18.

24 Mbiti, *African Religions and Philosophy*.

25 M. Alleyne, *Roots of Jamaican Culture*, London, Pluto Press, 1988.

26 Mbiti, *African Religions and Philosophy*, p. 29.

27 E. Foster, 'Out of this World: A Consideration of the Development and Nature of the Black-led Churches in Britain', in P. Grant and R. Patel, eds, *A Time to Speak: Perspectives of Black Christians in Britain*, Birmingham, CRRU/ECRJ, 1990, pp. 57–70.

28 I. Brooks in A. Jackson, ed., *Catching Both Sides of the Wind: Conversations with Five Black Pastors*, London, British Council of Churches, 1985, p. 25.

29 N. Thomas-Juggan, *Story of the Calvary Church of God in Christ*, Enfield, Norma Thomas-Juggan, 2000, p. 15.

30 Grant and Patel, eds, *A Time to Speak*, pp. 144–5.

31 Foster, 'Out of this World'.

32 D. Moore, 'Through a Black Lens: Telling our History and Understanding its Significance', in Grant and Patel, eds, *A Time to Speak*, pp. 17–21.

33 P. Grant and R. Patel, eds, *A Time to Act: Kairos 1992*, Birmingham, Black and Third World Theology Working Group/ ECRJ, 1992.

34 Grant and Patel, eds, *A Time to Act*.

35 J. D. Aldred, ed., *Praying with Power*, London, Continuum, 2000.

36 Aldred, ed., *Preaching with Power*.

37 Aldred, ed., *Preaching With Power*.

38 I. Sweeney, 'Skin Deep Christianity', in Aldred, ed., *Preaching with Power*, pp. 39–43.

39 See J. D. Aldred, ed., *Sisters with Power*, London, Continuum, 2000.

40 J. Edwards, ed., *Let's Praise Him Again: An African Caribbean Perspective on Worship*, Eastbourne, Kingsway, 1992.

41 Jackson, ed., *Catching Both Sides of the Wind*.

42 A. Lobo, ed., *Black Catholics Speak: Reflections on Experience, Faith and Theology*, London, Catholic Association for Racial Justice, 1991.

43 P. Thompson, I. Brown, E. Ellis and L. Lyseight, eds, *Here to Stay: A Collection of Stories by Women*, Oxford, Lion, 1990.

44 *Black Theology in Britain*, No. 1, 1998.

45 See R. Beckford, *Dread and Pentecostalism: A Political Theology for the Black Church in Britain*, London, SPCK, 2000.

46 Gerloff, *A Plea for British Black Theologies*.

47 Mohabir, *Building Bridges*.

48 I. Smith with W. Green, *An Ebony Cross: Being a Black Woman in Britain Today*, London, Marshall Morgan and Scott, 1989.

49 O. A. Lyseight, *Forward March: An Autobiography*, Wolverhampton, George Garwood, 1995.

50 R. L. Hyatt, *Walking with God in this Troubled World*, London, Minerva Press, 1999.

51 I. V. Brooks, *Where Do We Go From Here? A History of 25 Years of the New Testament Church of God in the United Kingdom – 1955–1980*, London, Charles Raper, 1982.

52 Thomas-Juggan, *Story of the Calvary Church*.

53 I. Brooks, *In Chains They Shall Come Over*, Birmingham, New Testament Church of God, c. 1970.

54 Centre for Caribbean Studies, *A Handbook of the Afro-Westindian United Council of Churches*, London, Globe Communications Enterprise, 1984.

55 J. D. Aldred and M. Sturge, eds, *Black Majority Churches UK Directory 2000*, London, ADP Services, 2000.

56 R. Milwood, *Liberation and Mission: A Black Experience*, London, African Caribbean Education Resource Centre, 1997.

57 P. Mohabir, *Pioneers or Settlers?*, London, Scripture Union, 1991.

58 P. Mohabir, *Worlds Within Reach: Cross Cultural Witness*, London, Hodder and Stoughton, 1992.

59 J. Edwards, *Lord Make Us One – But Not All the Same*, London, Hodder and Stoughton, 1999.

60 J. Edwards, *The Cradle, the Cross and the Empty Tomb: A Faith We Can Be Proud to Proclaim*, London, Hodder and Stoughton, 2000.

61 I. V. Brooks, *Another Gentleman to the Ministry*, Birmingham, Compeer Press, c. 1985.

62 A. G. Reddie, *Faith, Stories and the Experience of Black Elders: Singing the Lord's Song in a Strange Land*, London, Jessica Kingsley, 2001.

63 A. G. Reddie, *Nobodies to Somebodies: A Practical Theology for Education and Liberation*, Peterborough, Epworth Press, 2003.

64 S. A. Dunn, *Jehovah God in the Old Testament is Jesus Christ in the New*, Birmingham: Bethel United Church of Jesus Christ (Apostolic), c. 1980.

65 S. E. Arnold, *From Scepticism to Hope: One Black-led Church's Response to Social Responsibility*, Nottingham, Grove Books, 1992.

66 R. Beckford, *Jesus is Dread: Black Theology and Black Culture in Britain*, London, Darton, Longman and Todd, 1998.

67 Beckford, *Dread and Pentecostalism*.

68 P. Grant, 'Book Review', *Black Theology in Britain*, No. 6, 2001, pp. 110–11.

69 R. Beckford, *God of the Rahtid: Redeeming Rage*, London, Darton, Longman and Todd, 2001, p. 89.

Chapter 5

1 G. Gutiérrez, *We Drink from Our Own Wells: The Spiritual Journey of a People*, London, SCM Press, 1984; J. H. Cone, *Black Theology and Black Power*, New York, Harper and Row, 1989.

2 R. E. Brown, *The Anchor Bible: The Gospel According to John I–XII*, New York, Doubleday, 1966, p. 3.

3 G. R. Beasley-Murray, *Word Biblical Commentary: John*, Waco, Word Books, 1987, p. lxvi.

4 C. K., Barrett, *The Gospel According to St John*, 2nd edn, London, SPCK, 1978, p. 151.

5 Brown, *The Anchor Bible*, p. 3.

6 T. L. Brodie, *The Gospel According to John*, Oxford, Oxford University Press, 1993, p. 136.

7 Barrett, *The Gospel According to St John*, p. 152.

8 J. N. Sanders and B. A. Mastin, *The Gospel According to St John*, Black's New Testament Commentaries, London, A & C Black, 1977, p. 67.

9 A. Clarke, *The Bethany Parallel Commentary on the New Testament*, Minneapolis, Bethany House, 1983, p. 496.

10 Beasley-Murray, *Word Biblical Commentary: John*, p. 10.

11 R. V. G. Tasker, *John*, Tyndale New Testament Commentaries, Leicester, Inter-Varsity Press, 1995, p. 47.

12 Sanders and Mastin, *The Gospel According to St John*, p. 73.

13 D. M. Smith, *John*, Abingdon New Testament Commentaries, Philadelphia, Fortress Press, 1986, p. 53.

14 Sanders and Mastin, *The Gospel According to St John*, p. 74.

15 J. H. Bernard, *The International Critical Commentary on the Gospel According to St John*, Edinburgh, T & T Clark, 1969, p. 5.

16 Tasker, *John*, p. 46.

17 R. H. Lightfoot, *St John's Gospel: A Commentary*, Oxford, Clarendon Press, 1956, p. 80.

18 Barrett, *The Gospel According to St John*, p. 133.

19 Smith, *John*, p. 54.

20 Barrett, *The Gospel According to St John*, p. 133.

21 W. Barclay, *The Gospel of John*, Vol. 1, Edinburgh, Saint Andrew Press, 1955, p. 33.

22 Lightfoot, *St John's Gospel*, p. 82.

23 Barrett, *The Gospel According to St John*, p. 134.

24 Barclay, *The Gospel of John*, p. 33.

25 R. Bultmann, 'The History of Religions: Background of the Prologue to the Gospel of John', in J. Ashton, ed., *The Interpretation of John*, Edinburgh, T & T Clark, 1997, p. 29.

26 W. A. Elwell, ed., *Evangelical Dictionary of Theology*, Carlisle, Paternoster Press, 1984, pp. 1025–8.

27 D. Edwards, *Jesus the Wisdom of God: An Ecological Theology*, Maryknoll, Orbis Books, 1995, p. 57.

28 J. H. Walgrave, 'Incarnation and Atonement', in T. F. Torrence, ed., *The Incarnation*, Edinburgh, Hansel Press, 1981, pp. 148–76.

29 B. Hebblethwaite, *The Incarnation: Collected Essays in Christology*, Cambridge, Cambridge University Press, 1987, p. 21.

30 Lightfoot, *St John's Gospel*, p. 83.

31 Tasker, *John*, p. 48.

32 J. Strong, *The New Strong's Exhaustive Concordance of the Bible*, Tennessee, Thomas Nelson, 1984.

33 J. Begbie, ed., *Beholding the Glory: Incarnation Through the Arts*, London, Darton, Longman and Todd, 2000.

34 B. C. Raw, *Trinity and Incarnation in Anglo-Saxon Art and Thought*, Cambridge, Cambridge University Press, 1997, p. 54.

35 Tasker, *John*, p. 48.

36 Barclay, *The Gospel of John*, pp. 36–8.

37 Barrett, *The Gospel According to St John*, p. 195.

38 Tasker, *John*, p. 47.

39 Smith, *John*, p. 56.

40 G. S. Sloyan, *John*, Interpretation Bible Commentaries, Atlanta, Westminster John Knox Press, 1988, p. 14.

41 Lightfoot, *St John's Gospel*, p. 83.

42 Barclay, *The Gospel of John*, p. 42.

43 Barrett, *The Gospel According to St John*, pp. 136–8.

44 Smith, *John*, p. 64.

Chapter 6

1 A. Franklin, *Greatest Hits*, Randor Music Ltd/Warner Chappell Music Ltd, 1967.

2 R. Patterson and J. Dougall, eds, *Virtue's English Dictionary, Encyclopaedic Edition*, London, Virtue, 1977.

3 J. Strong, *The New Strong's Exhaustive Concordance of the Bible*, Tennessee, Thomas Nelson, 1984.

4 J. H. Cone, *God of the Oppressed*, San Francisco: Harper San Francisco, 1975, pp. 17–18.

5 P. Grant and R. Patel, eds, *A Time to Speak: Perspectives of Black Christians in Britain*, Birmingham, CRRU/ECRJ, 1990.

6 W. Hollenweger, 'Foreword: British and Black', in R. I. H. Gerloff, *A Plea for British Black Theologies: The Black Church Movement in its Transatlantic Cultural and Theological Interaction*, Frankfurt am Main, Peter Lang, 1992, pp. ix–x.

7 R. Brown, *Slaying Giants*, National Overseer's Address to Annual National Convention, New Testament Church of God.

8 M. Sturge, 'Don't Dis Me If You Don't Know Me: Rereading the Abraham–Lot Narrative', *Black Theology in Britain: A Journal of Contextual Praxis*, Vol. 4 No. 1, 2001, pp. 62–77.

9 Sturge, 'Don't Dis Me If You Don't Know Me'.

10 E. Foster, 'Out of this World: A Consideration of the Development and Nature of the Black-led Churches in Britain', in Grant and Patel, eds, *A Time to Speak*, pp. 57–70.

11 J. Edwards, *The Jamaican Diaspora: A People of Pain and Purpose*, Kingston, Morgan Ministries International, 1998.

12 I. V. Brooks, *Where Do We Go From Here? A History of 25 Years of the New Testament Church of God in the United Kingdom – 1955–1980*, London, Charles Raper, 1982, p. ix.

13 A. Trotman, 'Black, Black-led, or What?', in J. Edwards, ed., *Let's Praise Him Again: An African Caribbean Perspective on Worship*, Eastbourne, Kingsway, 1992, pp. 12–35.

14 E. Scobie, *Global African Presence*, New York: A & B Books, 1994, p. 13.

15 E. Lartey, 'Editorial', *Black Theology in Britain: A Journal of Contextual Praxis*, No. 1, 1998.

16 *Black Theology: An International Journal*, Vol. 1 No. 1, 2002.

17 J. D. Aldred, 'The Black Church in Britain and their Relations with the Ecumenical Movement', in *Pfingstkirchen und Okumene in Bewegung*, Frankfurt am Main, Verlag Otto Lembeck, 2001, pp. 181–98.

18 V. Alexander, 'Afrocentric and Black Christian Consciousness: Towards an Honest Intersection', *Black Theology in Britain*, No. 1, 1998, pp. 11–18.

19 Brooks, *Where Do We Go From Here?*, p. xiii.

20 N. Thomas-Juggan, *Story of the Calvary Church of God in Christ*, Enfield, Norma Thomas-Juggan, 2000, p. 13.

21 D. W. Baker, *Nahum, Habakkuk and Zephaniah*, Tyndale Old Testament Commentaries, Leicester, Inter-Varsity Press, 1988, p. 58.

22 Grant and Patel, eds, *A Time to Speak*.

23 Foster, 'Out of this World' .

24 *Black Theology in Britain: A Journal of Contextual Praxis*, issue 1, 1998.

25 W. E. Vine, M. F. Unger, W. White, Jr, eds, *Vine's Expository Dictionary of Biblical Words*, New York, Thomas Nelson, 1985, p. 493.

26 R. Beckford, *Jesus is Dread: Black Theology and Black Culture in Britain*, London, Darton, Longman and Todd, 1998, p. 42.

27 Beckford, *Jesus is Dread*, p. 45.

28 Beckford, *Jesus is Dread*, p. 58.

29 S. Muhammed, 'Religion is the Sigh of the Oppressed', in P. Grant and R. Patel, eds, *A Time to Act: Kairos 1992*, Birmingham, Black and Third World Theology Working Group/ECRJ, 1992, pp. 97–9.

30 D. Moore, 'Through a Black Lens: Telling our History and Understanding its Significance', in Grant and Patel, eds, *A Time to Speak*, pp. 17–21.

31 R. Milwood, *Liberation and Mission: A Black Experience*, London, African Caribbean Education Resource Centre, 1997, p. 90.

32 C. Amjad-Ali, 'Religious Demand for Justice: An Ecumenical Challenge for Today', in Grant and Patel, eds, *A Time to Act*, pp. 101–8.

33 Milwood, *Liberation and Mission*, p. 105.

34 L. Dixon, 'A Reflection on Black Identity and Belonging in the Context of the Anglican Church in England: A Way Forward', *Black Theology in Britain*, No. 4, 2000, pp. 22–37.

35 D. Isiorho, 'Black Theology in Urban Shadow: Combating Racism in the Church of England', *Black Theology: An International Journal*, Vol. 1 No. 1, 2002, pp. 29–48.

36 Dixon, 'A Reflection on Black Identity'.

37 A. G. Reddie, *Nobodies to Somebodies: A Practical Theology for Education and Liberation*, Peterborough, Epworth Press, 2003.

38 J. H. Cone, *Black Theology and Black Power: Twentieth Anniversary Edition*, San Francisco, Harper and Row, 1989, p. 6.

39 Cone, *Black Theology and Black Power*, p. 8.

40 J. Johnson, 'Cultural Spiritual Recovery: A Black Woman's Experience in the Church', in J. D. Aldred, ed., *Sisters with Power*, London, Continuum, 2000, p. 97.

41 S. E. Arnold, *From Scepticism to Hope: One Black-led Church's Response to Social Responsibility*, Nottingham, Grove Books, 1992, p. 63.

42 A. Sarkis, 'The Professional Woman', in Aldred, ed., *Sisters with Power*, pp. 65–74.

43 Brooks, *Where Do We Go From Here?*.

44 Thomas-Juggan, *Story of the Calvary Church of God in Christ in England*.

Glossary

Afro Caribbean An outmoded term for people of African and Caribbean heritages.

African Caribbean People of African and Caribbean heritages.

Black a) People of African heritage; b) Dark-skinned people, usually of African and Asian descent; c) 'Non-White', a social-political indicator.

Black Christianity Corporate identity of all Black Christians of all denomination, affiliation and tradition.

Black Church Movement A reference to the dynamism and diversity of churches that have sprung up in Britain since the 1950s, led by Black people.

Black-led church A local congregation or wider church that is led solely or substantially by Black people.

Black majority church A local congregation or wider church that has a majority of Black members.

Caribbean a) Etymologically, from 'Carib', one of the native inhabitants of the region; b) Geographically, those islands and continental enclaves in and around the Caribbean sea; c) Ethnically, the people of or from the region.

Creolization The co-mingling of ethnicities that occurred in the Caribbean.

Caribbean British Ethnic designation of people of Caribbean and British heritages.

Caribbean British Christianity The various forms of Christian traditions in Britain that have their roots in the Caribbean experience.

Caribbean British Christians Christians of Caribbean and British ethnic and religious heritage.

Respect From the Latin *respicio*, meaning 'to look back or again': to be informed, to know, or to understand.

Bibliography

Aldred, J. D., 'The Black Church in Britain and their Relations with the Ecumenical Movement', in *Pfingstkirchen und Okumene in Bewegung* (Frankfurt am Main: Verlag Otto Lembeck, 2001).

Aldred, J. D., *A Black Majority Church's Future*, unpublished Masters Thesis, University of Sheffield, 1994.

Aldred, J. D., ed., *Praying with Power* (London: Continuum, 2000).

Aldred, J. D., ed., *Preaching with Power: Sermons by Black Preachers* (London: Cassell, 1998).

Aldred, J. D., ed., *Sisters with Power* (London: Continuum, 2000).

Aldred, J. D., and Parris, G., 'The Bible and the Black Church', in Rowlands, C., and Vincent, J., eds, *Bible and Practice: British Liberation Theology – 4* (Sheffield: Urban Theology Unit, 2001).

Aldred, J. D., and Sturge, M., eds, *Black Majority Churches UK Directory 2000* (London: ADP Services, 2000).

Aldred, J. D., and Sturge, M., eds, *Black Majority Churches UK Directory 2003/4* (London: ACEA/CTBI, 2003).

Alexander, V., 'Afrocentric and Black Christian Consciousness: Towards an Honest Intersection', *Black Theology in Britain: A Journal of Contextual Praxis*, No. 1, 1998.

Alexander, V., *Breaking Every Fetter: To What Extent has the Black Led Church in Britain Developed a Theology of Liberation?*, unpublished PhD Thesis, University of Warwick, 1996.

Alibhai-Brown, Y., *Who Do We Think We Are? Imagining a New Britain* (London: Penguin, 2001).

Alleyne, M., *Roots of Jamaican Culture* (London: Pluto Press, 1988).

Amjad-Ali, C., 'Religious Demand for Justice: An Ecumenical Challenge for Today', in Grant, P., and Patel, R., eds, *A Time to Act: Kairos 1992* (Birmingham: Black and Third World Theology Working Group/ECRJ, 1992).

Arnold, S. E., *From Scepticism to Hope: One Black-led Church's Response to Social Responsibility* (Nottingham: Grove Books, 1992).

Augier, F. R., Gordon, S. G., Hall, D. G., and Beckford, M., *The Making of the West Indies* (Essex: Longman, 1960, 1994).

Baker, D. W., *Nahum, Habakkuk and Zephaniah*, Tyndale Old Testament Commentaries (Leicester: Inter-Varsity Press, 1988).

Barclay, W., *The Gospel of John*, Vol. 1 (Edinburgh: Saint Andrew Press, 1955).

Barrett, C. K., *The Gospel According to St John*, 2nd edn (London: SPCK, 1978).

Barrett, L. E., *The Rastafarians* (Edinburgh: Sangsters Book Stores, 1977).

Beasley-Murray, G. R., *Word Biblical Commentary: John* (Waco: Word Books, 1987).

Becher, V., and Breiner, M., *Black Christians: Black Church Traditions in Britain* (Birmingham: Centre for Black and White Christian Partnership and Westhill RE Centre, 1995).

Beckford, R., *Dread and Pentecostalism: A Political Theology for the Black Church in Britain* (London: SPCK, 2000).

Beckford, R., *God of the Rahtid: Redeeming Rage* (London: Darton, Longman and Todd, 2001).

Beckford, R., *Jesus is Dread: Black Theology and Black Culture in Britain* (London: Darton, Longman and Todd, 1998).

Beckford, R., *Macpherson and the White Church*, talk given to the Christian Network for Racial Justice Conference at the Centre for Black and White Christian Partnership, December 2001.

Beckles, H., 'Columbus and the Contemporary Dispensation Within the Caribbean', in Grant, P., and Patel, R., eds, *A Time to Act: Kairos 1992* (Birmingham: Black and Third World Theology Working Group/ECRJ, 1992).

Begbie, J., ed., *Beholding the Glory: Incarnation Through the Arts* (London: Darton, Longman and Todd, 2000).

Bernard, J. H., *A Critical and Exegetical Commentary on the Gospel According to St John*, Vol. 1 (Edinburgh: T & T Clark, 1969).

Bernard, J. H., *The International Critical Commentary on the Gospel According to St John* (Edinburgh: T & T Clark, 1969).

Bevans, S. B., *Models of Contextual Theology: Faith and Culture* (New York: Orbis Books, 1992).

Bhogal, I. S., *On the Hoof: Theology in Transit* (Sheffield: Penistone Publications, 2001).

Bisnauth, D., *History of Religions in the Caribbean* (Kingston: Kingston Publishers, 1989).

Black, C. V, *History of Jamaica* (Kingston: Carlong Publishers Caribbean, 1958, 1983).

Boesak, A., *Black and Reformed: Apartheid, Liberation and the Calvinist Tradition* (Maryknoll: Orbis Books, 1986).

Boff, C., 'Methodology of the Theology of Liberation', in Sobrino,

J., and Ellacuria, I., eds., *Systematic Theology: Perspectives from Liberation Theology* (London: SCM Press, 1996).

Boff, L., and Elizondo, V., *The Voices of the Victims, 1492–1992* (London: SCM Press, 1991).

Bosch, D. J., *Transforming Mission: Paradigm Shifts in Theology of Mission* (New York: Orbis Books, 1991).

Brereton, B., 'The British and French West Indies', in Knight, F. W., and Palmer, C. A., eds, *The Modern Caribbean* (London: University of North Carolina Press, 1989).

Brierley, P., *Christian England: What the Church Census Reveals* (London: MARC Europe, 1991).

Brierley, P., *The Tide is Running Out: What the English Church Attendance Survey Reveals* (London: Christian Research, 2000).

Brodie, T. L., *The Gospel According to John* (Oxford: Oxford University Press, 1993).

Brooks, I. V., *Another Gentleman to the Ministry* (Birmingham: Compeer Press, c. 1985).

Brooks, I. V., *In Chains They Shall Come Over* (Birmingham: New Testament Church of God, c. 1970).

Brooks, I. V., *Where Do We Go From Here? A History of 25 Years of the New Testament Church of God in the United Kingdom – 1955–1980* (London: Charles Raper, 1982).

Browder, A. T., *Nile Valley Contributions to Civilization* (Washington: Institute of Karmic Guidance, 1996).

Brown, R. E., *The Anchor Bible: The Gospel According to John I–XII* (New York: Doubleday, 1966).

Brown, R., *Slaying Giants*, National Overseer's Address to Annual National Convention, New Testament Church of God (Brighton Conference, Audio from Sapphire Video Services, July 2002).

Bulmer, M., ed., *Social Research Ethics* (New York: Holmes & Meier, 1982).

Bultmann, R., *The Gospel of John* (Oxford: Blackwell, 1971).

Bultmann, R., 'The History of Religions: Background of the Prologue to the Gospel of John', in Ashton, J., ed., *The Interpretation of John* (Edinburgh: T & T Clark, 1997).

Burgess, S. M., and McGee, G. B., eds, *Dictionary of Pentecostal and Charismatic Movements* (Michigan: Zondervan, 1988).

Centre for Caribbean Studies, *A Handbook of the Afro-Westindian United Council of Churches* (London: Globe Communications Enterprise, 1984).

Cheetham, J., 'Immigration', in Halsey, A. H., ed., *Trends in British Society since 1900* (London: Macmillan, 1972).

Christian Life Across the City: The Birmingham Christian Directory,

1997 (Birmingham: Birmingham Christian Media Services, 1997).

Clarke, A., *The Bethany Parallel Commentary on the New Testament* (Minneapolis: Bethany House, 1983).

Cone, J. H., *Black Theology and Black Power: Twentieth Anniversary Edition* (San Francisco: Harper and Row, 1989).

Cone, J. H., *For My People: Black Theology and the Black Church* (Maryknoll: Orbis Books, 1992).

Cone, J. H., *God of the Oppressed* (San Francisco: Harper San Francisco, 1975).

Cone, J. H., *Martin & Malcolm & America* (London: HarperCollins, 1993).

Conn, C. W., *Like a Mighty Army: A History of the Church of God 1886–1976* (Cleveland, TN: Pathway Press, 1977).

Davidson, C. T., *Upon This Rock*, Vol. 1 (Cleveland, TN: White Wing Publishing, 1973).

Davis, K., *Emancipation Still Comin': Explorations in Caribbean Emancipatory Theology* (Maryknoll: Orbis Books, 1990).

Dayfoot, A. C., *The Shaping of the West Indian Church* (Florida: University Press, 1998).

De Gruchy, J. W., 'The Nature, Necessity and Task of Theology', in De Gruchy, J. W., and Villa-Vincencio, C., eds, *Doing Theology in Context: South African Perspectives* (Maryknoll: Orbis Books, 1994).

Dixon, L., 'A Reflection on Black Identity and Belonging in the Context of the Anglican Church in England: A Way Forward', *Black Theology in Britain: A Journal of Contextual Praxis*, No. 4, 2000).

Douglas, D., *The Handbook of the International Ministerial Council of Great Britain* (Watford: IMCGB Publications, 1990).

Dragas, G. D., 'The Eternal Son', in Torrence, T. F., ed., *The Incarnation* (Edinburgh: Hansel Press, 1981).

Dube, M. W., and Staley, J. L., eds, *John and Postcolonialism: Travel, Space and Power* (London: Sheffield Academic Press, 2002).

Dunn, S. A., *Jehovah God in the Old Testament is Jesus Christ in the New* (Birmingham: Bethel United Church of Jesus Christ (Apostolic), c. 1980).

Dyson, M. E., *Making Malcolm: The Myth and the Meaning of Malcolm X* (New York: Oxford University Press, 1995).

Edwards, D., *Jesus the Wisdom of God: An Ecological Theology* (Maryknoll: Orbis Books, 1995).

Edwards, J., *The Cradle, the Cross and the Empty Tomb: A Faith We Can Be Proud to Proclaim* (London: Hodder and Stoughton, 2000).

Edwards, J., *The Jamaican Diaspora: A People of Pain and Purpose* (Kingston: Morgan Ministries International, 1998).

Edwards, J., ed., *Let's Praise Him Again: An African Caribbean Perspective on Worship* (Eastbourne: Kingsway, 1992).

Edwards, J., *Lord Make Us One – But Not All the Same* (London: Hodder and Stoughton, 1999).

Elwell, W. A., *Baker Encyclopaedia of the Bible*, Vol. 1 (Michigan: Baker Book House, 1988).

Elwell, W. A., ed., *Evangelical Dictionary of Theology* (Carlisle: Paternoster Press, 1984).

Ferguson, S. B., and Wright, D. F., eds, *New Dictionary of Theology* (Leicester: Inter-Varsity Press, 1988).

Field, F., and Haikin, P., eds, *Black Britons* (London: Oxford University Press, 1971).

Ford, D. F., ed., *The Modern Theologians: An Introduction to Christian Theology in the Twentieth Century* (Oxford: Blackwell, 1997).

Foster, E., 'Out of this World: A Consideration of the Development and Nature of the Black-led Churches in Britain', in Grant, P., and Patel, R., eds, *A Time to Speak: Perspectives of Black Christians in Britain* (Birmingham: CRRU/ECRJ, 1990).

Fryer, P., *Staying Power: The History of Black People in Britain* (London: Pluto Press, 1984).

Gates, B., ed., *Afro Caribbean Religions* (London: Ward Lock Educational, 1980).

Gelder, A., and Escott, P., eds, *Church in Life: A Snapshot of Church Life in Britain at the Beginning of the Twenty-first Century* (London: Churches Information for Mission, 2001).

Gerloff, R. I. H., *A Plea for British Black Theologies: The Black Church Movement in its Transatlantic Cultural and Theological Interaction* (Frankfurt am Main: Peter Lang, 1992).

Gilroy, P., 'Steppin' Out of Babylon – Race, Class and Autonomy', in the Centre for Contemporary Studies, *The Empire Strikes Back: Race and Racism in 70s Britain* (London: Hutchinson Education, 1982).

Gilroy, P., *There Ain't No Black in the Union Jack* (London: Routledge, 1987).

Goodridge, M., 'In Our Churches All Are Welcomed', in *A Handbook of the Afro-Westindian United Council of Churches* (London: Centre for Caribbean Studies, 1984).

Grant, J., *White Woman's Christ and Black Woman's Jesus: Feminist Christology and Womanist Response* (Atlanta: Scholars Press, 1989).

Grant, P., 'Book Review', *Black Theology in Britain: A Journal of Contextual Praxis*, No. 6, 2001.

Grant, P., and Patel, R., eds, *A Time to Act: Kairos 1992* (Birmingham: Black and Third World Theology Working Group/ECRJ, 1992).

Grant, P., and Patel, R., eds, *A Time to Speak: Perspectives of Black Christians in Britain* (Birmingham: CRRU/ECRJ, 1990).

Guthrie, D., *New Testament Theology* (Leicester: Inter-Varsity Press, 1981).

Gutiérrez, G., *We Drink from Our Own Wells: The Spiritual Journey of a People* (London: SCM Press, 1984).

Hannaford, I., *Race: The History of an Idea in the West* (Maryland: Johns Hopkins University Press, 1996).

Harris, C., 'Post-War Migration', in Harris, C., and James, W., eds, *Inside Babylon: The Caribbean Diaspora in Britain* (London: Verso, 1993).

Hastings, A., *A History of English Christianity 1920–1990* (London: SCM Press, 1991).

Hayes, D., 'Emerging Voices, Emerging Challenges', in Schultenover, D. G., ed., *Theology Toward the Third Millennium: Theological Issues for the Twenty-first Century* (Lampeter: Edwin Mellen Press, 1991).

Haynes, A., *The State of Black Britain* (Antigua: Root Publishing, 1983).

Hebblethwaite, B., *The Incarnation: Collected Essays in Christology* (Cambridge: Cambridge University Press, 1987).

Hesselgrave, D. J., and Rommen, E., *Contextualization: Meanings, Methods and Models* (Leicester: Apollos/Inter-Varsity Press, 1989).

Hollenweger, W., 'Foreword: British and Black', in Gerloff, R. I. H., *A Plea for British Black Theologies: The Black Church Movement in its Transatlantic Cultural and Theological Interaction* (Frankfurt am Main: Peter Lang, 1992).

Holmes, C., *John Bull's Island: Immigration and British Society, 1871–1971* (Basingstoke: Macmillan, 1988).

Howell-Baker, M., and Bolton, T., *Am I My Brother's and Sister's Keeper: Black Majority Churches and Development* (London: Christian Aid/Centre for Black Theology, 2003).

Hyatt, R. L., *Walking with God in this Troubled World* (London: Minerva Press, 1999).

Isiorho, D., 'Black Theology in Urban Shadow: Combating Racism in the Church of England', *Black Theology: An International Journal*, Vol. 1 No. 1, 2002).

Jackson, A., ed., *Catching Both Sides of the Wind: Conversations with Five Black Pastors* (London: British Council of Churches, 1985).

Jagessar, M., 'Pan Recipe: Philip Potter and Theology in the Caribbean', *Black Theology in Britain: A Journal of Contextual Praxis*, No. 5, 2000.

James, C. L. R., *The Black Jacobins: Toussaint L'Ouverture and the San Domingo Revolution* (Reading: Cox and Wyman, 1938, 1963, 1980).

Johnson, J., 'Cultural Spiritual Recovery: A Black Woman's Experience in the Church', in Aldred, J. D., ed., *Sisters with Power* (London: Continuum, 2000).

Karn, V, ed., *Ethnicity in the 1991 Census, Vol. 4, Employment, Education and Housing Among the Ethnic Minority Population of Britain* (London: The Stationery Office, 1997).

Kinnamon, M., and Cope, B. E., eds, *The Ecumenical Movement: An Anthology of Key Texts and Voices* (Geneva: WCC, 1997).

Knight, F. W., and Palmer, C. A., eds, *The Modern Caribbean* (London: University of North Carolina Press, 1989).

Lamont, D., 'Deconstructing Patriarchy', in Aldred, J. D., ed., *Sisters with Power* (London: Continuum, 2000).

Lewis, G. K., *The Growth of the Modern West Indies* (New York: Monthly Review Press, 1968).

Lightfoot, R. H., *St John's Gospel: A Commentary* (Oxford: Clarendon Press, 1956).

Lindars, B., *New Century Bible: The Gospel of John* (London: Marshall, Morgan & Scott, 1972).

Lobo, A., ed., *Black Catholics Speak: Reflections on Experience, Faith and Theology* (London: Catholic Association for Racial Justice, 1991).

Lyseight, O. A., *Forward March: An Autobiography* (Wolverhampton: George Garwood, 1995).

Manley, M., *Jamaica: Struggle in the Periphery* (London: Writers and Readers Publishing Co-operative Society Ltd, 1982).

May, T., *Social Research: Issues, Methods and Process* (Philadelphia: Open University Press, 1993).

Mbiti, J. S., *African Religions and Philosophy* (Oxford: Heinemann Educational, 1990).

McGrath, A. E., *Christian Theology: An Introduction* (Oxford: Blackwell, 1995).

Milwood, R., 'How is Theology Political?', in *A Handbook of the Afro-Westindian United Council of Churches* (London: Centre for Caribbean Studies, 1984).

Milwood, R., *Liberation and Mission: A Black Experience* (London: African Caribbean Education Resource Centre, 1997).

Mohabir, P., *Building Bridges* (London: Hodder and Stoughton, 1988).

Mohabir, P., *Pioneers or Settlers?* (London: Scripture Union, 1991).

Mohabir, P., *Worlds Within Reach: Cross Cultural Witness* (London: Hodder and Stoughton, 1992).

Moore, D., 'Through a Black Lens: Telling our History and Understanding its Significance', in Grant, P., and Patel, R., eds, *A Time to Speak: Perspectives of Black Christians in Britain* (Birmingham: CRRU/ECRJ, 1990).

Morris, L., *Luke*, Tyndale New Testament Commentaries, revised edition (Leicester: Inter-Varsity Press, 1995).

Morrison, D., 'Resisting Racism – By Celebrating "our" Blackness', *Black Theology: An International Journal*, Vol. 1 No. 2, 2003.

Muhammed, S., 'Religion is the Sigh of the Oppressed', in Grant, P., and Patel, R., eds, *A Time to Act: Kairos 1992* (Birmingham: Black and Third World Theology Working Group/ECRJ, 1992).

Nathan, R., 'Caribbean Youth Identity in the United Kingdom', *Black Theology in Britain: A Journal of Contextual Praxis*, No. 1, 1998.

Nelson, C. T., 'The Churches, Racism and the Inner Cities', in Grant, P., and Patel, R., eds, *A Time to Speak: Perspectives of Black Christians in Britain* (Birmingham: CRRU/ECRJ, 1990).

Nettleford, R., *Jamaica in Independence: Essays on the Early Years* (London: James Currey, 1989).

Parry, T., *Black-led Churches in West Yorkshire* (Leeds: Churches and Neighbourhood Action Project, 1993).

Patterson, R., and Dougall, J., eds, *Virtue's English Dictionary, Encyclopaedic Edition* (London: Virtue, 1977).

Patterson, S., *Dark Strangers: A Study of West Indians in London* (Middlesex: Penguin, 1963).

Pemberton, D., 'Foreword', in *A Handbook of the Afro-Westindian United Council of Churches* (London: Centre for Caribbean Studies, 1984).

Pemberton, E., '1492: An Evaluation of the Evidence', in Grant, P., and Patel, R., eds, *A Time to Act: Kairos 1992* (Birmingham: Black and Third World Theological Working Group/ECRJ, 1992).

Pemberton, E., 'African Slave Religions in the Caribbean', *Black Theology in Britain: A Journal of Contextual Praxis*, No. 2, 1999.

Pemberton, P., Pemberton, E., and Maxwell-Hughes, J. R., eds, *History of the Wesleyan Church in the British Isles* (Birmingham: The Wesleyan Holiness Church, 1983).

Petersen, R., 'Theological and Religious Pluralism', in de Gruchy, J. W., and Villa-Vincencio, C., eds, *Doing Theology in Context: South African Perspectives* (Maryknoll: Orbis Books, 1994).

Phillips, M., and Phillips, T., *Windrush: The Irresistible Rise of Multi-Racial Britain* (London: HarperCollins, 1998).

Potter, P., 'Report of the General Secretary: Sixth Assembly of the WCC, Vancouver, 1983', in Kinnamon, M., and Cope, B. E., eds, *The Ecumenical Movement: An Anthology of Key Texts* (Geneva: WCC, 1997).

Raw, B. C., *Trinity and Incarnation in Anglo-Saxon Art and Thought* (Cambridge: Cambridge University Press, 1997).

Reddie, A. G., *Faith, Stories and the Experience of Black Elders: Singing the Lord's Song in a Strange Land* (London: Jessica Kingsley, 2001).

Reddie, A. G., *Nobodies to Somebodies: A Practical Theology for Education and Liberation* (Peterborough: Epworth Press, 2003).

Reddie, A. G., 'Peace and Justice Through Black Christian Education', *Black Theology in Britain: A Journal of Contextual Praxis*, No. 6, 2001.

Roberts, J. M., *A History of Europe* (Oxford: Helicon, 1996).

Royal Institute of International Affairs: Board of Studies on Race Relations, *Report on Jamaican Migration to Great Britain* (London: Chatham House, 1956).

Runnymede Trust and the Radical Statistics Race Group, *Britain's Black Population* (London: Heinemann Educational, 1980).

Sanders, J. N., and Mastin, B. A., *The Gospel According to St John*, Black's New Testament Commentaries (London: A & C Black, 1977).

Sarkis, A., 'The Professional Woman', in Aldred, J. D., ed., *Sisters with Power* (London: Continuum, 2000).

Scobie, E., *Global African Presence* (New York: A & B Books, 1994).

Selltiz, C., Jahoda, M., Deutsch, M., and Cook, S. W., *Research Methods in Social Relations* (London: Methuen, 1965, 1977).

Sherlock, P. M., *West Indian Nations: A New History* (Kingston: Jamaica Publishing House, 1973).

Simmonds, M. H., *A Portrayal of Identity: A Study of the Life and Worship of the First United Church of Jesus Christ, (Apostolic) UK*, unpublished Thesis, Department of Theology, University of Birmingham, 1988.

Sloyan, G. S., *John*, Interpretation Bible Commentaries (Atlanta: Westminster John Knox Press, 1988).

Small, S., *Racialised Barriers: The Black Experience in the United States and England in the 1980s* (London: Routledge, 1994).

Smith, D. M., *John*, Abingdon New Testament Commentaries (Philadelphia: Fortress Press, 1986).

Smith, D. T., *Lives of Service: Obeying God's Call* (Cleveland, TN: White Wing Publishing, 1996).

Smith, I., with Green, W., *An Ebony Cross: Being a Black Woman in Britain Today* (London: Marshall, Morgan and Scott, 1989).

Smith-Cameron, I., *The Church of Many Colours* (London: Jeyaram Press, 1998).

Solomon, N., 'The Third Presence: Reflections on the Dialogue', in Byfield, T., and Braybrooke, M., eds, *Dialogue with a Difference* (London: SCM Press, 1992).

Sondhi, R., 'Diversity and Equality', *Connections*, Spring 1998 (London: Commission for Race Equality).

Stewart, R. J., 'Religion in the Anglophone Caribbean: Historical Overview', in Pulis, J. W., ed., *Religion, Diaspora and Cultural Identity: A Reader in the Anglophone Caribbean* (Amsterdam: Gordon and Breach, 1999).

Strong, J., *The New Strong's Exhaustive Concordance of the Bible* (Tennessee: Thomas Nelson, 1984).

Sturge, M., 'Don't Dis Me If You Don't Know Me: Rereading the Abraham–Lot Narrative', *Black Theology in Britain: A Journal of Contextual Praxis*, Vol. 4 No. 1, 2001.

Sturge, M., *Look What the Lord Has Done: An Exploration of Black Christian Faith in Britain* (Bletchley: Scripture Union, 2005).

Sweeney, I., 'Skin Deep Christianity', in Aldred, J. D., ed., *Preaching with Power* (London: Continuum, 1998).

Tasker, R. V. G., *John*, Tyndale New Testament Commentaries (Leicester: Inter-Varsity Press, 1995).

Thomas, H., *The Slave Trade: The History of the Atlantic Slave Trade 1440–1870* (London: Macmillan, 1997).

Thomas-Hope, E., 'The Patterns of Caribbean Religions', in Gates, B., ed., *Afro-Caribbean Religions* (London: Ward Lock Educational, 1980).

Thomas-Juggan, N., *Story of the Calvary Church of God in Christ* (Enfield: Norma Thomas-Juggan, 2000).

Thompson, P., Brown, I., Ellis, E., and Lyseight, L., eds, *Here to Stay: A Collection of Stories by Women* (Oxford: Lion, 1990).

Torrance, T. F., ed., *The Incarnation* (Edinburgh: Hansel Press, 1981).

Trotman, A., 'Black, Black-led or What?', in Edwards, J., ed., *Let's Praise Him Again: An African Caribbean Perspective on Worship* (Eastbourne: Kingsway, 1992).

Tschuy, T., *Ethnic Conflict and Religion* (Geneva: WCC, 1997).

Turner, H., 'New Religious Movements in the Caribbean', in Gates, B., ed., *Afro-Caribbean Religions* (London: Ward Lock Educational, 1980).

Vincent, J., 'Developing Contextual Theologies', in Duffield, I. K., Jones, C., and Vincent, J., eds, *Crucibles: Creating Theology at UTU* (Sheffield: Urban Theology Unit, 2000).

Vine, W. E., Unger, M. F., and White Jr, W., eds, *Vine's Expository Dictionary of Biblical Words* (New York: Thomas Nelson, 1985).

Walgrave, J. H., 'Incarnation and Atonement', in Torrence, T. F., ed., *The Incarnation* (Edinburgh: Hansel Press, 1981).

Wallerstein, I., 'The Construction of Peoplehood: Racism, Nationalism, Ethnicity', in Balibar, E., and Wallerstein, I., eds, *Race, Nation, Class: Ambiguous Identities* (London: Verso, 1991).

Walvin, J., *Black Ivory: A History of British Slavery* (London: Fontana, 1993).

Wang, H.-C., 'Some Perspectives on Homeland Theology in the Taiwanese Context', in Sugirtharajah, R. S., ed., *Frontiers in Asian Christian Theology: Emerging Trends* (Maryknoll: Orbis Books, 1994).

Weller, P., ed., *Religions in the UK: A Multi-Faith Directory* (Derby: University of Derby/Interfaith Network for the United Kingdom, 1997).

Wilkinson, J. L., *Church in Black and White* (Edinburgh: Saint Andrew Press, 1993).

Williams, E., *From Columbus to Castro: The History of the Caribbean, 1492–1969* (London: Andre Deutsch, 1970).

Williams, L. L., *Caribbean Theology* (New York: Peter Lang, 1994).

Woods, W., 'The Black Church Movement in Britain', in *A Handbook of the Afro-Westindian United Council of Churches* (London: Centre for Caribbean Studies, 1984).